Statistics and the Quest for Quality Journalism

Statistics and the Quest for Quality Journalism

A Study in Quantitative Reporting

Alessandro Martinisi

Jairo Lugo-Ocando

ANTHEM PRESS

Anthem Press
An imprint of Wimbledon Publishing Company
www.anthempress.com

This edition first published in UK and USA 2022
by ANTHEM PRESS
75–76 Blackfriars Road, London SE1 8HA, UK
or PO Box 9779, London SW19 7ZG, UK
and
244 Madison Ave #116, New York, NY 10016, USA

First published in the UK and USA by Anthem Press in 2020

British Library Cataloguing-in-Publication Data
A catalogue record for this book is available from the British Library.

Library of Congress Control Number: 2020946150

ISBN-13: 978-1-83998-583-6 (Pbk)
ISBN-10: 1-83998-583-6 (Pbk)

This title is also available as an e-book.

To our beloved parents, always source of inspiration and love

CONTENTS

LIST OF ILLUSTRATIONS

Figures

Tables

Chapter 1

INTRODUCTION

In his 1903 book *Mankind in the Making*, the British science-fiction novelist and social commentator Herbert George Wells (1866–1946) argued for a new type of political system in which society renounced any claim of absolute truths and people's ideas were based on presented facts – a system in which overall policy and public affairs in society were scientifically examined in the light of mathematical and statistical reasoning. Wells would go on to argue that

> The great body of physical science, a great deal of the essential fact of financial science, and endless social and political problems are only accessible and only thinkable to those who have had a sound training in mathematical analysis, and the time may not be very remote when it will be understood that for complete initiation as an efficient citizen of one of the new great complex world-wide States that are now developing, it is as necessary to be able to compute, to think in averages and maxima and minima, as it is now to be able to read and write. (Wells,[1903] 2014)

Wells, who was a biologist by training and one of the top science-fiction writers of the time, lived in the age of modern scientific utopias, marked by the rise of industrialization and workers' struggles. However, what makes Wells' contribution so relevant today is that he was standing up against Eugenics at a time when other intellectuals, including some fellow socialists, were siding with this racist pseudoscientific idea.

Wells was not opposed to a science of heredity, nevertheless he rejected the notion of Francis Galton (1822–1911), the father of modern statistics, that the state should intervene in order to breed human beings selectively. Positive traits such as beauty, health, capacity, and genius, as well as supposed negative traits such as criminality and alcoholism, says Wells, are in fact such complex entanglements of characteristics that ignorance and doubt bar our way. Still today at the Rijksmusem Boerhaave of science and medicine in Leiden, the Netherlands, the visitors can see some drawings of a facial angle, a geometrical system invented by the Dutch scientist Petrus Camper (1722–1789) and later used to justify slavery and racism. Wells' extensive writings on equality and human rights would gain him the rare distinction of his work being incinerated in the Nazi book burnings of 8 April 1933 only to be taken in later years by the United Nations as a source of inspiration for the Universal Declarations of Human Rights (James, 2012; Partington, 2017 [2003]).

In the age of Big Data, when statistics and the use of numbers in general are becoming increasingly essential in the practice of journalism (Baack, 2015; Borges-Rey, 2016), it is easy to forget that the very same numbers that today we prize as the culmination of the Enlightenment as a political project have served both to elucidate as well as to obscure our own understanding of society and its problems. We live in a time in which mathematical thinking has overwhelmingly taken over great chunks of our lives. Decisions set by algorithms determine for us the outcomes of credit checks, access to housing and even whom we could meet on a dating site – all this while influencing voters or exposing us to particular fake news items (Briant, 2018; O'Neil, 2016).

However, contrary to common assumptions, the relationship between journalists and statistics is neither new nor unique. Instead, it is part of a long and broad historic tradition where numbers have been used to create social reality and reassert authorial control over what is said to the public. It is a tradition that has both a history and politics of its own and that has played a pivotal role in asserting and challenging simultaneously the authority of certain narratives of power.

One of the most important aspects of this relationship is the way journalists have engaged and used statistics in perusing quality; a quest that has not only proven to be elusive and complex but also problematic at times, particularly in relation to how journalism has engaged with power. In this book, we explore the relationship between journalism and statistics in relation to how the former has used numbers to establish authority over truth while establishing its own legitimacy as an agent of power (Mattelart, 2019b; Nguyen & Lugo-Ocando, 2016). In so doing, numbers have become an instrumental piece of the jigsaw puzzle to set journalists apart as 'custodians of conscience' (Ettema & Glasser, 1998).

We argue that beyond normative claims of just 'seeking quality', news people have used, and continue to use, numbers to reassert their own credibility and therefore claim authority over what is truth in society. Moreover, as their authority is becoming increasingly challenged in recent years, journalism in general as a political institution in the West has responded by moving further towards the use of data and numbers to re-establish that authority. The thesis is that sub-disciplines such as data-driven journalism are a manifestation of this wider trend of reasserting legitimacy and part of a historical, positivist tradition of making the journalistic profession 'scientific',one that continues today with its engagement with Big Data in order to become 'Apostles of certainty' (C. Anderson, 2018).

We argue that by engaging with statistics and data, journalists are constructively and systematically trying to exercise their authority as guarantors of truth in society. It is a premise that is increasingly relevant in an age of the so-called Big Data, when journalists' engagement with numbers is seen by many in the industry and the academy as the Holy Grail that could save quality journalism (Miller, 2017; Narisetti, 2013).

This is particularly the case as the news media faces a perfect storm created by declining streams of revenues, hyper-fragmentation of audiences and the de-politicisation of society in general. For many, the interaction between journalists and numbers is the future of the face of Data Journalism. To be sure, these voices often refer to the 'datafication' of news – and society in general – and vehemently call for the incorporation of statistics and data into journalism practice as a way of improving the quality of news (Cervera, 2017; Renó & Renó, 2017; Seth C Lewis & Westlund, 2015). For others, storytelling remains exclusively a creative act and therefore to be included in the genre of literature.

This is not to say that the incorporation of data and statistics in journalism is just a cynical effort to re-establish authorial power upon truth. On the contrary, the 'data revolution' presents to us a real possibility to revolutionize the way journalism is done, making news stories more comprehensive, relevant, accessible and engaging. It is an opportunity to enhance journalism and provide better public service. Indeed, as many journalists are now expected to deal with and examine big and small numbers almost on a daily basis, at least in ways that they were not asked to do in the past, they have had to up their game. This against the challenges raised by time pressures in the 24-hour cycle of news, declining resources in the mainstream newsroom and growing masses of quantitative information related to economic, political and social phenomena (including scientific and academic research reports, public opinion data, political polls, and official and non-official datasets, among others).

Therefore, it is impossible today to disassociate the discussion about quality and power in the news from the use of numbers and data. Therefore, the question remains as to how journalists use statistics to articulate news. What are the reasons and rationales behind incorporating numbers in the news stories? Are news stories really *better* – a term that in itself is problematic – because they present the audience particular numbers or data? Does the incorporation of statistics make news stories more comprehensive and accessible? The book is an attempt to answer some of these questions including among other more fundamental ones, such as: What do we understand by quality in the news? Is data really the future for journalism?

What this book is about

In this book, we aim at challenging some common assumptions about how journalists engage and use statistics in their quest for quality news. In so doing, it seeks to improve our general understanding about the usage of data and statistics as a primary means for the construction of social reality. Our work incorporates data from a series of primary sources and triangulates it, allowing us to draw a great deal of our analysis. The idea is to provide an explanatory framework as to how journalists engage and use statistics in the articulation of news.

This, we believe, is an urgent task given the hopes and aspirations placed upon data and statistics to solve what we believe are far more structural problems facing the news reporting structures. Indeed, in light of the rapid deterioration that the news media ecology is facing in an age of 'post-truth' politics and the rise of 'fake news', we call for a sound understanding of what numbers and data can do for journalism as a political institution. It is an endeavour, nevertheless, that requires examining also the decline in trust towards journalism as a Fourth Estate in society, which is linked not only to the profound changes in the media ecology but also to the erosion of resources within the newsroom to carry out the type of journalism that guarantees depth, impartiality and overall quality in what is disseminated.

Given this context, there has been a renewed emphasis to produce 'quality' news (P. J. Anderson, Williams, & Ogola, 2013; Pennycook & Rand, 2019), and efforts have been displayed by both mainstream legacy media and new digital-native ones across the globe. Particularly, resources have been poured into developing investigative capabilities around data analysis methods and incorporating statistics in the process of gathering, producing and disseminating news stories that are relevant to society at large. However, as we will also argue here, this engagement with data, as laudable and straightforward as it sounds, is instead far more problematic and complex than what is often accounted for. This is not only because the process of datafication of journalism brings with it a long positivist tradition that is in itself problematic but also due to the fact that the aspirations to quality are so vaguely defined within journalistic practice.

To be sure, the notion of 'quality' in the news remains not only elusive but also contentious. On the one hand, the notion of 'quality news' and 'quality news providers' has centred on the normative claims of journalism being a public service to society; something that, as we will argue, is questionable both factually and historically. On the other hand, there is ample evidence to suggest that statistics and data do not necessarily bring accessibility, reliability, validity or credibility to the news stories.

Our own research, which draws on original data, suggests that the use of data and statistics within the practice of journalism is deeply associated with a pressure for authorial control and self-legitimization and used as a ritual to ascertain objectivity in similar ways in which Gaye Tuchman (1972) suggested for all news sources. Through the lenses of five quality dimensions: Relevance, Accuracy, Timeliness, Interpretability and Accessibility, we explore this ritual in which reporters engage and use statistics. In so doing, we seek to understand how statistics are articulated to achieve quality in news stories.

In analysing this process, we highlight the dichotomy between the normative and professional aspirations of journalism; one whereby statistics seek to support the quality of news and, at the same time, to strengthen the storytelling authority of journalists through the use of these numbers. The book tries to underpin the tensions and issues around journalism and statistics. The central point to make is that while the concept of quality and its dimensions remains a normative aspiration among journalists, what they really aim to achieve is ultimately trustworthiness and authority. Hence, drawing from this last dichotomy we argue that not only the use of statistics does not automatically translate into quality journalism, but that on some occasions it even hinders the possibility of greater civic engagement with the news by becoming elements of gatekeeping rather than the liberation of information.

Journalists use data and statistics to ensure that their stories are authoritative and trustworthy – this against increasing pressure of time, decreasing resources in the newsrooms and overall depoliticization of society (which translates in declining interest in news overall). In other words, journalists increasingly are drawn into data and statistics to address issues of quality and trust. To examine this usage, our research offers an explanatory theoretical framework that sees quality of the news through a series of five dimensions. We then explore how journalists make use of numbers in their attempt to achieve – successfully or otherwise – these dimensions, and the strategies and approaches journalists undertake in that process. The research has adopted a multidisciplinary approach that integrates a series of qualitative and quantitative research methods to allow a holistic examination of the role statistics play in the articulation of quality news and to ask what this means for an informed and democratic citizenship.

Our rationale

Media scholars such as Manuel Castells (2011) and Armand Mattelart (2003) have argued that ours is an 'Information Society'. One of the forms that this 'information' takes is numeric data, which both conveys and creates the meaning of things (Mattelart, 2019a). Indeed, today we are witnessing an increase in the type of information that is translated into data and numbers, one type that drives our daily lives for decision-making, from health data to educational data and crime data and beyond. Thus, it is cogent to understand not only the role statistics play in society but also how news stories that convey these numbers legitimate and contribute to the "mutual construction" of social reality.

In this regard, philosopher Luciano Floridi (2011) has said that if information is the vital breath of democracy and that the quality of such information is the element that keeps our society in good health by helping citizens to make sound and safe decisions, then, we can add, those who mediate this information and how it is mediated are increasingly relevant actors in the reshaping of our society. Consequently, there is a growing need of a data-driven awareness. In order to understand society at both practical and theoretical levels, our empirical research explores precisely this, the articulation of statistical information in journalism practice by focusing on journalists as the main sense-makers of the data in the information landscape (which we later refer to as *Infosphere*). By doing so, we examine the practical use of such quantitative information in the articulation of quality news stories. As such, this research proposes to build an innovative account of how statistical information is used in news reporting, specifically through a mixed-methods analysis. The analysis will make use of the background of the Philosophy of Information as theorised by Luciano Floridi (2011) as this philosophical construct was crucial to address the issue of quality when applied to the journalistic workflow.

Therefore, our inquiry is based on the triangulation of quantitative and qualitative methods that allowed us to explore these issues in depth. However, we have limited the study to the scope of crime and health news beats, mainly as this would allow us to focus on particular news beats that tend to be detached from political debates to a greater degree than others – which avoids methodological distortions in the amount of data collected and because these areas provide important evidence to the type of gaps between normative claims and practice that we aim to explore (J Lugo-Ocando, 2017).

Our data suggests that, among other things, a lack of interpretability and coherence within the narration causes an over-emphasis on numbers that leads to the paradox 'more numbers = less quality'. It also suggests an emphatic use of numbers, often mixing together different statistical sources demonstrating a lack of understanding of the difference between official and non-official sources. The semi-structured interviews we carried out highlight the awareness and confidence towards the numerical skills of journalists, their opinions about the usage of statistics and their criticism against statistics driven by politics. Most importantly, it looks at their understanding of quality. Our focus groups explored audience perceptions, which were very often over-reactions mixed with hyper-criticism, when the readers dealt with news that makes use of numbers. Broadly speaking, this research found that statistics bring authority and trust to the news but not necessarily quality.

All these findings are contextualised in relation to a broad range of literature taken from media and communications studies, journalism studies and information studies with the purpose of highlighting how these areas of research overlap when dealing with quantitative information. A technique of comparing and contrasting was adopted as a means of observing points of strength and of weakness in each area of the literature. It was shown that the notion of quality, because of its ambiguity, is the most common concern among readers, but it is also often underestimated and perhaps 'snubbed' by journalists in favour of a more approachable, down-to-earth, widely accepted notion of credibility.

We suggest that even if the quality of statistics does not impact directly on the overall narrative quality of news articles, the results of a poor understanding of its dimensions can spark confusion and doubts and inspire unnecessary over-scepticism among readers. This is a kind of reaction that is detrimental, if not for the storytelling itself, which is a creative act, but for the journalistic mission of informing the public. We argue that by being aware of the five dimensions of quality both in statistics and in news, which are later detailed in this work, journalists could successfully achieve the journalistic mission to inform and educate their readers.

Our findings also highlight a general deficiency in the training of journalists regarding the interpretation of statistical releases and their databases, and this deficiency is now corroborated by our findings as one of the key issues to be addressed. Indeed, one of the innovative contributions of this book is to pinpoint unequivocally that it is not only time pressures nor access to data – key culprits in relation to flaws and pitfalls – but the educational background of reporters that needs to be addressed. While traditional explanations have blamed journalists' ability to manage datasets and verify critically statistical sources on the current speed of the news cycle, our work suggests instead that blame lies in a lack of skills among journalists. Therefore, the main question around how journalists use statistics to deliver quality in their work is ever more pertinent as a guide for the research rationale.

Definitions of main terms

Some of the key concepts used throughout the book are grounded upon journalistic practices and are distinctive from the conceptualisation or interpretation given to the same term in a different context. Yes, we have adopted conventional notions to ease the understanding of the study. However, we have done so exploring the meaning within the context of field under analysis. In other words, terms such as 'quality', 'statistics' and 'philosophy of Information' are dissected under a very different magnifying glass than if they were to be used by, let us say, a statistician.

In this sense, the term *quality* is at the centre of this study. Many attempts have been made over the last decades to define 'quality' in general terms. There is a wealth of research which will be extensively analysed in this book, but for the present purposes two notions are proposed: that of (1a) quality statistics and of (1b) quality journalism. For the authors, the term (1a) quality statistics can only be applied to official statistics. We have tried to offer a comprehensive review of the most important reports and government white papers related to this topic. According to the website of the Office of National Statistics (ONS, 2020) the quality of a statistical product can be defined as the 'fitness for purpose' of that product. More specifically, it is the fitness for purpose with regards to the European Statistical System dimensions of quality. The dimensions of quality statistics, for which we have developed five dimensions, are of extreme importance in the articulation of numerical information in news reporting. On the other hand, the notion of (1b) quality journalism is a highly contested one, and it has been at the centre of debate for at least 50 years. However, for the purposes of this book, we argue that quality journalism is achieved through the use of quality statistics. Therefore, quality journalism is guaranteed if, and only if, all five dimensions we set as a threshold at the beginning of the analysis are satisfied in the outcomes.

The starting point of this research stems from three recent studies. The first two were conducted by the Reuters Institute for the Study of Journalism based at the University of Oxford: *What Is Quality Journalism* by Johanna Vehkoo (2010) and *Quality Journalism, the View from the Trenches* by Jarmo Raivio (2011). The third is *Defining and Measuring Quality Journalism* by Stephen Lacy and Tom Rosenstiel (2015) under the School of Communication and Information at Rutgers University. These three studies are the most up-to-date researches on quality journalism, organically collecting and analysing, through qualitative semi-structured interviews, the opinions and reflections of a broad range of professionals. All three studies aim to find a possible definition of quality journalism and common points of agreement among respondents.

Overall, let us start by acknowledging that statistics is a fundamental concept. According to the Royal Statistical Society (2020), it is all about turning numbers into information. Statistics is the art and science of deciding what are the appropriate data to collect, deciding how to collect them efficiently and then using them to answer questions, draw conclusions and identify solutions. This study uses the term *statistics* often in conjunction with the word 'information'. 'Statistical information' is used interchangeably with 'numerical information' and 'numbers'. Statistics may be presented also by mean of visual graphs, formulae or written narratives (Franzosi, 2017). Also, we will consider as statistics the sources related to stories of crime and health as key datasets for journalists when they communicate a specific set of statistics or make a statistical claim.

Another very important aspect being discussed in this book is around the Philosophy of Information, which refers specifically to the work of Luciano Floridi (2011) who coined the term in the 1990s and who has published extensively in this area with the aim of elaborating a unified and coherent conceptual framework for the whole field of Philosophy of Information. It is our intention to apply, wherever possible, this theoretical approach to the topics addressed in this book.

According to the Stanford Encyclopaedia of Philosophy, the Philosophy of information historically

> deals with the philosophical analysis of the notion of information both from a historical and a systematic perspective. With the emergence of empiricist theory of knowledge in early modern philosophy, the development of various mathematical theories of information in the twentieth century and the rise of information technology, the concept of 'information' has conquered a central place in the sciences and in society. (Ladyman, 2014)

However, Luciano Floridi puts an emphasis on the rise of computers that are at the centre of the information revolution. He states that 'the UNESCO Observatory on the Information Society have well documented that the information revolution has been changing the world profoundly, irreversibly, and problematically since the fifties, at a breath-taking pace, and with unprecedented scope, making the creation, management, and utilisation of information, communication, and computational resources vital issues' (Floridi & Illari, 2014). As we will explain later in the book, it is our opinion that this philosophical approach is more now than ever before of extreme importance in the practice of a type of journalism which aims at being data-driven.

Modernity and cybernetics as projects

Initial efforts behind the introduction of numbers into the public sphere were state-led (Desrosières, 2002; S. M. Stigler, 1986). They were part of a larger project of social engineering in order to both consolidate hegemonic power by means of culture and be able to deliver more effectively coercion. It is part of a broader effort of governing by trace, numbers, data, files or algorithms.

It is, according to Mattelart (2019a, 2019b), a new rationality of government based on the market economy and is focused on the quantifiable individual. However, the idea of a society governed by numbers is not new. It goes back long before cybernetics unveiled its potential and the notion of information made its way into the language or culture of modernity.

Indeed, the concept of cybernetics is central in explaining how the agenda of numbers has been advanced in modern society. The concept refers to a transdisciplinary approach to exploring regulatory systems, their structures, constraints and possibilities. The word *cybernetics* was originally used by Norbert Wiener (1948) as the study of control and communication. The term *cybernetics* stems from the Greek but draws its origins from the mechanicist philosophy forged during the Enlightenment. It is the belief that natural wholes – principally living things – are like complicated machines or artefacts, composed of parts lacking any intrinsic relationship to each other. This view understood the universe as a clockwork in which each piece geared with the other (Crowe, 2007). Indeed, over the years and into the 20th century, mechanics became cybernetics and as such it had mathematical thinking as its core.

The push to reduce social reality to binary numbers is part of a broader historical process, part of the Scientific Revolution, from which the thought of the quantifiable and measurable became the prototype of any true discourse in the West (Mattelart, 2019a). The use of numbers was part of an effort to use mathematical models in the social sciences. This in itself was part of the zeitgeist in the 1940s and 1950s in which a variety of new interdisciplinary scientific innovations occurred, such as information theory, game theory, cybernetics and mathematical model building, in the social and behavioural sciences (Lazarsfeld & Henry, 1966).

The original attempts to use numbers for societal control had a colonial nature, as they were closely linked to the consolidation of European Empires and their efforts to assert their dominance by means of asserting quantitative control over society and project cultural hegemony through scientific and technical superiority. This was a period of 'Statistical Enlightenment', which ran roughly between 1885 and 1935, which was a distinctive epoch in the annals of statistical thought. Key in this was Francis Galton and his efforts to justify racist theories through the use of statistics (S. Stigler, 2010) and collaterally support the British Empire.

More recent approaches to organize society using numbers had as its backdrop also broader issues of power and possibilities offered by the application of the principles of cybernetics in general aspects of society's governance. In the classical book *The Nerves of Government* (Deutsch, 1985 [1963]), social and political scientist Karl Wolfgang Deutsch (1912–1992) argued that the concepts of the theory of information, communication and control could be applied to address the key problems of political and social sciences. Based on Norbert Wiener's use of the concepts of feedback, channel capacity and memory, Karl Deutsch advanced these concepts to underpin the development of the computer-based political world models that we use today. Hence the study of journalism's use of statistics to achieve quality needs to be appreciated in this particular historical and political dimension.

Overview of the book

Hence, we start with a review of existing literature about quality journalism and focus on the ambiguity and convergence of the concept among scholarly writings/research. However, we do so in the context of the historical construction of news reporting as a political institution and hegemonic civil society. We then go to focus upon the problems of defining and measuring the concept of quality for research in the wider context of cybernetics and societal control over truth. Consequently, we have linked the concept of quality to that of objectivity, the latter seen as a way to overcome subjective approaches. The chapter concludes by exploring how scientific methods are used in journalistic practice as a means to convey credibility and authority.

Chapter 2 introduces some philosophical challenges that take into account the branch of philosophy known as Logic. Adopting such a philosophical approach to the main question and how this relates to the concept of quality allows us to embrace a more critical approach to the topic under analysis, and we then contextualise it into journalistic performance. In so doing, we make the link between Enlightenment, Positivism and the Information Society and learn how this link has defined the relationship between journalism and numbers over the years.

In Chapter 3, we move on to consider some philosophical views, mainly taken from the branch of Logic, known as Philosophy of Information in relation to how it applies to data and quality in journalism. We discuss the normative importance of the concept of quality in democratic life and how the scientific aspirations of journalism as a political institution have come to determine the way reporters understand, engage and use numbers. Chapter 4 is about how statistics have come to set the quality standards for journalism practice and principles and their power of persuasiveness by means of mathematical rationale and argument. Chapter 5 discusses the normative aspirations around 'quality' in journalism and how these have incorporated frameworks and practices in the daily routines of reporters.

Chapter 6 provides empirical evidence from our fieldwork about statistics in journalism in terms of quality. It presents the key-findings divided by method: content analysis, close-reading rhetorical structure analysis, semi-structured interviews, focus groups and Q-test. Chapter 6 outlines general conclusions based on them. Furthermore, it highlights their implications on how journalists manage statistics and more specifically how numbers are articulated by journalists to legitimate their stories through a scientific lens. This chapter concludes with suggestions for future research and how we, as researchers, should engage with questions about the role of statistics in producing quality journalism. In Chapter 7 we discuss what we call the 'ideology of statistics in the news where we offer not only some final reflections around these issues but also explore future for scope for future research'.

We need to warn readers that the book has some very important limitations that need to be highlighted here. They are mostly the product of time and resource restrictions and contextual issues which perhaps narrow our discussion in terms of geography and time. Firstly, we cannot assume that the findings and contributions explored here in relation to newspaper journalism in the United Kingdom can be extrapolated and have universal applicability. We recognize that, despite important overlaps among journalists from all over the world in relation to their practices and around their news cultures, there are nevertheless equally important differences among them as the Worlds of Journalism Study Project has recently highlighted (Hanitzsch, 2016). Thus one of the key challenges in future works will be to examine how these results and conclusions compare across the globe and speak in comparative terms to the ideal of what David Randall once called a 'universal journalist' (Randall, 2000).

The other area to further this research is in relation to news audiences and how they perceive, engage and use this statistical information. Although our book provides some initial insights by carrying out some exploratory research, this only proves the need to advance more empirical investigation in this area. Given how neglected the area is, this is perhaps one of the biggest challenges of all in the media and communication studies.

As with all works such as this one, it was never going to be an isolated and single enterprise. We received the support and help of many people across the research path that led us to this point. However, we cannot but assume that any flaws and gaps are ours and ours alone. The credits, nevertheless, need to be shared with a variety of people and institutions across the board. Firstly, three great colleagues and friends at the University of Sheffield in the United Kingdom who signed off the start of this project, Prof. Martin Conboy, John Steel and Scott Eldridge II who from the start were emphatically positive and supportive of us; equally important in that initial support was our friend and colleague Julie Firmstone at the University of Leeds, also in the United Kingdom. We wish to thank also Arnoud Versluis and Bruce McLean Hancock, friends and colleagues at Breda University of Applied Sciences in the Netherlands; Dr Giulio Alvaro Cortesi of the University of Paris 1 Pantheon-Sorbonne, France; Prof. Micheal Hofmann at Florida Atlantic University; Prof. Pietro Ghezzi at Brighton and Sussex Medical School and Prof. Eddy Borges-Rey at Northwestern University in Qatar.

Finally, we would want to thank our publisher at Anthem Press, who has been supportive, brilliant and overall patient with what was a much more diffi-cult task than we originally envisaged. He understood what we were trying to do with this project but also saw its potential to open important discussions in our field. We hope to have met his and others' expectations in the following pages.

Chapter 2

NUMBERS AS INFORMATION IN THE INFORMATION SOCIETY

To understand how journalists use statistics to achieve quality, we need first to contextualize news reporting practice within the wider ideological context of professionalization. In this sense, Professor Mark Deuze (2005) has argued that the professional identity of journalists is held together by an occupational ideology of journalism. Historically speaking, a person's occupation exerts important influence in determining their role and their family's position in society, and in the past even the place the individual would live (Mack, 1957), which also underpins the more general ideologies that these individuals embraced as part of their beliefs (Dibble, 1962). However, the great reconfiguration of society that took place in the West due to deindustrialization, the growth of the service and financial sectors and the creation and incorporation of a set of Information and Communication Technologies (ICTs) that alter most people's daily lives have meant that all professionals now operate under very different occupational ideologies.

These transformations can be encapsulated within the notion of the Information and Network Society about which several authors have referred to over the years (D. Bell, 1973; Castells, 2011; Drucker, 2012; Mattelart, 2000, 2003). It is a concept that reflects specific trends in the capitalist society and that has had an important impact in particular areas such as the media industry. Perhaps no other profession has had to endure such significant changes as journalism given not only the dissemination of the political economy that used to sustain the media industry but also the development of a completely new media ecology that has transformed working conditions and professional practices around news reporting.

Therefore, the use of statistics in journalism should be understood within the context of the Information Society. The notion of the Information Society took shape during World War II with the invention of 'thinking' machines (Dyson, 2012). However, it only became a standard reference in academic, political and economic circles from the 1960s onwards, thanks to promotion of the idea by scholars such as Daniel Bell (1973, 1976), who is recognized as

the foremost writer on the Information Society, developing a robust argumentation around the subject from the 1960s to the 1990s (Duff, 1998).

This neologism became popular among certain circles at that time of the
Cold War, as it described a new forthcoming capitalist society, which would
emerge from the advent of the 'information revolution', one that many saw
being realized with the arrival of the Internet as a dissemination of ICTs
across society (Mattelart, 2000, 2003). The notion was, from the start, linked
to the ideas of a knowledge-based economy that would supplant the existing
industrial-based economic paradigm of development and progress that had
dominated the war and post-war until then. It was also deeply connected to
the idea of depoliticization although not explicitly. Instead, Daniel Bell spoke
of *The End of Ideology* (1960), an idea that he drew from Karl Mannheim's pre-
diction in *Ideology and Utopia* (2015 [1929]) of the exhalation in the ability of
traditional ideologies to mobilize the masses. For Bell, the grand old ideologies
such as Marxism and Fascism, derived from the nineteenth and early twentieth centuries, were exhausted. Instead, society would see more 'parochial'
ideologies and witness how ideology in general would be irrelevant among
'sensible' people. His view would be a techno-deterministic one, claiming
that the polity of the future would be driven by piecemeal technological
adjustments of the extant system.

Bell's position would be revived later by US political scientist Yoshihiro
Francis Fukuyama (1989, 2012 [1992]) in the face of the collapse of the Soviet
Union and the Fall of the Berlin Wall. He would go on to argue, in a Hegelian
tone, that the worldwide spread of liberal democracies and free-market capitalism of the West and its lifestyle may signal the end point of humanity's
sociocultural evolution and become the final form of human government.

Information technology enthused Western society because of its ability
to underpin the triumph of capitalism and the end of ideology. With its
technodeterministic nature, the neologism provided the key argument for
1980s' and 1990s policies such as that of deindustrialization that took place
under the Reagan administration in the United States and the Thatcher government in the United Kingdom, therefore giving impulse to the disarticula-
tion of workers' rights guised now as the creation of 'portfolio workers', the
process of deregulation of telecommunications and media and the increasing
'financialization' of the Western economy, where industries and jobs were
being relocated to China, India and other places in the world. For many
authors, indeed, the Information Society was by all means a mantra to dis-
guise neoliberalism (Fuchs, 2010; Neubauer, 2011).

As we mentioned above, journalism – both as a social practice and political institution – did not escape this trend, as the political and organizational
context in which it operated changed rapidly and dramatically in a matter of

just a few years (J. Blumler & Gurevitch, 2002; Lugo-Ocando, 2013; Russial, Laufer & Wasko, 2015). In the face of these multiple challenges, journalists and news organizations have had to change and adapt over the years. This meant, among other things, incorporating new or revitalizing old reporting techniques such as Computer-Assisted Reporting (CAR), which can be traced back to the 1980s (C. W. Anderson, 2018; Garrison, 1998; Maier, 2000). The rise of CAR happened in conjunction with the development of computer softwares by the American IBM and the Italian company Olivetti and having in the background the development of precision journalism as a new branch of practice that incorporated social science research techniques into the art of news reporting (Meyer, 2002). The techniques and technologies were able to harness the power of calculation in order to produce a new form of journalism based on quantitative information. All these developments, over the past recent years, have converged in a way and evolved into what is today referred to as data-driven journalism (Borges-Rey, 2017; Borges-Rey, Heravi & Uskali, 2018; Fink & Anderson, 2015).

Enlightenment, society and information

By now it ought to be clear that the process of change that has led journalism into becoming increasingly more data-driven has not happened in a vacuum but instead as part of the wider context of the changes encapsulated in the neologism of the Information Society. The concept of Information Society is deeply rooted in the spirit of the Enlightenment, which was itself inspired by a blind belief in numbers (Mattelart, 2003, p. 5). This approach dates back to the seventeenth and eighteenth centuries, where scientific thinking took hold in society. In part, it embraced the idea that the natural world was quantifiable and measurable and that numbers could help us reach a universal truth through a 'universal language' (Mattelart, 2003), which many believed to be mathematics (Martinisi & Lugo-Ocando, 2015; Martišius & Martišius, 2008) (or standard measures).

Hence, scientific reasoning and mathematics, in particular, were seen as the paths for the perfectibility of human society (Elliott, 2010; Lugo-Ocando, 2017; Mattelart, 2019a). In this respect, it was the French Revolution and the Napoleonic era that followed that marked a high point in the quest for a 'geometrical certitude' in society by bringing statistics to the centre of government and official planning (Desrosières, 2002; S. M. Stigler, 1986) and setting the basis for what would be later called modernity (Williams, 1989). It was this period that really placed statistics at the centre of the state and society's governance as a whole (Perrot & Woolf, 1984). An example of this is the Netherlands in the eighteenth century. Until the end of the eighteenth century, every region used its own weights and measures, which were often based on human proportions such as inches, ells and feet. This meant that trade between countries, regions or cities involved a lot of recalculating. To put an end to this confusion, the French revolutionary government commissioned a committee of mathematicians and physicists to design a universal system of weights and measures: the metric system. In the end, Napoleon's imperial mandate was needed to effectively implement the system. Nowadays, the National Statistical Offices of many governments have similar problems despite ample efforts made to 'harmonise statistics' around the world.

The Enlightenment meant the consolidation of modernity as a fundamental historical category. One marked by developments such as a questioning or rejection of tradition, the prioritization of individualism and by faith in the inevitability of social, scientific and technological progress (Foucault, [1975] 2012). At the centre of the push for modernity were numbers and the need to count things. It had, however, two slopes; one conservative towards individuality and another one progressist and more favouring egalitarianism.

On the conservative side, numbers were in fact instrumental in advancing particular narratives that underpinned power and private property, consequently allowing Thomas Robert Malthus, for example, to develop the argument set in *An Essay on the Principle of Population* (1798), which not only warned against overpopulation but also advocated in favour of quantifying and controlling natural resources and restricting access to common land and human goods (Harkins & Lugo-Ocando, 2016; Ross, 1998). Statistics also enabled the systematic and orderly enslavement and transatlantic transport of millions of people from Africa into the New World, as the registration of numbers was a fundamental element in commerce and exchange of human beings. These numbers were also later used to justify empire and the implementation of eugenic-driven policies and remain today embedded in science in relation to broad assumptions about IQ and race (Roberts, 2011; Saini, 2019; S. Stigler, 2010; Zuberi, 2001). The categorization of human beings undoubtedly brought up a number of dark sides. We cannot forget however that nineteenth-century Europe witnessed a rapid spread of cholera, which was a mystery to scientists. A group of hygienists gathered in Amsterdam and started to analyse the causes of the deadly cholera epidemics. They used statistics to learn for the first time how the epidemics were related to sickness-inducing environmental and living factors. Even today, at the beginning of 2020, to understand the spread of the coronavirus, scientists implement similar inferential calculations.

Also historically, numbers had a more progressive role within the Liberal political framework that derived from modernity. By 1789, for example, the T-square and the level had become the two emblems of Equality and attributes of the goddess Philosophy, the incarnation of Reason. The ideal of egalitarian 'levelling' that would bring men closer together inspired by the Declaration of Human Rights led to the introduction of a new system of planning and organizing statistics (Saetnan, Lomell & Hammer, 2010). Numbers were used to highlight poverty by journalists such as Henry Mayhew (1812–1887) during the Victorian (Lugo-Ocando, 2014; Maxwell, 1978) era, as well as to highlight the unnecessary deaths of British servicemen in the Crimean War due to poor hygienic conditions (Knightley, 2000 [1975]; Kopf, 1916).

If well statistics have been around for a long time (M. Anderson, 1992; Freedman, 1999; S. M. Stigler, 1986), they are by all means a 'modern' phenomenon, at least as we know them today. Statistics stemmed from a philosophical grounding and a political context in the modern times, and the use of the word 'statistics' is rooted in the concept of the modern nation-state and that of stable borders. From 1660 the notion of *Staatkunde*, or 'state knowledge', was promoted after the Treaties of Westphalia (1648) as a way of meeting the increasing demands of state as a centralized organization and gave the lexicon the later word 'statistics'.

The etymology of statistics also comes from the Latin *statisticum collegium*. Subsequently the notion was defined by Gottfried Achenwall (1719–1772) as the 'state science' or *Staatwissenschaft*. The aim was 'illustrating the excellences and deficiencies of a country and revealing the strengths and weaknesses of a State' (S. M. Stigler, 1986). The philosophical ground behind the notion of statistical information can be synthetically found in the works of two philosopher-mathematicians: Gottfried Leibniz (1646–1716) and Nicolas de Condorcet (1743–1794).

Indeed, Leibniz is extremely important in our understanding of the Information Society because he believed the nature of logic to be an essential step in developing the idea that it is possible for thought to manifest itself in a machine. Leibniz came very close to automating the thinking process by implementing binary arithmetic and a *calculus ratiocinator* or 'arithmetic machine'. For Leibniz and his contemporaries, more efficient methods of calculation were needed to meet the requirements of modern capitalism. The German philosopher laid the foundations of the algorithmic writing that allowed the British mathematician George Boole (1815–1864) in 1854 to find the beginning of an autonomous discipline of computer sciences that would appear on the technology landscape only hundreds of years later.

In an effort to 'establish a universal language', a language of signs that would bring 'geometrical certitude', the Marquis de Condorcet proposed a new way 'to bring to bear on all the objects embraced by human intelligence, the rigour and accuracy required to make the knowledge of truth easy and errors almost impossible' (Mattelart, 2003). This language was expected to have made broad use of charts, tables, methods of geometrical representation and descriptive analysis. It related to the perfectibility of human society as Condorcet elaborated a view based on a new relationship with history that ought to offer universal and demonstrable knowledge based on empirical evidence. By observing the frequency with which an event occurred, it was then possible to predict the future based on the probability of it happening again. Therefore, probability theory became a new means of objectivizing human society, and it proposed a method for making choices in the event of uncertainty. This was a decisive step forward that distanced the Modern Age from the Ancient Age of the Greeks and Romans (Bernstein, 1996).

As a matter of fact, at the beginning of the Enlightenment, the quarrel between the Ancients and the Moderns, pivotal for the History of Ideas and an essential feature of the European Renaissance, began to transform and shape the view of history that would lead to modernity itself. Condorcet, in his *Sketch for a Historical Picture of the Progress of the Human Mind* (1794), analysed some issues that arose with the Modern Age, such as the impact of printing on scientific development, the formation of democratic opinion and the growth of the ideal of equality. This was taking place in the face of the first Industrial Revolution, which would bring numbers to the forefront of the public discourses, as they would become a language of power on their own.

Reporting numbers as information

Quantification through numerical information was pivotal in the construction of a 'new' Western society. Alfred Crosby, in his sharp investigation of the role of quantification, gives a beautiful example of the complexity of trading some 800 years ago. It involves the Italian merchant Francesco di Marco Datini (Crosby, 1997):

> On November 1394 he transmitted an order for wool to a ranch of his company in Mallorca in the Balearic Isles. In May of the following year the sheep were shorn. Storms ensued [...] Then the wool was divided into thirty-nine bales, of which twenty-one went to a customer in Florence and eighteen to Datini's warehouse in Prato. The eighteen arrived on 14 January 1396. In the next half year his Mallorcan wool was beaten, picked, greased, washed, combed, carded, spun, then woven, dried, teasled and shorn, dyed blue. Napped and shorn again, and pressed and folded. These tasks were done by different groups of workers [...] At the end of July 1396, two and a half years after Datini had ordered his Mallorcan wool, it was six cloths of about thirty-six yards each and ready for sale. (1997, p. 35)

This quote is interesting for the purpose of this book, since Crosby (1997) draws attention to the care, the precision and the quality that Marco Datini needed to keep track of things, but also notes that each step of the above, each exercise involving a task by some other actor, had to be paid for, and in the end Marco Datini needed to know that he was going to make a profit. No wonder there was a need for bookkeeping. Interestingly, it was only during Datini's career that Hindu-Arabic numbers began to be used. Prior to 1383 his books have all the numbers written out in words. This is one of the major achievements in Western society and the most important intellectual break-through. One that also had a huge impact on the way our civilization has come to understand itself.

Having briefly mentioned bookkeeping, there is a need to stress the importance of it for the origin of numbers reported in the news. The beginning of the double-entry bookkeeping system is often associated with the name of the Italian Luca Pacioli (1445–1517) described as the 'father of modern accounting'. In his 600-page book *Summa de Arithmetica, Geometria, Proportioni et Proportionalia* (1494 and re-edited in 1994), we see the beginning of what Max Weber would call the 'rationalisation of society' (Ritzer, 1983) or what modern sociologists have labelled 'bureaucratisation' (Blau, 1956; Cochrane, 2018).

It is our opinion that as bookkeeping gives us eyes to see what others cannot, akin to news reporting, we can then make sound decisions and have informed opinions. Such rigorous accounting procedures formed one of the necessary foundations of the Industrial Revolution. If this would be regarded as the genesis of a way of 'reporting numbers' for large consumption, the genesis of statistics, as we conceive it today, can be traced back only to the seventeenth and eighteenth centuries. Yet, it was not until the Victorian period that numbers began to circulate on a systematic basis, and this was thanks to the considerable expansion of the British press.

Newspapers were the most important vehicle during the late Georgian and Victorian periods; but other media have also experienced considerable growth during this time, including pamphlets, periodicals and novels. As Mark Hampton from Lignan University in China (Hampton, 2008, 2010) has argued, during the mid-Victorian period, the press was conceived as an instrument of 'popular enlightenment', as it aspired to what he terms an 'education ideal', later replaced by a 'representative ideal' (Mitchell, 2009). The dailiness of modern news has been traced back to the seventeenth century, but it became rooted in political life only in the late eighteenth and early nineteenth centuries.

Perhaps one of the most notable examples of this early engagement with statistics was the work of Henry Mayhew (1812–1887) and the reporting he did to document poverty in England based on the statistical numbers available at the time (Lugo-Ocando, 2014; Woodcock, 1984). Although Charles Dickens (1812–1870) in the 1830s had brought to the public agenda the issue of poverty, it was really Henry Mayhew who as a journalist undertook this subject as a comprehensive and serious study on street-folk, and it became a subject worth four volumes and sixteen hundred pages (Maxwell, 1978). Some refer to him as 'the statistical Dickens' and point out that his *London Life and the London Poor* (Mayhew, 2010 [1851]) is still very relevant today. By using data in the way he did, Mayhew was able to provide a vivid picture of the experiences of working people in the London of the nineteenth century. It was one of the few works with any statistical content to still be in print 150 years after it first came out (Champkin, 2007).

The flow of statistics into the newsrooms gradually intensified after 1800. Numbers as facts in the news became subject to systematic collection, circulation and consumption. The development of telegraphy and the rise of news agencies such as the British Reuters and the French Agence Havas, which were particularly focused on disseminating data from the markets, brought a more global dimension in the dissemination of numbers. Statistical numbers became an institution within society and were seen as a pivotal element in underpinning empire by means of technology and science. It was at that time that Belgian astronomer and mathematician Adolphe Quetelet (1796–1874) would help to set up the Statistical Society of London (Wessler & Rinke, 2014) with the design of the British census (Saetnan et al., 2010). He later organized the International Congress of Statistics in Brussels in 1853, bringing together the heads of statistical agencies from across Europe, who agreed to harmonize standards and set up the International Institute of Statistics.

Political arithmetic and public sphere

The idea that statistics is strictly related to the notion of state was underlined by Sir William Petty (1623–1687) who, as an English economist, coined the term 'political arithmetic' in his 1685 *Five Essays on Political Arithmetic*, suggesting the division of statistical records, elections and opinion polling. Since then, statistics as a knowledge system has become inseparable from its political occurrences (Saetnan et al., 2010). Some authors have widely considered the interrelation between statistics and political life (Porter, 1986, 1996). In addition to this, Alain Desrosières' 'History of Statistics' (2002) highlighted the 'co-constructive interaction' between, on the one hand, the scientific process of description, coding, categorizing, measurement and analysis, and on the other hand, the administrative and political world of action, decision-making, intervention and improvement. Desrosières points out how different actors, tools, techniques, structures, events, actions and so on contribute to the establishment of a Foucauldian 'regime of truth' (Hall, 2001; Taylor, 1984). In relation to this, there was emphasis placed on the political power of numbers in modern societies:

> Received wisdom has long been that quantitative methodologies won a place in the social sciences and in governance thanks to their demon-strated effectiveness within the natural sciences, and that their effective-ness there is due in large part to the natural ability of numbers to imitate and describe nature. (Saetnan et al., 2010, p. 4)

Theodor Porter (1986, 1996) for his part has underlined how statistics underpin credibility, impartiality and, above all, objectivity in the context of public life. For him and others, objectivity meant 'withholding judgments and resisting subjectivities when accounting for the outside world', and he notes how many statistical practitioners in the nineteenth century were embedded within the public sphere, self-consciously trying to transform society at large. Porter stressed how statistical science transformed the very meaning of 'public reason' as soon as statistical science began to develop an ethos of detachment rather than engagement, which we refer later to as an 'engagement-detachment game'.

Over the years, a torrent of numbers accompanies both bureaucratic communication and the public discourses that are characteristics of moder-nity (Tooze, 2001, 2006), one that is defined by detachment. The same that underpins normative values in journalism such as impartiality and objectivity. To be sure, as Alain Badiou (2008) suggests, the hegemony of statistics and the way numbers 'immobilise' any proper critical engagement are central to debates in modern society. An example of this 'immobilisation' is in the past, in Fascist Italy. Italian statistics were seen as a mere instrument of the total-itarian strategy aimed at immobilizing public opinion. For Badiou, 'we live in the era of number's despotism, something which means we have become incapable of posing more abstract questions concerning freedom, justice, and the true nature of citizenship' (1994, p. 14). In other words, numbers help to 'objectify' society and by doing so set the groundwork for the emergence of the modern notion of state and bureaucratic power.

The argument that instead of engaging in rational-political debate, members of the public are forced to become consumers of 'manufactured' forms of opinion and culture, including statistics, has been a valid argument among Habermas (1991) and others, who viewed the application of numer-ical information in the public sphere – such as opinion polling – as part of its degeneration during the twentieth century (1996) as also the French philoso-pher René Guénon prophesized in his *The Reign of Quantity and the Sign of Time* (2017 [1945]), when he talked about 'the obsessions of quantification'.

Numbers and public sphere

Habermas (1978) defined the public sphere as a realm of our social life in which something approaching public opinion can be formed and also a sphere which mediates between society and the state forming a principle of public information, which once had to be fought for against the arcane policies of monarchies and which since that time has made possible the democratic control of state activities. What was called public opinion was increasingly used by statesmen and politicians as a form of authority and then eventually 'decayed' into a series of battles between groups of interests.

Today media historians tend to make a distinction between different types of public spheres, based on gender, politics and class. We can say that the history of the modern public sphere follows the same complex destiny of statistics and modern governance, showing this way that numerical information has various applications within the public sphere itself and in the evolution of public reason. Historically, the key medium for the modern public sphere were the newspapers, which during the Victorian period expanded their sales exponentially over the late nineteenth century and early twentieth century (Conboy, 2002; Saetnan et al., 2010).[1]

Those years witnessed what Ian Hacking (1982) called 'an avalanche of printed numbers' and marked a threshold with respect to the breadth of issues suitable for enumeration. Population was the first concern but also other modern administrative domains such as the judicial, military, economic, educational, medical, criminal and others. If well words and not numbers seemed to dominate the debates and narratives in the public sphere in the late nineteenth and early twentieth centuries, numbers complemented words as a vehicle for persuasion (Yalch & Elmore-Yalch, 1984). In that age, statistics became an instrument to convey truth and to underpin the explanatory framework provided by journalists.

Using statistics to inject scientific rigour into journalism however received criticism from commentators such as Walter Lippmann (1889–1974), who in his article 'Elusive Curves' (1935) warned against attempts to predict the future by employing statistical curves (Seyb, 2015). An over-reliance on statistical manipulations, Lippmann observed, could cause analysts to give the statistical curve an authority that it did not deserve, an authority that could suspend reason and common sense in deference to the stature of the findings.

---

[1] The press was regarded as a significant source of popular accountability. Popular titles flourished between the 1830s and mid-1850s. In the 1880s, the *Star* quickly established a circulation of 200,000, and in 1911 the *Daily Mirror* became the first paper to reach a circulation of one million (Conboy, 2002, 2006).

'The best statisticians', Lippmann cautioned, 'are very sceptical. They respect their tools but they never forget that they are tools and not divining rods' (Seyb, 2015). Statistical findings, according to him, must be measured against the standards of 'common sense and general knowledge'. A failure to do so was to engage in a positivism, whose insistence on pattern and order could generate a picture of the world that was so misleading that it could thwart rather than inform (Bevir & Rhodes, 2015).

This intellectual heritage would be further developed many years later by journalism Professor Philip Meyer in the 1970s in his seminal book *Precision Journalism* (Meyer, 2002). In it he addresses concepts and methods from the quantification approach to understanding social trends by suggesting that journalism should widely engage with social science methods. Meyer's aim was to drive journalism towards a more scientific approach, which is why the term 'precision' refers to quantifiable facts measurable through statistical performance and data analysis.

Meyer's contribution marked distancing from a literary-humanistic approach that some associate with journalists as storytellers. This because his work meant a reconciliation with social science and a new impetus to reduce uncertainty (C. W. Anderson, 2018). His contributions and suggestions, which many saw vindicated in the rise of data journalism, aimed at pushing for a greater use of social science techniques by reporters in the United States, and overall a realization that in order to be better and sound, reporters had to embrace the use of this type of data,

> When well used, numbers can draw attention to the relevant conditions among all the noisy buzz and glare of the Information Age. In a world where not much is certain beyond death and taxes, we are sometimes tempted to give up on quantification, preferring instead to rely on intuition and story-telling. But the advantages of numbers, used properly, is that their strength can itself be quantified. (Meyer, 2002)

Precision journalism was seen both as a theory of news and as a set of observation techniques focused on reporting and analytical skills. It has also been a way of advancing the norm of objectivity among reporters. This as statistics have been seen as a further instrument for impartiality and a way of introducing social sciences into news reporting,

> While journalists talk of 'objectivity' and 'impartiality', social scientists hold the ideals of 'reliability' and 'validity'. However, just like journalists, social scientists rely on certain rules of procedure, both in terms of methodology and presentation of findings. (Fawcett, 1993)

Quality in a quantified world

One of the main reasons as to why this push for journalism to embrace social sciences in the pursuit of 'quality' is embedded in the idea of 'precision'. Historically speaking, quality has been underpinned worldwide by numbers across different societies. For example, precision in the measurement of length, mass and time was achieved in the ancient Hindu Valley around 3000 BC (Plofker, 2009) as a way of determining quality. In ancient Egypt and the pre-Columbus civilizations of America also, the dimensions of the pyramids and other constructions show a high degree of accuracy related to precision (Burton, 2011). The pursuit of quality by means of measurement can also be traced back to medieval Europe (Crosby, 1997), when craftsmen began organizing into unions called guilds in the late thirteenth century. This was followed by standards set in manufacturing in the industrial world by the European empires in the eighteenth century.

Objective methods of measuring and ensuring dimensional consistency evolved over the years. Henry Ford's moving automobile assembly line was introduced in 1913, and the use of statistics to set standards and design assembly lines was central to the increase in productivity to assure consistently good-quality products.

The introduction of scientific management to improve workflows and economic efficiency, especially labour productivity in the industries, brought in by Frederick Winslow Taylor (1856–1915) during the 1880s and 1890s within manufacturing industries, demanded the need for quality standards. By 1924, Walter A. Shewhart (1891–1967) would introduce the basic ideas of statistical quality control, something that would be further developed during World War II, which brought recognition to the need to use statistics to assure quality in manufacturing industries for the military. After the war, industries in the United States and Japan saw the emergence of a movement known as Total Quality Management (TQM). Several individuals made significant contributions in this direction. Worth mentioning are the American engineer W. Edwards Deming (1900–1993), the Romanian-born American management consultant and quality evangelist Joseph M. Juran (1904–2008), the businessman Philip Bayard Crosby (1926–2001) and the American engineer and theorist of the TQM (Total Quality Management) Armand V. Feigenbaum (1920–2014).

This trend invaded the newsrooms and by the late 1980s it started to be used to measure reporters' work through a numerical 'grid system' in many newsrooms having in the background the spread of managerialism across the media landscape (Nerone & Barnhurst, 2003; Osborn, 2001; Underwood, 1988). Media organizations defended such codified evaluation systems as

necessary for reducing inefficiency, managing costs and encouraging performance together with professional growth. However, many reporters found this
inappropriate for a professional activity; reducing reporting to only scores or
grades or statistical measurements can be 'traumatic' for journalists. Quality
needed to be quantified and standardized in order to be understood. The situation can be easily summarized as follows:

> If you overlay some factory model onto newsroom, you begin to detract
> from the thing that makes for a good newsroom: creative freedom. You
> can put a quantified system into any newsroom, but good journalists
> won't work there. (Osborne, 2001, p. 23)

The implementation of TQM and other managerial approaches did not
manage to save the newspaper industry, nor did it stop the disruption in the
media sector created by the technological and societal changes of the subsequent years. Soon, merger after merger and cuts after cuts later, many
directors and managers inside the news media – in the face of the futility of
their actions – moved away from these managerial ideas as a way of implicitly recognizing that when it came to quality, the news media industry was an
entirely different beast to others. However, the belief that numbers could not
only improve the 'quality' of the news stories being produced but also provide
a leaner manner of reporting did stay.

Quality as a precision tool

Many segments of the journalism establishment have over the years embraced
the notion that statistical information is a key tool to represent the world outside
in a more objective and scientific manner. One that reflected the normative
aspiration of being objective and scientific in the pursuit of truth. If well since
the 1970s journalism – as a 'gate' between official bodies and citizens – had
taken possession of mathematical tools in a decisive way to improve the accuracy and credibility of news reporting in, then the new millennium brought
data to the centre of news reporting by promising a totally new way of doing
journalism. The underlining rationale behind it was that journalists could
make their work far more relevant and a central element for the advancement
of a democratic society if they could effectively embrace data in their news
stories. This was seen, therefore, as a way of ensuring quality in the news.

Despite this, the notion of quality in the news remains largely elusive
although crucial in the aspiration for authorial control. Quality is seen as the
bonding element that holds together trust and credibility in journalism, which

are seen as part of the sort of unspoken 'social contract' between journalists and society.

There have been a number of important works referring to quality in the news (Abramson, 2010; P. J. Anderson et al., 2013; J. Lewis, Williams & Franklin, 2008; Vehkoo, 2010), which have offered ample discussions around the conceptualization and nature of what quality in the news looks like. These works have, nevertheless, a problematic nature of quality in the news. Since Umberto Eco wrote *Apocalyptic and Integrated* (Eco, 2000), scholars have been cautious about setting cultural standards or using existing ones to define quality in relation to any type of cultural industries. This because what is quality for one community might not be so for another. Nevertheless, there is some broad agreement that if journalism is considered as a public service then this could be taken as a common denominator of quality. As statistics have intrinsic relation to governance and delivery of public service, then it is more than expected that statistical information would be used in journalism.

Mayo and Leshner (2000) have conceptualized 'quality' as a rating of superiority applied to communication messages, and define 'quality' as an evaluation of how informative, important, interesting and well-written a news story is. Slater and Rouner (1996), for their part have defined 'message quality evaluation' as an overall assessment of the stylistic quality of the message, while Chaiken and Eagly (1989) and Tormala, Briñol and Petty (2006) identified adjectives such as good, interesting, enjoyable and important, all of them grouping together to form what they named 'story quality'. According to these authors, readers tend to assume that 'story quality factor' is distinct from factors relating to credibility evaluations.

Other works remind us how much the quality of information is crucial in the journalistic workflow (J. Lewis et al., 2008; J. M. W. Lewis, Williams, Franklin, Thomas & Mosdell, 2008). Methodological issues in this work are addressed by means of mindful discussions around theory and practice, theoretical frameworks and pragmatic implications.

One topic worth discussing here is the importance of quality dimensions and their definitions. This is because in relation to news consumption, readers (audiences) may consider different aspects of quality. Media and communication research show that 'quality' has a series of dimensions, and these are an integral part of the overall evaluation of content. In this book we identify and work with five quality dimensions. This because different dimensions of quality matter to different people at different times depending on their cultural contexts, needs and expectations. One quality dimension is that of credibility or trust, whereas the present research aims to be more complete in covering all dimensions (Floridi & Illari, 2014). The dimensions with which we work here are set to serve as a foundation upon which this research is built, namely: (1) Relevance; (2) Accuracy; (3) Timeliness; (4) Interpretability; (5) Accessibility. We used these dimensions as conceptual thresholds to explore how journalists have used data and numbers to try to uphold certain standards that they associate with quality. In exploring these dimensions, we hope to throw new light on how the statistical information is understood by journalists and the role data has in defining Information Quality (Abdi & Valentin, 2007) and underpinning power over discourses and narratives in the news.

Chapter 3

THE NEVER-ENDING DEBATE ON QUALITY IN JOURNALISM

As suggested previously, an agreed-upon definition of quality journalism has been, over the years, an ambiguous and problematic issue for both scholars and practitioners. Trying to define what is quality newsgathering and production is a post-modernist labyrinth that can lead to many dead ends as well as mirrors, not least because quality journalism can be conceptualized in a variety of different ways. Moreover, this ample variety of definitions can themselves be more relevant than others within specific national and cultural contexts.

Basically, different people in different countries perceive the concept of quality in the news very differently, and attempting to impose a universal quality criteria carved in stone is a futile exercise in a media industry that defines success largely upon very distinctive economic, cultural and political criteria.

In addition to this, judgements of quality are often culture-specific or related to one's socio-economic background and level of education. Interestingly enough, not even the Pulitzer Prize, one of the world's best-known awards for journalistic excellence, has a set of criteria for judging what makes a piece of journalism distinguished enough to win the prize.[1] Nowadays journalists have come to accept that they compete on a global scale with other citizen-journalists (Allan & Thorsen, 2009) in the so-called 'information marketplace' or market of ideas, and their knowledge contributes to the quality of their work (Shapiro, 2010). It is still debatable among scholars how this role of 'adding value' to ubiquitous information can be described and evaluated also in light of a rational choice theory (Russ-Mohl, 2006).

This question is rather problematized by the fact that journalists are an interpretative community (Zelizer, 1993), which creates social reality for media

---

[1] On the website www.pulitzer.org it is explicitly written, under point 6, that only the Nominating Juries and the Pulitzer Prize Board can determine exactly what makes a work 'distinguished'.

audiences that in turn are also interpretative communities (Rlindlof, 1988). Yet, journalists are 'information workers' rather than 'knowledge workers',[2] as they use information to assist in making decisions or taking actions, or a person who creates information that informs the decisions or actions of others (Drucker, 2012, p. 5).

Indeed, as predicted by some, the more that audiences have been gaining an increasing number of choices in their access to information, journalists have had to change in turn "from an unavoidable to an avoidable link in the chain of information possession" (Bardoel, 1996, p. 61). In this sense, US sociologist Leo Bogart, who researched journalists' views on quality standards over two decades, concluded that while 'the hallmark of any craft or profession is an adherence to certain generally accepted standards of performance and a respect for meritorious achievement' (Bogart, 2004, p. 40), the assessment of quality in journalism remains 'as murky as critical judgment of poetry, chamber music or architecture' because the abilities of the field are 'as intangible as those of any art' (Bogart 2004, p. 44). Likewise, the influential media economist Robert G. Picard (2000) pointed out that quality is a central element in achieving the social, political and cultural goals asserted for journalism in democratic societies. He argues that this concept becomes problematic when applied to journalism, because measurability is difficult.

This link between the delivery of quality journalism and service democracy had been already highlighted many decades ago by Ray Anderson who framed the issue of quality in a broader democratic process, suggesting that it is possible for the function/role of the fourth estate to be a characteristic of quality news providers, or better, of 'information providers',

> The specific understandings of it can be seen to be core requirements for the functioning of democracy to the fullest extent that it would appear is possible in a considerably less than perfect world. Quality will therefore be broadly measured according to the extent to which journalism performs the information provider role. (R. L. Anderson, 1970, p. 371)

---

[2] When Peter Drucker originally articulated the idea of a 'knowledge worker' in 1959, he was proposing a classification with the primary goal of describing the work of people who applied knowledge directly, and in a unique way, to the tasks assigned to them. As computing technology infused within organizations, it became a new tool for understanding an organization's data. Over time, though, computer programming became more sophisticated. Some of the knowledge workers found their way into computer programming, and computers became more capable of applying knowledge to data without human intervention. More details: www.seriousinsights.net.

Over the years, a variety of authors from political science have also referred to the levels of news information or 'Levels of Abstraction', as they will be referred to in further parts of this work. These are argued to be the necessary aspects for a well-functioning democracy, or rather for democracies in general. In this regard, Jesper Strömbäck (2005) has identified a four-fold typology of democracy. One of the four which is worth mentioning is the competitive democracy where journalism should meet the democratic need for an in-depth 'information provider' and 'watchdog' for those in power, with particular emphasis on the platforms and records of political parties and the key political players with a fair use of numbers and statistics.

In the context, as it is becoming increasingly clear, quality of news and quality of journalism practice itself are highly problematic topics. Indeed, as Ivor Shapiro's (2010) extensive literature review suggests, the notion of quality requires rationalizing a variety of definitions and concepts around journalism, media and communication in ways in which quality should be evaluated and conceptualized at a diversity of levels and in relation to specific organizational and cultural contexts. In other words, quality in journalism will always be a relative notion despite its attempts to universalize standards and approaches.

However, this has not stopped multilateral institutions from attempting to do so. For example, significant research about quality journalism was conducted in 2010 by the United Nations Educational, Scientific and Cultural Organization (UNESCO), which produced a series of three documents aimed at comprehensively setting a matrix of quality indicators in the Brazilian journalism scenario. In spite of very different journalism cultural differences, UNESCO has kept advocating for universal terms of references, including a preset curriculum, which has now been approved and published by the organization.

Indeed, despite some criticism, attempts to universalize and standardize the journalism education syllabus have continued, and a generic model has been proposed to be adapted according to each country's specific needs. The effort aimed at incorporating 'full cognizance of the social, economic, political and cultural contexts of developing countries and emerging democracies, highlighting the connection between democracy and journalism and arguing for a more cross-disciplinary approach within journalism training centres' (UNESCO, 2017).

Following this evolution of the concept of quality, UNESCO researchers highlighted the formulation of Quality Journalism Indicators, defined and applied within a Quality Management System, which may help to monitor journalistic companies and allow media companies to identify more accurately quality attributes and practices in journalism. In the analysis of Guerra (2010), quality supposes, as a basic premise, the fulfilment of demands from clients and society. Quality is an organizational resource that links the spheres of the production of goods and services and their consumption. For producers, the effective consolidation of quality management and its implementation has competitive advantages for the organization. The sphere of consumption and the indication of quality seem to guarantee that the product really does contain those features the customer wants. It offers security about consumption, due to the 'quality' label's credibility with consumers. The commitment to quality is therefore a central part of the discourse of many organizations, and newsrooms often include this in their daily routines as news producers. Indeed, as reported by American researchers Slack, Chambers and Johnston (2010), business newspapers and management magazines are dominated by articles about quality. To them it seems that we as society have experienced a 'quality revolution'.

As a matter of fact, in the wake of this 'quality revolution', the International Standardization and Accreditation Services and the Media and Society Foundation carried out some very insightful investigations.[3] The former is a private organization dedicated to certification and accreditation services whose mission is to support private, public and government institutions in establishing and maintaining quality standards in the public interest and then verifying their commitment to those standards. The latter is a Swiss non-profit organization whose mission is to encourage the development of standards for communication organizations.

The outcomes of their research are summarized in 13 dimensions: (1) quality of information; (2) quality of content; (3) ethics; (4) independence; (5) relations with advertisers; (6) relations with the public; (7) relations with public officials; (8) transparency; (9) audience surveys; (10) human resource management; (11) work organization; (12) infrastructure; and (13) relations with contractors and suppliers. These investigations aimed to merge the quality dimensions of assessment, management criteria of firms and companies, and the sphere of journalistic activity together.

After that, UNESCO also commissioned 'experts' for the initial development of the journalism education curricula initiative, who then solicited a response to their first draft from 20 senior journalism educators 'who were deemed to have considerable experience working in developing countries and emerging democracies'. The revised draft design thus featured a list of courses for both undergraduate and post-graduate levels, a brief description of each course and an outline of fundamental journalism competencies. Journalism

---

[3] Reports can be downloaded from www.media-society.org.

instructors with experience working in developing countries or emerging democracies were then 'carefully selected from Africa, Asia, Europe, the Middle East, and North and South America' to write the syllabuses for 17 core courses. The draft curricula were then reviewed by other 'experts' in Paris.

It is worth reminding ourselves that this is not a new attempt although perhaps the first one that is so explicitly organized. Journalism curricula in the Global South, for example, were originally copied from journalism degrees in the Global North and thereafter transferred to media systems and political frameworks in very different contexts. This has led to accusations that journalism curricula in the Global South reflected values and practices grounded in Western normative ideas of the role and function of journalism (Rodny-Gumede, 2018). Consequently, goes the argument, these impositions ignore the particular realities and contexts in the countries where they are implemented. Moreover, the efforts reflect a top-bottom approach and an aspiration to 'standardise' journalism education.

In Latin America, for example, this included both programmes deployed directly by the United States and also through multilateral institutions such as the Organization of American States (OAS) – which launched in the early 1960s as a programme to train science journalists – and, training in more general terms delivered by the Centro Internacional de Estudios Superiores de Comunicación para América Latina (CIESPAL) in Ecuador financially backed by UNESCO in times in which its own policies and approaches were driven by the United States as its main donor (Dellamea, 1996; Mellado Ruiz, 2010).

Regardless of these efforts, Josenildo Guerra (2010) claims that in places such as Latin America the culture of quality evaluation similar to the one existent in other areas, such as industry, commerce or service, has not been entirely adopted in newsrooms. According to Guerra (2010), quality is a linking resource between the sphere of production and the consumption of goods and services, stressing in this way the origin of the idea of quality, as we understand it nowadays comes from the Industrial Revolution and its development of the mass production processes.

Shapiro's (2010) position in this regard is also sceptical, as he advocates the existence of considerable hostility by journalists in accepting corporate or institutional concepts such as 'quality assurance/assessment' or even 'best practices'. However, this hostility is not proven or substantiated yet by sufficient academic research. Robert Picard (2000), on the other hand, sees attempts to stipulate quality attributes and measure journalistic performance in line with meeting particular attributes and as part of a broader process of continual improvement. For him, it is *intuitively appropriate* for both journalism and communication scholars. If Picard's intuition is right, we should add, then the pragmatic question to ask is: What, therefore, are the quality requirements for products in journalism? The answer, however, is not straightforward.

Ambiguity and convergence

Within the sphere of journalistic activity, on the one hand, it could be argued that from the public's point of view there are two basic requirements for news: *truth* and *relevance*; *truth*, because it is expected to inform the public of the facts; *relevance*, because not all facts are newsworthy. On the other hand, from the journalistic point of view, the two requirements are *accuracy* and its *estimation*. In both cases we encounter the first difficulty: justifying such attributes as being quality standards and substantiating them both scientifically and theoretically. However, there are ambiguities and some converging points on the aforementioned concepts, which will be addressed in the following section.

Referring to the quest for quality journalism, Ivor Shapiro (2010) argues that frequently, almost daily, the practice of journalism is evaluated through different lenses. One is in the newsroom, where the reporter's work is assessed in the editorial management's workflow. A second is through the audiences' lenses that evaluate journalists' performance. The third lens of daily evaluation is the journalism school classroom where the production work of students is assessed for pedagogical purposes. Ultimately there are studies of those involved in journalism scholarship, media criticism, and other academic investigations of the journalistic production.

For him, to evaluate is a thorough understanding of the existing paradigms upon which three distinct approaches converge: (1) the study of the professional culture of journalists; (2) reflections on journalism as an art form to be located within the field of arts and humanities; and (3) sociological surveys of journalists' criteria of 'quality' and 'excellence'. Below we briefly summarize the key points made by Shapiro. The question that then arises is whether or not journalists possess a common and definable set of traits or values. According to Mark Deuze the answer is affirmative, thanks partly to a common "occupational ideology" characterized by a "collection of values, strategies and formal codes" (2005, pp. 445–47). For Einar Thorsen and Stuart Allan, 'the news values of newspapers were being recast by a new language of "dailiness", one which promoted a peculiar fascination for facts devoid of "appreciation" to communicate a sense of an instantaneous present' (Thorsen & Allan, 2014).

This ideology can be summarized under five headings: (1) *Public service*: journalists provide a public service (as watchdogs or 'newshounds', active collectors and disseminators of information); (2) *Objectivity*: journalists are impartial, neutral, objective, fair and (thus) credible; (3) *Autonomy*: journalists must be autonomous, free and independent in their work; (4) *Immediacy*: journalists have a sense of immediacy, actuality and speed (inherent in the concept of news); and (5) *Ethics*: journalists have a sense of ethics, validity and legitimacy.

In 1993 Stuart G. Adam released a Poynter Institute monograph titled *Notes toward a Definition of Journalism: Understanding an Old Craft as an Art Form*, in which he defined journalism as a form of expression used to report and comment on the final result of the individual production of journalists and the culture in which they work. This product is marked by five 'principles of design': (1) news or news judgement; (2) reporting or evidentiary method; (3) linguistic technique; (4) narrative technique; and (5) method of interpretation or meaning. Adam explained that his ideas on what constitutes and differentiates journalism began when, as a juror in an awards programme, he was obliged to invent his own 'scoring system'. He therefore suggested it was possible to 'locate journalism in the territory of art and the humanities' (Adam, 2006, p. 344). We cannot stress enough here two schools of thought: one that claims that journalism is a form of literature, the other that maintains there must be a convergence of journalism towards the social sciences. This divisive debate is still vivid among journalism scholars.

The roots of survey research on how quality is articulated and substantiated in journalism can be seen in the study *The Elite Press: Great Newspapers of the World* by John C. Merrill (1968). Merrill's quality indicators included expansion of readers' education and intellect; good writing/editing; independence and financial stability; integrity; power to influence opinion leaders; social concern; staff professionalism and intelligence; strong opinion and interpretative analysis; world consciousness; and emphasis on politics, international relations, economics, social welfare, culture, education and science. A few years later, the same author (Merrill & Lowenstein, 1971) proposed more detailed internal and external criteria, such as editing and proofreading care, frequency of quotation and allusion. With regard to the three points above there is no indication on how to ensure such concepts in future research and it seems to remain at a theoretical level only.

Philip Meyer, on the contrary, is less theoretical and paves the way to a more pragmatic approach in the *Vanishing Newspaper*. In his words,

If we can agree on enough interesting elements of quality that are measurable, and if there is statistical evidence that they are driven by some common underlying force not directly measured, we can make a good claim that the underlying force, even though it might be latent, is in fact quality. (Meyer, 2009, p. 68)

He does not exactly give us a definition of quality journalism, but he attempts to define quality as credibility (Vehkoo, 2010), even if it is still not clear what he means when he talks about a 'common underlying force'.

Johanna Vehkoo (2010), who has summarized Meyer's viewpoint, says that Meyer produced a cogent, empirically tested case for the link between quality journalism and profitability called 'the profit controversy'. Meyer offers news organizations a practical way of looking at their business from the point of view of quality and public service, and how this is perceived by the end users – namely the readers. Accordingly, quality journalism materializes itself only when readers' reactions are under analysis. Meyer looks specifically at *credibility* and *influence* in local communities; *accuracy* in reporting; *readability*; and the impor-tance of *editing*. The main conclusion is what became famous as the *Influence Model* – this theory claims that quality in journalistic content increases the per-ception of readers in relationship to other people and to society in general.

> If entrepreneurs learn anything from newspaper history, it should be that trust has economic value, and that trust is gained through quality content. If the influence model works, the successful transitions will be by newspapers that use savings in production and transportation to improve their content. (Meyer, 2009, p. 188)

Later Meyer extracted from the responses of editors four broad dimensions of quality: ease of use, editorial vigour, news quantity and interpretation (Meyer & Kim, 2003). According to Winfried Schulz (2000) there are basically three conditions that determine quality and performance of journalism in a free, open society. First, the resources; second, the legal and political order; third, the professional standards, behaviour and values. In addition to that, there are different methods to approach these three conditions. With specific regard to the methodology, some studies start by interviewing people in the profession and trying to uncover their insights based on experience (Albers, 1992). Other studies survey audiences and ask them to assess media quality (Ebert, 2003). A third approach proceeds from media laws and extracts the standards for a norm-compliant media performance and journalism of high quality (Schatz, Hoßfeld, Janowski & Egger, 2013). Also, Denis McQuail has highlighted that the criteria for journalistic quality are closely connected with basic values of a free, democratic society, values like freedom, equality, social security and order (McQuail, 1992).

It is also worth citing communication sciences professor George Albert Gladney (1996), who abstracted from the literature 18 standards of journalistic excellence paradigms and divided them into 9 'organisational standards' and 9 'content standards'. Through a survey of newspaper editors, he found that the top-ranked content category standards were in the following order: strong local news coverage; accuracy; good writing; visual appeal; strong editorial page; community focus; news interpretation; lack of sensationalism; and comprehensive coverage. The top organizational standards were set by integrity; impartiality; editorial independence; staff enterprise; editorial courage; community leadership; staff professionalism; influence; and impartiality (Bovaird & Löffler, 2003).

At a different level, Northwestern University in the United States launched a resource guide called *Managing for Excellence – Measurement Tools for Quality Journalism* (2000) in which they answer questions like the following: How well are the readers served, and how can this be improved? The outcomes are built around five all-embracing ideas: mastery of the basics; developing consistency; learning from mistakes; developing self-corrective actions; developing value propositions, what the Centre calls 'unique, relevant value' (Media-Management-Centre, 2000, p. 22).

In light of this we can argue that even if there are some convergences on existing paradigms, there is no single common framework for measuring quality journalism. Yet it is possible to suggest that the frameworks based on the existing paradigms are all intellectually coherent and 'intuitively appropriate', even if each seems either too complex or not comprehensive enough to meet the needs of 'insider' and 'outsider' evaluators. In this sense, Shapiro (2010) again suggests some indicators that could be ascribed to the practice of journalism under specific topics. This means that quality refers to an attribute that can, in principle, be tested factually, even measurably, in order to assess if this work constitutes quality journalism or not. In this point, he suggests an evaluative 'standard' through a performative test for determining whether or not quality journalism exists.

Shapiro higlights aspects such as 'discovery', which includes the nature and the scope of journalistic curiosity, the choice of subject matter, its focus and angles, the potential and social benefit of the investigation and the extent to which it might further journalism's democratic functions. In sum, discovery is the identification of an event, issue or question as 'newsworthy'. It also includes issues related to research methodology, such as sourcing procedures and values, promises to sources, reliance on official and secondary sources, as well as interviewing methods.

He then mentions examination, which is strictly related to methods of verification. Documentary evidence and bibliographic research methods; data-mining techniques and statistical analysis; and reliability of Web resources either from 'closed' or from 'open' sources. In his following rationale, he underlines interpretation that is associated with in-depth analysis;

breadth of context; and ideas like fairness, proportionality and emphasis. Then style, which refers to the faculty of written and spoken clarity, ease of reading, viewing or navigation; engagement, interactivity and significance; word choices, image choices, data visualisation, infographics, packaging and structure. Finally, he argues, we have 'presentation' a topic that is related to the collective effort involved in producing, packaging and collating works of journalism. All of them include the relationship of form to content, packaging and labelling; placement, design and layout; the separation of fact and opinion (if any); a publication's range of subjects and genres; and the difference between 'grabbiness' and sensationalism. Other issues might include harm-avoidance; legal constraints; and the actual impact of a work on its audience. (Shapiro, 2010, pp. 152–54)

What this discussion has highlighted is that given such disparities and lack of homogeneity at three levels – terminological, theoretical and cultural, there is an imperative need to develop a suitable framework to address key research questions around journalism and quality in general and particularly in relation to how news reporters engage with numbers. This could be, however, a challenging but, optimistically speaking, not impossible endeavour.

The problem of measuring

Indeed, most of the definitions of quality asserted by observers of journalism present remarkable problems for those who attempt to measure quality. Taking as an example the list of topics summarized by Shapiro (2010), it is evident that the intrinsic problem resides in measurability. How can we measure veracity, emotional proximity and comprehensibility? According to media economist Robert G. Picard (2000), when we focus specifically on journalism, the issue of intangibility of the product and the difficulty of measurement are problematic. Consequently, we are forced to rely on representative measurements for performance. Accordingly, measuring *completeness, breadth, truthfulness, reliability* or *context* is never possible or practical because no person is in a position of full knowledge in which to make such evaluations:

> One cannot even set an effective standard for the types of stories or new mix that make up quality because the standard would become invariable and the events and issues of coming days cannot be forecasted because no one can foretell the future. (Picard, 2000, p. 99)

This leaves us with the impossible position of wanting to set measurable standards but finding it impossible or meaningless to evaluate journalists' efforts towards quality journalism. Hence, any possible answer to this dilemma is not as straightforward as it seems.

One possibility to solve this is to consider the journalistic workflow rather than just the outcomes. Journalism is not in itself a product or service but a very complex set of cultural practices defined by a professional ideology and engagement with the political context outside.

We have to carefully consider, for example, the mental activity of journalists that produces *values* in the forms of news, features and commentary. In our view, journalists react as if they were *Inforgs*,[4] organisms that bear information and make sense of it by their activity, literally immersed in what the philosopher Luciano Floridi calls *Infosphere* (2002, 2011). It is the intellectual labour that creates additional value by editing, drawing parallels between stories and numbers and, above all, as Plato in *Cratylus* would say, 'knowing how to ask and answer questions' (Silverman, 1992, p. 51).[5]

Following Picard's (2000) suggestions, it is possible to measure those activities that make these mental activities possible and therefore affect its quality. In so doing, one can produce representative measurements of quality journalism. This happens because journalism is not merely a function of the active brain. It results in the brain *processing information* collected for the purposes of creating journalism.

The better the information obtained, the more effort is placed in developing knowledge and understanding, and the more journalists can *process* the information better and thus produce quality journalism. In other words, journalistic quality is a function of journalistic activity, and those activities that *process* and produce information can be measured. These activities can be illustrated in the Figure 3.1.

The entire range of activities in the process cannot be obviously measured but it is possible to assess the activities that abstract major elements. Circled below are those elements that could be a matter for careful analysis.

In order to complement and substantiate Picard's viewpoint, it is useful to apply to Figure 3.2 the concept of *mind boxes*. This concept comprises all of the

---

[4] *Inforgs* is a neologism coined by Luciano Floridi to describe what constitutes an infosphere. The usage of the word describes organisms that are made up of information rather than 'standalone and unique entities'. This description of inforgs allows them to exist in the infosphere as natural agents alongside artificial agents. Inforgs can be part of a hybrid agent, that is, for example, a family with digital devices such as digital cameras, cell phones, tablets and laptops.

[5] Plato's quote lies at the core of the *Interviewing Principles* paper released by the Columbia Journalism School. See http://www.columbia.edu/itc/journalism/isaacs/edit/MencherIntv1.html (accessed on 14 January 2018).

Figure 3.1 The process of producing quality news.

Figure 3.2 Measurable elements of the process of producing quality journalism.

factors that 'box' ideas and information into a specific composition or shape within the minds of both news reporters and their audience. They include the frames that result from the 'boxing' process. The notion of mind boxes, according to H. J. R. Anderson, sees the mind 'at the heart of the box' in a dynamic, often unpredictable, interpretative role, trying to get to grips with a reality that is mediated frequently by inaccurate or incomplete information. The same has the advanced idea of mind boxes and conveys more effectively than pre-existing analytical tools the way that individuals' views of the world are limited and constrained by a wide and still growing variety of influences:

> They are to a considerable extent the other side of the coin to story boxes and story boxing processes, insofar as the latter are the means by which stories are shaped for presentation to the interpretative minds of the audience and can become part of the mind boxing process. (J. R. Anderson, 2014, p. 16)

The 'mind boxing process' is an innovative theory and seems to tangentially refer to the broad philosophical area of logic and its ultimate attempt to distinguish good reasoning and bad reasoning. As we will see in the next paragraph, the concept of quality has been deconstructed into several dimensions.

A brief review of the literature in the area will help our readers to find the thread to unravel the skein of such a complex topic.

Manifold dimensions of quality

An important feature of the literature on quality journalism as well as on information quality (Abdi & Valentin, 2007) is an attempt to categorize quality in dimensions. Stepping quickly back to ancient philosophy, one could find useful the definition of quality made by Aristotle. The Greek philosopher analyzed the idea of quality (from Latin *qualitas*) in his seminal work, the *Categories*. Aristotle divides quality as follows: habits and dispositions; natural capabilities and incapabilities; affective qualities and affections; shape. Aristotle's categories of quality idea have had its supporters, like Saint Thomas Aquinas, who affirmed that

> We take into account whether a thing be done with ease or difficulty; whether it be transitory or lasting. But in them, we do not consider anything pertaining to the notion of good or evil: because movements and passions have not the aspect of an end, whereas good and evil are said in respect of an end. (Ackrill, 1988, p. 198)

We think that a pure philosophical reflection on the polarity 'quality/qualities' is extremely important because it creates a connection with the pre-Industrial Revolution Age, and it highlights how this polarity of concepts is historically dear to humanity because it is also linked to the metaphysical and ontological 'realm'. Journalism is a sort of 'realm', which is particularly important given the fact that journalism as we know it today is a by-product of both the Enlightenment and the Industrial Revolution. Philosophy sees *qualities* as related to subjective feelings and *quality* to objective facts. For this reason, this kind of philosophical debate appears relevant for both journalists and communication scholars always hovering between the concepts of objectivity and subjectivity.

According to media scholars Shoemaker and Reese (1996), the quality of something depends, on the one hand, on the criteria being applied to it and from a neutral point of view, on the other hand, not determining its value (the philosophical value as well as economic value). Under a subjective point of view, something might be of quality because it is useful, because it is beautiful or simply because it exists. Establishing and searching the binary polarity 'quality/qualities' involves therefore the *understanding* not only of what is useful but also of what is beautiful and what exists in accordance to our needs and wants. In this line, the authors Hazel Henderson and Fritjof Capra (2009) debate on the very nature of quality whose concept can be scientifically formulated and divided in two different meanings: objective and subjective. According to them, growth and development are deeply intertwined to the concept of quality that can be understood under a new systemic view of life that aims to reframe the conceptual basis of Classical Liberalism under the new lenses of a sustainable and ecological economy.

The father of Classical Liberalism, John Locke (1632–1704), wrote in his 'Essay Concerning Human Understanding' (1689) about the importance of making a distinction between primary and secondary qualities. Primary qualities are intrinsic to an object, a thing or a person, whereas secondary qualities are dependent on the interpretation of the subjective mode and the context of appearance. In this sense and following Aristotle's steps, Robert Pirsig (1999) analysed a sort of Metaphysics of Quality,[6] and he has tried to solve the never-ending debate reconciling those views in terms of non-dualistic holism in the attempt to dissolve such a polarity. *Qualities* versus *quality* is therefore an inspirational debate which has seen a radical change in recent history especially when humanity passed through the Age of Masses towards the Digital Age, also known as the Age of Information when the very concept of quality seems inseparable from its opposite, that of *quantity*. Over the ages the attempt to categorize the qualities, and to fit the concept of quality into categories, has been declined by both academia and practitioners into what is best known as *quality dimensions*.[7]

Scholars across disciplines have identified four, five, six, seven and even eight dimensions, each of which has complementary, similar or different definitions depending on either the area they apply to or the cultural context they are moving within. We will review here the commonly accepted eight-fold and seven-fold dimensions, and then consider those dimensions in the context of Information Quality (Abdi & Valentin, 2007) research, which is supportive of the main theoretical argument presented in this work.

The following tables show definitions and dimensions of quality as they are theorized by David Garvin (1988) in Table 3.1, and by Roberta Russell and Bernard Taylor (2005) in Table 3.2.

---

[6] More details about the *Metaphysics of Quality* on www.moq.com.

[7] The best interpretation of all dimensions of IQ is affected by purpose. Purpose is a *relational* rather than relative concept: something has (or fails to have) a purpose for something else. We shall refer to this as the 'purpose problem', otherwise called 'fit-to-purpose' or 'fitness for purposes'. In the online section *Quality in the Office of National Statistics* in the United Kingdom is written: 'the quality of a statistical product can be defined as the fitness for purpose of that product'.

Table 3.1 Dimensions of quality according to D. Garvin (1988).

DIMENSION	DEFINITION
Performance	The primary operating characteristics of a product.
Features	The 'bells and whistles' of a product.
Reliability	The probability that a product will fail within a specified period of time.
Conformance	The degree to which the design or operating characteristics of a product meet pre-established standards.
Durability	The amount of use a product can sustain before it physically deteriorates to the point where replacement is preferable to repair.
Serviceability	The speed, courtesy, competence and ease of repair.
Aesthetics	The look, feel, taste, smell and sound of a product.
Perceived Quality	The impact of brand name, company image and advertising.

Table 3.2 Dimensions of quality according to R. Russell and B. Taylor (2005).

DIMENSION	DEFINITION
Time & Timeliness	Customer waiting time. On-time completion.
Completeness	Customers get all they ask for.
Courtesy	Treatment by employees.
Consistency	Same level of service for all customers.
Accessibility & Convenience	Ease of obtaining service.
Accuracy	Performed correctly every time.
Responsiveness	Reaction to special circumstances or requests.

Drawing a parallel between quality dimensions in business and information quality dimensions can help to properly frame the debate around the issue. In Table 3.3 below, it is possible to make a useful comparison between category and dimensions.

Above, we have taken into consideration one of the earliest and still most influential categorizations of IQ dimensions made by Wang (1998). One can see a slight discrepancy between the three tables (such as for the dimensions of *accuracy* and *timeliness*, for example) but this gives the measure of how views differ from one to another. Paraphrasing Illari Illari and Floridi (2014), the concern is clear: there is no settled agreement even on the most deeply embedded dimensions and, as a consequence, categorization appears to be

Table 3.3 Comparison between IQ category and IQ dimensions.

Information Quality CATEGORY	Information Quality DIMENSIONS
Intrinsic IQ	Accuracy, objectivity, believability, reputation, relevance.
Accessibility IQ	Access, security.
Contextual IQ	Relevancy, value-added, timeliness, completeness, amount of data.
Representational IQ	Interpretability, ease of understanding, concise representation, consistent representation.

problematic. However, this lack of convergence may not be a problem, but now it is necessary to contextualize at least three dimensions such as those of *objectivity*, *relevance* and *accuracy* in the context of journalism practice.

Pursuing objectivity and quality

In a traditional fashion, the notion of objectivity (Maras, 2013; Ward, 2015) was for a long time closely associated with quality. The former is undoubtedly important when the latter is the goal of newsrooms driven by moral choices (Knowlton & Reader, 2009). The success of delivering objectivity therefore impacts on the overall quality of a specific product, whether it is a TV programme or a newspaper article. We can assume that the greater the objectivity in quality initiative, the easier the decision whether an article is ready to be published or not. However, the concept of objectivity in journalism is far more complex and deeply rooted in its practices and culture.

Michael Schudson argues that 'the belief in objectivity is a faith in "facts", a distrust in "values", and a commitment to their segregation' (1978, p. 6). He said that this concept had fully emerged as a guiding principle by the 1890s. The experience of World War I, and its logic of propaganda, changed the course of the concept. Thus, from the 1920s on, the idea that humans, either individually or collectively, build the reality they deal with has held a central position in social thought and encouraged a more sophisticated ideal of 'objectivity' among journalists (Schudson, 1978).

What is more, as scientific progress acknowledged advancements in each field of science and technology, the notion of 'scientific objectivity' was conceived as freedom from personal biases. According to this view (Wien, 2005), science is objective to the extent that personal biases are absent from scientific reasoning, or that they can be eliminated in a social process. The consequences do not depend on researchers' personal preferences or idiosyn-cratic experiences. That, among other things, is what distinguishes science from the arts, for example.

Objectivity is therefore the most problematic quality criterion because it stimulates associations with a highly controversial philosophical concept as Figure 3.3 shows. However, there are ways of deconstructing the objectivity concept in more concrete terms, which are linked to rules of everyday practice in journalism, as Westerstahl (1983) has demonstrated.

A first-level subdivision of objectivity (Figure 3.4) makes a distinction between *factuality* and *impartiality*. While the former can be further differenti-ated into the aspects of *truth* and *relevance*, the latter comprises the aspects of balance (or non-partisanship) and of neutral presentation.

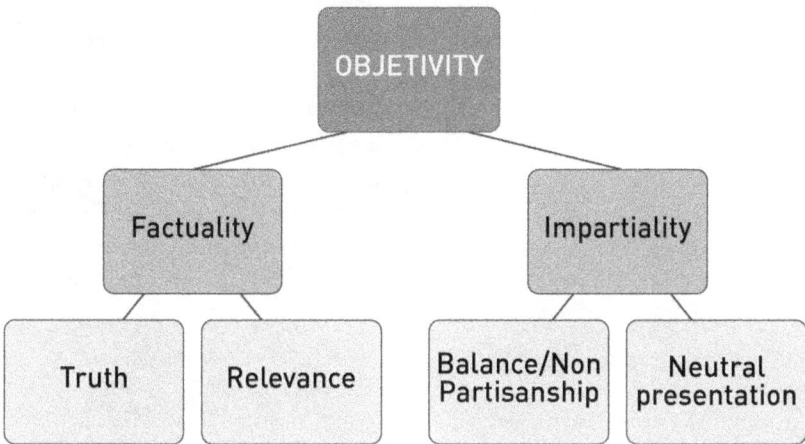

Figure 3.3 Features of objectivity.

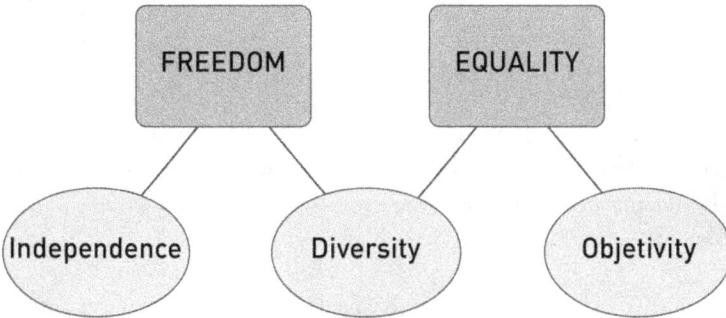

Figure 3.4 First-level subdivision of objectivity.

Figure 3.4 shows the logical interrelations of these concepts. *Independence*, *diversity* and *objectivity* are abstract norms and they are also, to a certain degree, interconnected with each other (Wien, 2005).

In this sense, 'independence' has two meanings: independence *from* and independence *for*. The former includes not only independence from the state but also from pressure groups, advertisers and the owners of mass media. The latter means, above all, independence for advocacy and for taking a 'watchdog' role.

On the other hand, 'diversity' comprises two aspects, which are partly interdependent: diversity of content and diversity of access. Diversity (or plurality) of content relates to several different dimensions, like opinions, topics, issues, persons and groups, and geographic regions. The demand of diversity of access means that all relevant social groups and political actors must have access to mass media. Two different principles are considered: equal access and proportional access. Equal access means that each group receives equal attention in the media, in terms of space or time. Proportional access means that the attention is allocated according to the importance or size of different groups in reality.

We will later in the book show how these two principles are pivotal for statistical information, principles that play a crucial role in election campaigns when the attention given to different political parties in the news and in election broadcasts is a critical matter (Wien, 2005). Objectivity and its fundamentals and its meaning for journalism will be summarized in the next paragraph.

Scientific methods in journalism

The first course in journalism was set at the University of Missouri in the United States, and the first trade union of journalists was founded in England; the discipline resembled to a great extent what Elizabeth Blanks Hindman in *Spectacles of the Poor* (1998) calls 'mainstream journalism', which according to Wien (2005) remains the type of journalism the vast majority of journalists perform today:

> Mainstream Journalism is represented by professional norms and uses certain techniques of news-gathering and construction. A mainstream journalist tries to be objective, remains distant from her or his subject, finds information in official places, and presents that information in particular ways. (Hindman, 1998, p. 177)

The modern scientific breakthrough and the growing complexity of society brought new questions for those 'particular ways through which information is presented' (Hindman, 1998, p. 178).

According to Walter Lippman – as summarized by Henrik Petersen (2003) – 'the general citizenry had neither the time, the ability nor the inclination to inform itself on important questions [...] The remedy had to be boards of experts who could distill the evidence and offer the residue facts'. Those experts could be those *inforgs* (Floridi, 2010), namely journalists, who are able to acquire certain information about specific topics. The idea is that if journalists borrow most of their tools from the scientific methodological toolbox, they can declare themselves as having the same degree of objectivity as scientists. Richard Streckfuss explains the reason why Lippmann argued that journalism should utilize scientific methods in order to achieve objectivity:

> Lippmann's usage of the words objective, science, and scientific are significant. Adapting scientific method for human affairs, including journalism, was central to the thought of the decade. [...] Objective reporting, as he [Lippmann] envisioned it, would not create passive justification for the status quo, as is often assumed now. Those advancing the idea of applying scientific methods to human affairs – in all areas, not just journalism – were political liberals. They attempted to create a system of values using scientific method, borrowing from the philosophy of pragmatism expounded by William James and its variant, instrumentalism, set forth by John Dewey. (Streckfuss, 1990, p. 979)

With the clear connection to the positivist scientific ideal, one could have expected that the 'lippmannian' attempt to save and improve the journalistic concept of objectivity would be quietly forgotten. To a certain degree, it may be argued that this seems not to have been the case – Philip Meyer is widely cited for having invented precision journalism. Meyer (2002) observed that

> A better solution is to push journalism toward science, incorporating both the powerful data-gathering and -analysis tools of science and its disciplined search for verifiable truth. This is not a new idea. Walter Lippmann noted seventy years ago that journalism depends on the availability of the objectifiable objects [...] Scientific method offers a way to make happenings objectified, measured and named. (2002, p. 4)

Later, Meyer noted that precision journalism 'means treating journalism as if it were science, adopting scientific method, scientific objectivity and scientific ideals to entire process of mass communication' (2002, p. 5). Meyer points out that the social science methodological apparatus should include statistical data processing. As Wien argues, Meyer's book is an easy-to-read version of a textbook in statistics and much more, we should add.

Paraphrasing Meyer, in pursuing objectivity beyond objectivity precision journalism demonstrates the applicability of social science research methods to the very real problems of newsgathering in an increasingly complex society. It produces work that both the researchers and the craft people could appreciate. The tools of sampling, computer analysis and statistical inference increased the traditional power of the reporter without changing the nature of his or her mission: 'to find the facts, to understand them and to explain them without wasting time' (Meyer 2002, p. 3).

However, in Meyer's idea, the objectivity model was designed for a simpler world, a world still untouched by the deluge of data that the Internet has brought in less than a decade. According to Wien, during the 1960s American journalism failed to meet the essence of the concept and the consequent frustration led the media to embrace a 'new journalism', which freed journalists from the constraints of objectivity by granting them artistic licence to become *storytellers*, but this was exactly what Philip Meyer feared, as the following suggests:

This [failure] pushes journalism toward art. Its problem is that journalism requires discipline, and the discipline of art may not be the most appropriate kind. A better solution is to push journalism toward science, incorporating both the powerful data-gathering and – analysis tools of science and its disciplined search for verifiable truth. (2002, p. 4)

Following the first edition of *Precision Journalism*, in 1989 the physicist Lawrence Cranberg said: 'journalism itself is a science, and a properly qualified, responsible journalist is a practicing scientist' (1989, p. 47). As a matter of fact, knowing what to do with data and information is the essence of the new precision journalism. The problem may be thought of as having two phases: the input phase, where data is collected and analysed, and the output phase, where the data is prepared for entry into the reader's mind. This point will be useful later in our work when discussing our data. Journalists who adopt the two phases and adapt the tools of scientific methods to their own work can be in a position, Meyer assures us, 'to make useful evaluation with the more powerful objectivity of science' (2002, p. 10).

The positivist ideal seems to pervade both precision journalism and computer-assisted reporting (Wien, 2005), and this is perhaps the most important philosophical point made so far. Great emphasis is placed on instructing and training journalists in the use of the computer, still a sore point when it comes to journalism courses in the United Kingdom and continental Europe. Even though in a newly revised edition of *Precision Journalism* the emphasis is

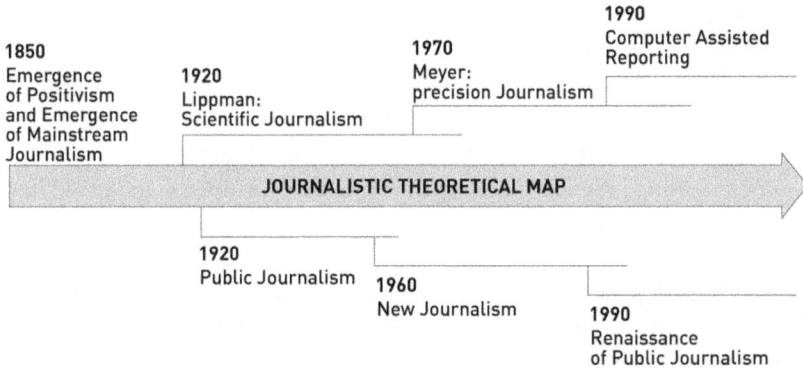

Figure 3.5 Theoretical map (Westherstal, 1983).

placed more on scientific methods, while the computer aspect is downplayed, the importance of the relationship between journalists and computer language processes still remains a hot topic not sufficiently addressed by academia. The map shown in Figure 3.5 exemplifies the theoretical schools of journalism and how they developed over a century.

Rosenberg (2008) enriches the debate further by introducing the concept of pragmatism in journalism, first developed by American philosopher and logician Charles Saunders Pierce. Pragmatism was particularly important because it did not consider science as a realm apart that could dictate what we had to accept. On the contrary, pragmatism cast science as common sense made more rigorous and systematic, but still, fundamentally, common sense.

Rosenberg believes that the key to all of this was that pragmatism said we have to evaluate things in terms of how well they work *in relation to a given purpose*, and did not presume to dictate which purposes were legitimate and which were not:

> Science itself does not have a single purpose. It has one purpose when we are trying to form a hypothesis, and an altogether different process when we are trying to test that hypothesis. 'Seek truth' and 'shun error' are two sharply contrasting imperatives, each with its own logic, shared with a myriad of other, non-scientific endeavours, a vast multitude of which are simple, everyday, mundane. (2008, p. 32)

The two approaches of Positivism and Pragmatism had direct consequences for journalism. Beginning with an example: the status of expert knowledge and how lay people relate to it are taken to follow the *prototypical model* of the scientist/layperson duality:

> If one takes the positivist approach, the scientists are priest-like figures with special access to truth, and the same is true of all the experts whose understanding journalists rely on to create true pictures of the world, in order to explain it to the masses. (Rosenberg, 2008, p. 34)

These contrasting views on the nature of knowledge translated into the nature of journalism are at the core of a great debate between Walter Lippmann and John Dewey. On one hand, Lippmann (*Public Opinion*, 1922, then 1948) argued that it was an expert-guided process, in which journalists relied on experts to set the parameters for the great mass of people. It describes a process in which unquestioned knowledge flows down from above.

On the other hand, Dewey argues that it is a process in which questions rise up from below. In Dewey's viewpoint (*The Public and Its Problems*, 1927; *The Quest for Certainty*, 1929), there is no division between facts and opinions, but neither is there pretence that some are purely factual, while others are 'trapped' in mere opinion: 'we all have partial knowledge, we all are embedded in our points of view, but we can all gain a broader understanding by engaging in a common quest for understanding' (Rosenberg, 2015, p. 37). The debate lies at the foundation of the 'idea' of journalism itself, but at the same time it is a sort of archaeological showcase where the great concepts dear to journalism are displayed.

Over the years, society and technology have changed quickly, together with old views. We are living in the hyperhistory[8] now, as stated by Luciano Floridi, and the roles of journalism practices and journalism business have also changed dramatically in less than a decade. Indeed, looking at journalism through the lenses of the Philosophy of Information (PI) could cast both a vivid and a renewed light on the main concepts at the heart of the journalistic profession and at the same time complement and integrate old views with new ones. In the next chapter we will try to explain in detail how the PI might contribute to enrich the debate on quality journalism.

----

[8] According to Luciano Floridi, humanity has passed through three ages of development: prehistory, history and hyperhistory. In prehistory there are no Information and Communication Technologies (ICTs); in history there are ICTs, which record and transmit information, but human societies depend mainly on kinds of technologies concerning primary resources and energy; in hyperhistory, there are ICTs, which record, transmit and, above all, process information, increasingly autonomously, and human societies become vitally dependent on them and on information as a fundamental resource in order to flourish.

Chapter 4

STATISTICS IN JOURNALISM PRACTICE AND PRINCIPLE

There seems to be uniqueness to the logic of journalists' way of thinking. That is, news reporters have their own way of interpreting the world outside and developing a close system upon which social reality is constructed in the public sphere. The power of journalism as a political institution to define the terms of reference for discursive regimes and narratives that frame people, places and events has been analysed and dissected by sociologists, media scholars and political scientists. However, insufficient engagement has happened with logic and cognitive psychology, which we believe is essential in the analysis regarding the use of statistics in the context of journalism.

To be sure, early calls by Holly Stocking and Paget Gross (1989) highlighted the failure of journalism studies to employ research by cognitive psychologists with regard to the kinds of errors and biases that can negatively alter the processing of information. According to Stocking and Gross, there is a lack of academic research that looks explicitly at the way journalists mentally process information when reporting and gathering the news because there are a number of specific errors and biases that 'have been found in a variety of professions across a variety of tasks' as well (Josephi, 2009).

Interestingly, if errors and biases are examined from the perspective of cognitive psychology, several of the errors and biases are also studied in the branch of philosophy known as Logic. Philosophy of Information also belongs to this branch. As Elliot Cohen writes:

> Since the latter discipline is directly concerned with providing standards for assessing the adequacy of reasoning, it may prove helpful to keep in mind certain of its fundamental concepts [*sic*]. Reasoning itself can be understood as a process of making inference. That is, when people reason, they come to conclusions on the basis of evidence. (1985, p. 7)

In information processing, factors like prejudices, prior expectations, values, poor insight, visual conditions and emotional stress affect the 'quality' of this inferential reasoning. Stocking and Gross are clear in warning journalists about committing 'the eyewitness fallacy', that is, the fallacy of overestimating the reliability of eyewitness reports as compared with other sources of information.

In Logic there are three kinds of inferences (Minnameier, 2010). Firstly, *deduction*, known as 'top-down' logic, is the process of reasoning from one or more general statements (premises) to reach a certain logical conclusion. Secondly, *induction* is a reasoning in which the premises supply strong evidence for the truth of the conclusion. While the conclusion of a deductive argument is supposed to be certain, the truth of an inductive argument is supposed to be probable, based upon the evidence given. Finally, *abduction* is a form of logical inference that goes from observation to a hypothesis that accounts for the reliable data (observation) and seeks to explain relevant evidence. In abductive reasoning, unlike in deductive reasoning, the premises do not guarantee the conclusion. The fields of law, computer science and artificial intelligence research have renewed interest in the subject of abduction. Diagnostic expert systems frequently employ abduction.

Stocking and Gross (1989) articulate their analysis in seven steps: (1) underutilization of statistics, (2) confirmation bias, (3) misperceptions of risk, (4) sample errors and biases, (5) misunderstanding of regression, (6) hindsight bias and (7) illusory correlation. In particular, 'underutilization of statistics' clarifies to some extent people's tendency to give more weight to eyewitness accounts more than other types of evidence. In so doing people tend to favour anecdotal or case history information over base rate statistical information. The reason why people favour anecdotal information over base rate information still remains unclear.

What the study of Stocking and Gross suggests for journalists who routinely use anecdotes to 'personalise' the news is a need to handle anecdotal information with considerable caution:

> Some sources are masters of the anecdote. Intentionally or unintentionally, they may present anecdotal data that do not square with more abstract statistical information. If reporters fall victim to the tendency to favour vivid anecdotal information over pallid but reliable statistics, they, and their audiences in turn, may be misled. (1989, p. 6)

Psychologists such as Nestor and Schutt (2014) conducted research which proved that preconceived ideas can be very powerful in shaping what we see, understand and remember. The tendency for people to seek, select and recall data according to pre-existing expectations or theories is called 'confirmation bias'.

On the other side, Victor Cohen and Lewis Cope (2011) identify five areas where journalists fail: (1) journalists sometimes overstate, oversimplify and over-interpret; (2) journalists work too fast; (3) journalists often omit necessary caution and perspective; (4) seeking balance in reporting a controversial issue, journalists sometimes forget to emphasize where the scientific evidence points; and (5) journalists are influenced by intense competition.

Mathematician Allen Paulos (2013) also highlights two kind of side-effects: the *halo effect* and the *anchoring effect*, which state that the availability error is the tendency for people to make judgements or evaluations in light of the first thing that comes to mind. In other words, there are two reasoning procedures worth describing here. First of all, when people seek information related to one theory, they are resistant to seeking information with respect to another theory at the same time. People test hypotheses one at a time, or sequentially.

Secondly, as people seek information with which to test their hypotheses, they tend to use an acceptance/rejection strategy. For instance, a reporter who has hypothesized that there is a crime wave against the elderly may unconsciously seek out sources that confirm this; the potential and actual elderly victims in a bad part of town or the head of a crime prevention programme for the elderly. In addition, the reporter may ask questions of these sources (about increases in reported crimes, efforts to reduce crimes) that confirm the hypothesis, without asking probing questions that might disprove the hypothesis (Stocking & Gross, 1989).

Expectations may not just influence the sources to which reporters turn and the types of questions a reporter may ask, but they may also influence a journalist's evaluation and selection of data. One pervasive bias in perceivers' decisions about what information is most relevant or credible is the tendency to regard information that is consistent with one's a priori theories as the worthiest pieces of information. Finally, when one is testing a hypothesis between variables, the nature, causes or outcome of an event, the information that will be selected is, in the end, the most useful information coherent with one's theoretical framework.

Ars conjectandi in journalistic performance

Mathematics deals with certainty and statistics deal with uncertainty (Taylor & Pacelli, 2008). It is also widely accepted that journalists work routinely in information overload with uncertainty and time constraints. In this regard, Allen Paulos (2013) is very straightforward in saying that

> Newspapers are daily periodicals dealing with the changing details of everyday life, whereas mathematics is a timeliness discipline concerned with abstract truth. Newspapers deal with mess and contingency and

crime, mathematics with symmetry and necessity and the sublime. The
newspaper reader is everyman, the mathematician an elitist. (2013, p. 3)

Journalists must not only be able to navigate a landscape full of numbers but
also use statistical reasoning skills to make sense of the information they have
to handle. However, statistical literacy along with information literacy[1] 'is
unarguably critical to those who seek to explain scientific ways of knowing to
general audiences' (Dunwoody & Griffin, 2013, p. 529). Definitions of numerical literacy vary widely, but Diana Coben (2000) offers one useful definition:

> To be numerate means to be competent, confident, and comfortable
> with one's judgements on whether to use mathematics in a particular
> situation and if so, what mathematics to use, how to do it, what degree
> of accuracy is appropriate, and what the answer means in relation to the
> context. (2000, p. 35)

Dunwoody and Griffin agree that statistical reasoning[2] comes into play when
an individual meets decision-making situations in the context of incomplete
information. What is more, statistical literacy is viewed by many as distinct
from numeracy:

> Much of statistical reasoning combines ideas about data and chance
> which leads to making inferences and interpreting statistical results.
> Underlying this reasoning is a conceptual understanding of the impor-
> tant ideas, such as distribution, centre, spread, association, uncertainty,
> randomness and sampling. (Garfield, 1998, p. 783)

Other researchers (Gigerenzer et al., 2007) also argue that all citizens should
attain reasonable levels of 'statistical literacy' and take journalists to task for

---

[1] The *Prague Declaration* of 2003 states that Information Literacy 'encompasses knowledge
of one's information concerns and needs, and the ability to identify, locate, evaluate,
organise and efficiently create, use and communicate information to address issues or
problems at hand; it is a prerequisite for participating effectively in the Information
Society, and is part of the basic human right of lifelong learning'.

[2] It is the *ars conjectandi*, which is basically the capacity of doing mathematics without numbers. *La logique, ou l'art de penser*, published in 1713 by Jakob Bernoulli, concerned fundamental combinatorial topics such as his theory of permutations and combinations. The
book is the basis of what is now called the *Law of large numbers*.

communicating risk probabilities in ways easily misperceived by audiences. Garfield agrees on the value of these cognitive skills for 'journalists and science writers, who are interested in how to best explain and critique statistical information in the media' (1998, p. 785).

Victor Cohn and Lewis Cope (2011) point out that 'even when we journalists say we are dealing in facts and ideas, much of what we report is based on numbers' (p. 10). Although systematic evidence is sparse, journalists probably fare no better at either numerical or statistical literacy than do other segments of the population (Josephi, 2009). Yet much of the essential information that underlies today's news reflects decision-making under uncertain conditions.

> The secret language of statistics, so appealing in a fact-minded culture, is employed to sensationalize, inflate, confuse, and oversimplify. Statistical methods and statistical terms are necessary in reporting the mass data of social and economic trends, business conditions, "opinion" polls, the census. But without writers who use the words with honesty and understanding and readers who know what they mean, the result can only be semantic nonsense. (Huff, 1954, p. 6)

The above quote makes clear how the use of statistics in reporting is vital in the life cycle of information news. Since the 1970s we have been witnessing an authentic 'data analysis revolution' that is basically anti-probabilistic, according to Rolf Biehler (1994). John Tukey (1977) expresses the attitude to probability in the American Exploratory Data Analysis tradition as 'data analysis instead of statistics is a name that allows us to use probability where it is needed and avoid it where we should. Data analysis has to analyse real data' (p. 51). Similarly, we can argue that there are two different schools in a type of journalism driven by numbers, one coming from the area of engineering and the other one close to mathematics.

There are basically two cultures of statistical thinking related to considering 'paradigms' in Thomas Kuhn's sense as constitutive of science: 'among others, a paradigm contains techniques and methods, world views, attitudes and exemplars. Exemplars are prototypical examples showing to which cases and how theory is applied' (Kuhn & Hawkins, 1963, p. 45). According to Biehler, *probabilists* do not form such a clear-cut group with shared convictions. On the surface, we find the basic split into *personalists* (subjectivists) and *frequentists* (objectivists). Beneath that surface a rich structure of different meanings can be reconstructed in history and current practice, but a distinction could be made also between *realists* (or objectivists) and *relativists* (or historicists).

This opposition runs through many controversies in the epistemology of sciences, but for statistics it offers some original aspects once it is combined with the former – which distinguishes the languages of sciences and of action – in such a way to make visible four different attitudes in relation to statistical argument. (Desrosières, 1998, p. 336)

From a journalistic perspective, it would be meaningful for future research in this area focusing on these four different attitudes in relation to statistical arguments; something we will attempt to do over the following chapters. That is because, according to Alain Desrosières (1998), the realistic position postulates that there are objective things, existing independently of observers and exceeding singular contingencies:

This is, typically, the language of Quetelet: there are regularities and stable relationships. Statistics aims at 'approaching reality'. It sets itself problems of 'reliability of measurement'. [...] But, while remaining in the language of science, it is possible to reconstruct a genesis, and the social practices that have led to a solid statistical object. There are historical and social processes of constructing and solidifying equivalences and mental schemes. It is up to science to reconstitute them, by describing how social facts become things, through customs, law, or social struggles. The language of this position is that of social history, or of a constructivist sociology of knowledge. (1998, p. 336)

Probabilists led to the Probabilistic Revolution which summarizes the probabilistic developments in the sciences in the period between 1800 and 1930. The history of the Probabilistic Revolution (Romizi, 2012) is an interesting counterpart to the Data Analysis revolution that began in the 1970s (Biehler, 1994) because it is precisely in this historical stage that precision journalism is located, which is a type of journalism that bases its investigations on statistical analysis. Philip Meyer's words, the founding father of precision journalism, are significant to understand the change in journalism practice since the Probabilistic Revolution occurred:

It is the things that vary that interest us. Things that do not vary are inherently boring. [...] News writers and policy makers alike are always wondering how much of the variation is caused by heredity and how much by environment, whether it can be changed, and whether it correlates with such things as athletic ability, ethnic category, birth order, and other interesting variables. Variance, then, makes news. And in any statistical analysis, the first thing we generally want to know is whether the phenomenon we are studying is a variable, and, if so, how much and in what way it varies. Once we have that figured out, we are usually interested in finding the sources of the variance. Ideally, we would hope to find what causes the variance. (Meyer, 2002, p. 43)

Both journalism and science make use of statistical techniques to – in most cases – find causal, not casual, relationships. In such application of statistical methods, Meyer recommends a humble approach where 'modesty' seems to naturally lead to those 'unexplained variances' that make the journalistic quest for truth 'romantic'. How romanticism goes hand in hand with logical reasoning and statistics, Meyer does not say.

However, if we read the ancient Roman poet Virgil, it can be said that the 'meyerian' statistical reasoning applied to journalism helps to find 'the causes of things' (Gale, 2000), that *rerum cognoscere causas* aims at discovering the inherent and interesting variance of things because it is the variance itself that makes news, and particularly unexplained variance in any interpretation. In this sense, it becomes evident how revolutionary, profoundly positivist and thought provoking Meyer's message is.

To this definition we prefer to add the reflections given by Daniel Dorling (1999) who is one of the founders of the UK-based think-tank Radical Statistics. He specifies that

Statistics are a social product. [...] In a simple sense, statistics are a social product simply because they are produced by people. But they are also firmly located in the aims and tensions of the societies that produce them – whether expressed by organisations of government, trade or campaigns. In literature it is said that every text has a context. With statistics it is not just that what is discovered depends on the society from which those numbers are drawn [*sic*]. (1999, p. 48)

The viewpoint that social statistics are a product of their sociocultural context is widely applied in academic research. On the same line of thought, scholars Dot Griffiths, John Irvine and Ian Miles (1979) in *Demystifying Social Statistics* distinguish four different approaches of statistical practice and, more generally, scientific practice. Two approaches worth citing here are social responsibility and radical science.

The first approach sees statistics 'as ethically neutral, asocial, bodies of knowledge and techniques: they could be used for good purposes or abused for bad ones' (p. 68). This seems a widespread attitude among statisticians themselves: 'socially responsible statisticians argue for appropriate codes of practice for statistical work, aiming to limit the political misuse of statistics' (p. 68).

The second approach is called 'radical science', which recognizes the achievement of social responsibility in attaining changes to statistical policy or practice, and highlights that if statistics are a product of society, then they will never be neutral: 'they cannot be ignored nor can they be substantially changed unless society itself changed' (p. 69).

When dealing with statistics, on one end of the spectrum, we have the Meyerian modesty that adopts caution whereas at the other end of the spectrum we have 'radicality' in its social declination. On both ends, journalists and scientists alike are asked by society at large to act and make decisions, two approaches that indeed are not only apparently incompatible but surprisingly coexist with those tensions that our work attempts to bring to the surface.

Statistical agencies as information providers

Emeritus professor in information science at the University of California, Marcia Bates (1989), compared the actions of someone searching for information to those of someone picking berries:

> The metaphor of 'information landscape' and the conflation of information searching with nourishment seeking led to the emergence of several food-based metaphors, which were put forward to help researchers understand the problems of searching. (Olcott, 2012, p. 155)

This metaphor led other researchers to draw further outcomes. According to an analyst in open source information, Anthony Olcott (2012), information can be compared to food since for most creatures it is clumpy, with large empty or non-productive spaces in between areas where their food may be found, animals – compared to users – were found to engage in a constant struggle to strike the best balance among different variables.

Of the same opinion is Peter Pirolli (2007), 'founding father' of the Information Foraging Theory, who points out that 'the optimal forager is the one who has the strategies, mechanisms, diets, and so forth, that maximize the calories per unit of effort expended' (p. 31). By this analogy, the optimal information forager is one who maximizes the value of knowledge gained per unit cost of transaction.

Statistical agencies, one can argue, behave as information foragers and we think that the *statistical information = food* metaphor offers some suggestive elements to be considered. Interestingly, *some berries = statistical information* are available openly; others are kept under confidentiality agreements, considering confidentiality 'in terms of the tension between the rights of the respondent and the public's "right to know"' (Dale, 1999, p. 86).

In the current state of affairs, dissemination of official statistical information requires consumers. Such a simple statement can make the complex process of providing and using official statistics sound rather like selling berries: 'many national statistical institutes (NSIs) now have marketing sections that do indeed mimic many of the functions of the retail sector, although the extent to which the activity truly is marketing is debatable' (Blakemore, 1999, p. 61). Statistical agencies and governments are deeply intertwined. Government statistics, by their nature, address existing government policies. Therefore, governments and other bodies can decide to commission statistics 'as a means of doing nothing, or to give an image of doing something' (Dorling & Simpson, 1999, p. 34).

Officially, a fundamental role of the statistical agencies (Swanson & Van Dijk, 2006) is to provide relevant statistical information on the economic and social conditions of a country and its citizens. They represent the most trusted sources used by journalists. This activity is important to an open, democratic society, whether for developing government policy, making business decisions or helping individual citizens make their daily economic choices or in shaping news.

It can be suggested that their raison d'être lies in the production of high-quality and timely statistical information. Their effectiveness depends on its credibility, the relevance of their information, the *accuracy* and *accessibility* of their products and services, the attainment of high professional standards and the control of the burden on citizens as respondents to the specific surveys. Such information about the state, which is gathered by the state for policy purposes, is essential to enable citizens to evaluate government activities:

> Terms such as the 'information commons' hark back to the days when villagers could graze animals on common land which was a resource freely available to all. The 'information commons' are deemed to be analogous, all citizens having the right to access, process and analyse information. The 'information commons' are further protected in the USA through the freedom of information policy, which in essence states that all government information is to be accessible by citizens unless the information is explicitly deemed to be secret, sensitive or confidential. (Blakemore, 1999, p. 62)

These agencies publish and disseminate statistical information in a wide variety of forms and channels, and the media outlets play a crucial role in informing citizens about the latest release of official statistics. Most citizens get their statistical information from the media. The extent to which the agencies can gain access to the news media and communicate effectively through them has an enormous impact on how well they can inform the general population.

In other words, it is in the interest of these agencies to make every effort to ensure that the media report accurately and in a timely fashion on their news releases. Reports in the media have one objective to inform the general public about the population, society, economy and culture of the nation. This information will guide them in doing their jobs, raising their families, making purchases and in making a multitude of other decisions; and to demonstrate the relevance of the agencies to the government and the general public, so that they can anticipate greater public support for their programmes, as well as improve respondent relations and greater visibility of their products and services. To obtain media coverage, the agencies must develop a working relationship with journalists who are very much the 'gatekeepers' of access and meaning between statistical agencies and the general public. Most journalists recognize these agencies as a major news source. The clearer the communication to journalists, the more likely they will provide positive, accurate and informative coverage, not only of the data but the appropriate interpretation.

Therefore, it can be suggested that the main challenges of statistical agencies would be: (1) to prepare press releases which are understandable to journalists and thus understandable to the general public as the ultimate audience; and (2) to create an ongoing working relationship with journalists to ensure that they remain interested in reporting on such releases.

Two types of journalists may cover a statistical agency. There are 'beat' reporters who have expertise in fields such as business and economics – and are probably statistically literate – and there are reporters who are general news journalists. These latter individuals do not regularly cover an agency's releases and may not have expertise in any particular field such as economics. Consequently, they are probably not statistically literate.

In the context of informing the public through the media, 'statistical literacy' clearly implies the ability to understand the implications of the released statistical information. The challenge is therefore to ensure journalists get the story 'straight' and report the analysis in a statistically correct way. Consequently, it is beneficial that journalists have a certain degree of statistical literacy without being required to have a degree in statistics. In this regard, the study conducted by Sharon Dunwoody and Robert J. Griffin (2013) gives a very interesting insight, even if limited to the situation in Germany.

All things considered, the role of a statistical agency is not to create statisticians out of journalists, but to help journalists in whatever way possible to do their job. Today journalists face tremendous time constraints and do not have the capacity to analyze raw data independently, and to make things worse, reduced editorial budgets have made 'beat' journalists, who can build up specialized knowledge, a declining phenomenon.

Joel Best (2012) is very cautious in illustrating the problem, and he addresses the issue in a more opaque way. He presents a series of case studies of the way in which mass media report statistics so that social problems are constructed and sustained. Best argues that only by understanding certain regular ways in which journalists behave, and thereby improving quantitative literacy, can the general public have/obtain an informed and appropriately critical view of statistical data relating to public issues.

Best identifies 'number laundering' as a key feature of the media reporting of statistics. Here, a number appearing in one news report becomes a source for everyone interested in the social problem it describes: 'Its origins as someone's best guess are now forgotten and, through repetition, it comes to be treated as a straightforward fact' (Best, 2012, p. 35). But how exactly is this information gathered by journalists? One of the ways to gather information both in the United States and in the United Kingdom is through their Freedom of Information Acts. The Freedom of Information Act of the United States was introduced in 1966, becoming law on 4th July 1967. According to the *United States Department of Justice Guide to the Freedom of Information Act*, it 'firmly established an effective statutory right of public access to executive branch information in the federal government'.

Likewise, the UK's Freedom of Information Act 2000, which came into full force on 1 January 2005, extended the right of access by the public (individual or corporate) to information held by public authorities. In both cases, essentially every item of information must be made available on request (and on payment of an appropriate handling fee) unless it is specifically excluded from coverage, although:

> Of course, the acts do not apply to private bodies. Indeed, it is in the interests of competition between such bodies that they can keep their commercial data confidential. For this reason, and because of the universal use of electronic means of transferring data, sophisticated data encryption schemes are used. (Hand, 2007, p. 226)

In order to run efficiently, governments need to collect data about their people. Many other information-foraging bodies and governmental subsidiaries also need to make use of this data. However, business, people and other organizations will often only divulge data if they can be sure that it will remain confidential. This can pose a problem because this need for confidentiality requires some complicated legal manoeuvres. An alternative is to adjust the data to try to make it impossible to discover information about individuals. This topic is of particular concern for journalists who deal with statistical data analysis.

Leon Willenborg and Ton de Waal (2001) are experts in such 'adjustment' of data, defining *disclosure control* as 'the discipline concerned with the modification of statistical data, containing confidential information about individual entities such as persons, households, businesses, etc. in order to prevent third parties working with these data to recognise individuals in the data and thereby disclose information about these individuals' (p. 1). There would be little point in 'modifying' the data to the extent that it became useless for its intended 'fitness for purpose'. Measures of *information loss* are used to quantify the extent to which a particular adjustment compromises the quality of the information-forage, but unfortunately these measures are often an unfamiliar process for journalists. In conclusion, whatever way one looks at it, the current situation is just the same as with progress in any other scientific or technological area: progress cannot be stopped. All one can do is attempt to steer it in morally and ethically proper directions. American Congressman Jerrold Nadler made the same point when he appeared before the US Technology and Privacy Advisory Committee in November 2003 noting that 'the question isn't whether technology will be developed, but rather whether it will be used wisely'. This wisdom must be the priority for both statistical agencies and journalists in order to better serve the public interest.

Statistics as rhetorical device

On a conclusive note of this chapter, we deem it important to highlight the image of the journalist who deals with statistics can be conceived as a mixture of an honest lawyer and a good storyteller, with the virtues of a good detective. Putting these things together suggests that the purpose of statistics is to organize a useful argument from quantitative evidence using a form of rhetoric. Rhetoric in journalism, as well as in statistical presentation, is unavoidable and indeed acceptable as soon as it involves public participation, which is in its essence the formation of the idea of democracy. Journalists inside and outside schools or academies are concerned with encouraging public participation, bringing to life the 'publics' of 'public affairs'. Such concerns are especially apparent in the public or civic journalistic movement and its research.

Sociological approaches to journalism such as those represented in Dan Berkowitz's *Social Meanings of News* (1997) share same commonalities with rhetorical perspectives on writing processes, discourse communities, and scientific and technical discourse. These demonstrate the congeniality of several approaches to the study of communication processes and genres across disciplines (Dorling & Simpson, 1999). Whether statistics are used as stylistic devices or a rhetorical means that contribute to a melodramatic picture of the world (Abeslon, 2012) or to improve story credibility (Koetsenruijter, 2011), the purpose of this chapter is to locate the field of statistics with respect to rhetorical and journalistic narrative, numerical and narrative forms, 'figures of speech' and 'figures of arithmetic', as in one formulation from the 1830s. Moreover, numbers and narratives have maintained throughout history not just a complementary relationship as vehicles of persuasion, but also a strong antagonism over numerical and narrative modes of aggregation that manifest in forms of social realism. In conclusion, the central theme of this chapter is that quality statistical information involves arguments that convey an interesting and credible point.

The general public distrust statistics because media manipulation often confuses them with misleading statistical claims (Hutton, 2010; Nobels & Schiff, 2007). Politicians, for example, quote economic statistics (Avakov, 2010; Sabillon, 2005; Ullah, 1998), whereas their challengers cite evidence of coming bankruptcies and ruin. When people lie with words, the public can hypothetically detect false words with more ease than deceitful statistics, but blaming statistics themselves is neither reasonable nor useful.

When statistical analysis is carried out responsibly, public scepticism undermines its potentially useful application. A more mature response would be to learn enough about statistics to be able to discriminate between honest and clueless conclusions. From this consideration stems the importance of teaching statistics (Gelman & Nolan, 2017; Hulsizer & Woolf, 2009) that is also able to deepen the argumentative nature of statistical claims (Van Eemeren & Grootendorst, 2004).

According to Robert Abelson (2012), in the media we find the statistical claims that can be summarized in the following six points. First one being, 'stand-alone statistics' which comes in making a claim with an isolated number in which lies the problem that the audience may have no context with which to assess the meaning of the figure and the assertion containing it. Second, the 'simple comparison' used to make a point that is at all meaningful, statistical presentations must refer to differences between observations and expectation, or differences among observations. Third, 'standards of comparison', given a single statistic, many different observations or expectations may be used as standards of comparison: what is compared with what may have a substantial influence on the question asked and the answer given. The fourth is to 'choose among candidate explanations' which applies to any observed comparative difference and to choose from several possible candidate explanations that may occur to the investigator. In a given case, this set of explanations may include accounts varying widely in their substance and generality, ranging from a dismissal of the observed difference as a fluke or an artificial triviality to claims that the observations support or undermine some broad theoretical position.

It is the task of data analysis and statistical inference to help guide the choice among the candidate explanations. The chosen explanation becomes a claim.

Then there is also the fifth, the 'systematic versus chance explanations'. Indeed, to understand the nature of statistical argument, we must consider what types of explanation qualify as answers to certain questions. One characteristic type, the chance explanation, is expressed in statements such as 'these results could easily be due to chance' or 'a random model adequately fits the data'. Indeed, statistical inference is rare among scientific logics in being forced to deal with chance explanations as alternatives or additions to systematic explanations. Finally, we have the 'exaggeration of systematic factors'. This is applicable as journalists usually overestimate the influence of systematic factors relative to chance factors. To conclude, journalists exaggerate their ability to predict the behaviour of other people, and they have difficulty thinking statistically about human beings.

Chapter 5

THE NORMATIVE IMPORTANCE OF 'QUALITY' IN JOURNALISM

The assumptions that quality can be only asserted through numbers hold both within journalism and government. Particularly, as these numbers bring a sense of impartial and objective assessment to both formulate and evaluate policies. Moreover, at the centre of this assumption is the deep-rooted belief that statistics can bring about the type of scientific-based knowledge, transparency and trust needed to implement and analyse government policy. Nowhere was this more evident than during the Tony Blair-led New Labour government in the United Kingdom (1997–2001), when evidence-based policy became central to the way politicians sold their own agendas to the public (Hope, 2004, 2005). To be sure, the Command Paper[1] released under the title *Statistics: A Matter of Trust* (1998) made it clear that

> Quality needs to be assured. Official statistics must be sufficiently accurate and reliable for the purposes for which they are required. The production and presentation of official statistics needs to be free from political interference, and to be seen as such, so that the objectivity and impartiality of statistics is assured. (1998, p. 5)

In this sense, the UK Statistics Authority has adopted a structure broadly similar to that of the *European Code*, which sets out a number of high-level principles, each of which is further amplified by a series of more detailed practices (or 'indicators' in the European Code). Also, the UK *Code of Practice for Official Statistics*[2] and the assessment programme that follows have been

---

[1] Command Papers are considered by the UK government to be of interest to Parliament but are not required to be presented by law.

[2] See http://www.statisticsauthority.gov.uk/reports---correspondence/reports/report-2.pdf (accessed on 14 August 2020).

informed by, and are consistent with, both the *UN Fundamental Principles of Official Statistics*[3] and the *European Statistics Code of Practice*.[4]

According to Mark Pont, member of the board of directors of the UK Statistics Authority, the *European Code* has proved an effective basis for the international process of 'peer review' and 'the Statistics Authority believes that a similar approach will provide a sound foundation for the Statistics Authority's quality assessment function' (Code of Practice: 8). One of the strong points of the *Code* is its emphasis on the role of the user, and the need for statistical producers to consider the wider use that is – or may be – made of statistics. In addition to meeting specific policy needs within government, there is increasing demand by people working in research, academia and journalism for statistics in many aspects of social and economic life. This is the reason why official statistics should meet the high expectations of civil society without the propagandistic use made by politicians or elites. With regards to this, the *Code* is clear:

> Statistics must be as accurate and reliable as they reasonably can be, and free from political interference. In addition, they must also be planned to meet the future needs of society, and communicated in ways that are as helpful as possible to those who rely on them to inform their decisions. (*Code of Practice for Official Statistics*)

The strategy consultation paper *Measuring Quality as Part of Public Service Output*[5] substantiates this point further by urging that 'independent, authoritative and reliable information and methodologies are needed, in an area of political and public interest' (p. 15) and Mark Pont clarifies that:

> The term 'user' of statistics is used here to mean any organisation or person whose decisions or actions are beneficially influenced by official statistics; and similarly, 'potential user' is anyone who might be so influenced. This need not mean that the user directly inspects statistics or performs calculations. It may be more a matter of being influenced by messages derived from the statistics. For example, if crime statistics suggest that thefts are deemed to be a use of statistics; and such uses create

[3] See http://unstats.un.org/unsd/dnss/gp/FP-New-E.pdf (accessed on 14 August 2020).

[4] See http://ec.europa.eu/eurostat/documents/3859598/5921861/KS-32-11-955-EN.PDF (accessed on 14 August 2020).

[5] See http://www.ons.gov.uk/ons/guide-method/ukcemga/about-ukcemga/consultations/measuring-quality-as-part-of-public-service-output.pdf (accessed on 14 August 2020).

their own demand for statistical data to be available in particular forms and levels of detail. The interpretation is central to the Code. (2010, p. 4)

We employ the term 'user of statistics' to mean the ultimate consumer of statistical information (Gal & Ograjenšek, 2010; Taleb, 2007). In fact, the 'users of statistics' are both journalists and readers: the journalists when they manage official statistics and use them as primary sources; the readers as they consume statistical information provided by news reporting. Both are 'beneficially influenced' by using official statistics.

Normatively speaking, journalism and statistics share the same goal of serving the public interest. Both journalism and statistics claim normatively to provide objective and balanced information that can inform both the public and leaders in the process of designing, implementing and scrutinizing public policy. The interplay between journalism and statistics has to be assessed within the broader context of the interaction between professional news reporting approaches and practices and the incorporation of social science methods and methodology into news gathering and production.

In this sense, social scientists, more than journalists, have given special attention to refining their techniques of observation (Meyer, 2002). Indeed, one of the major criticisms sometimes made of social science is an excessive focus on the development of observation techniques and an underestimation of basic leading theory and questions. However, because social scientists have spent so much time improving and strengthening their techniques of observation and quantification, journalism can effectively borrow such techniques in order to increase the quality, accuracy and credibility of news reporting (Fawcett, 1993). In short, what has come to be called 'precision journalism' is the adaptation of such social science quantitative techniques to news reporting, the kind of journalism under analysis in this book.

Having said that, statistics have historically been used also – in daily news gathering practice – to underpin consensus around arguments and ideas expressed in the news. They have served the function of reinforcing rhetorical persuasion and not just informing and explaining issues to the public. Hence, journalists use these numbers to underpin and legitimize their own narratives as they advance in their stories.[6]

---

[6] According to the BBC Academy of Journalism: 'Journalists may sometimes breach an individual's legitimate expectation of privacy because it is in the public interest to tell people what they are doing – they may be corrupt, or anti-social. Incompetent or unethical doctors, plumbers – even journalists – can be a danger to the public. Indeed, the debate about the boundary between legitimate journalism and intrusion into the private life of individuals, and what might be justified in the public interest, has rarely been so

It is precisely in this context that 'quality' comes into play in defining journalism standards, that is, in its ability to accurately offer values, judgements and information that improve the overall democratic process and encourage civic engagement with public policy. If well, modern journalism as a social practice aims to 'assess' those in power it does so to underpin legitimacy and ultimately harbour trust from the public. This is not to say of course that everything in public policy can or should be measured, but to highlight that journalism's ability to evaluate outputs is at the core of its relationship with society in playing the role of 'watchdog' of power.

Trust is crucial in this exchange and is becoming particularly relevant in the era of mediatized politics and society (Hepp, 2013; Hjarvard, 2008). In the introduction to *Number and Numbers* (2008), philosopher Alain Badiou notes the abundance of statistics in contemporary Western societies and that this is in part due to the fact that 'the ideology of modern parliamentary societies, if they have one, is not humanism, law or the subject. It is numbers, the countable, countability' (Badiou, 2008, p. 32). He also noted that 'we live in the era of number's despotism' (Badiou & Sedofsky, 1994), which means we have become incapable of posing abstract questions concerning freedom, justice and the true nature of citizenship, something that journalism has the duty to question and 'assess' as 'watchdog' of the powerful.

Thinking in terms of what is countable and measurable became the prototype for truthful discourse, and it determined the scope of the quest for the perfectibility of human society. According to Armand Mattelart (2003), 'the idea of a society governed by information is inscribed, as it were, in the genetic code of the social project inspired by a blind belief in numbers'. Statistics and arithmetic, or political anatomy, opened up a new territory for practical science and the tools of statistical observation developed within the conceptual framework of political arithmetic, in which John Graunt saw 'a new light for the world' (Mattelart, 2003). However, as Chamont Wang (1992) says, 'statistics is infinitely rich in its subtlety and esoteric beauty [*sic*]' (1992, p. 6), showing how ambiguous statistics are in both covering and revealing 'facts' in accordance with those in power.

The idea of 'quality' does not escape this context but, on the contrary, can second the political agenda in terms of reporting outcomes. This was perfectly

---

much in the public eye or subject to a judge's scrutiny'. The Lib Dem leader Nick Clegg pointed out that journalists should not fear being prosecuted under computer misuse, data protection and bribery law: 'The amendments propose a new defence for journalists who unlawfully obtain personal data (section 55 of the Data Protection Act) where they do so as part of a story that is in the public interest, a public interest defence in the Computer Misuse Act, and a public interest defence in the Bribery Act'.

illustrated in the consultation paper *Establishing the Principles* (Scholar, 2009), which explained the role of quality in the context of public service output and its measurement, and further developed in the *Atkinson Report*,[7] which regards quality as an intrinsic part of output. Moreover, the UK Government Statistical Service[8] is committed to providing users with information on the quality and reliability of its statistical outputs, along with the methods that have been used to produce them, and the report *National Statistician's Guidance on Quality, Methods and Harmonisation*[9] provides readers with insightful guidelines. For some, principles 4 and 8 of the *Code* (January 2009, pp. 20–24) are the key foundational sections for those who want to be committed to quality issues.

Indeed, principle 4, Practice 2 ensures that official statistics are produced to a level of quality that meets users' needs, and that users are informed about the quality of statistical outputs, including estimates of the main sources of bias and other errors, and other aspects of the European Statistical System definition of quality while principle 8 provides information on the quality and reliability of statistics in relation to the range of potential uses, and on methods, procedures and classifications. Regarding this, Mark Pont underlines that

> Each organisation should have a policy, which states where and which quality output measures will be reported. For example, the organisational policy may state that all first releases will include a core set of quality measures or include a web link to quality information in their 'Notes to editors'. All key statistical outputs should have basic quality information as the minimum. The policy may also state that for each statistical product a reference report is produced which contains measures that do not change from one release to another. (2010, p. 6)

Strictly speaking, in order to enable users to determine whether outputs meet their needs, it is recommended that output producers report quality in

---

[7] *The Atkinson Review: Final Report* is the culmination of a year-long review of the measurement of UK government output and productivity. Sir Tony Atkinson from Nuffield College, Oxford, led the review supported by a team seconded from the Office for National Statistics, HM Treasury, Department of Health, and the Bank of England. A key objective of the review was to recommend methods and approaches that could be used to measure UK government output. In addition to recommending a general framework and principles, the report focuses on practical solutions for measuring the key functional areas of health, education, public order and safety and social protection.

[8] See https://gss.civilservice.gov.uk/ (accessed on 14 August 2020).

[9] See http://www.statisticsauthority.gov.uk/national-statistician/ns-reports--reviews-and-guidance/national-statistician-s-guidance/index.html (accessed on 14 August 2020).

terms of the five quality dimensions as set out by the European Statistical System (ESS),[10] namely: Relevance; Accuracy and Reliability; Timeliness and Punctuality; Accessibility and Clarity; and Coherence and Comparability. These dimensions can coincide with the same journalistic dimensions used in statistical news-driven narratives, if not in practice then at least in their theoretical components. For the sake of clarity, we refer to the definitions of what quality measures and quality indicators are, according to the 2013 *Guidelines for Measuring Statistical Output Quality*.[11]

In this sense, quality measures are defined as those items that directly measure a particular aspect of quality. For example, the time lag from the reference date to the release of the output is a direct measure. However, in practice, many quality measures can be difficult or costly to calculate. Instead, we can use quality indicators to give insight into quality. Meanwhile, quality indicators usually consist of information that is a by-product of the statistical process. They do not measure quality directly but can provide enough information to provide an insight into quality. For example, in the case of accuracy it is almost impossible to measure non-response bias, as the characteristics of those who do not respond can be difficult to ascertain. In this instance, response rates are a suitable quality indicator that may be used to give an insight into the possible extent of non-response bias (2013, p. 7).

Along with the ESS dimensions, the *Atkinson Report* usefully summarizes the approaches to measuring quality by using quality indicators (showing the successful delivery of outputs), or alternatively to use evidence on change in outcomes, which can be attributed to the incremental contribution made, for example, by public services in the public interest. On the other hand, quality measures based on user surveys may be helpful for some quality domains, but there are issues about whether 'subjective' measures from successive sample surveys can be used as a chronological series – they may be distorted by changing expectations. According to Karen Dunnell, national statistician, and Peter Smith, chairman of UKCeMGA Advisory Board (2007), the Office of National Statistics (ONS)[12] is working with experts to develop further practical

---

[10] See http://ec.europa.eu/eurostat/web/main/home (accessed on 14 August 2020).

[11] We wish to highlight here the remarkable work on rankings, quantification and indicators carried out by Wendy Espeland, professor of sociology at Northwestern University in the United States. She is presently writing a book about the effects of commensuration, the process of translating qualities into quantities. In it she aims to investigate how media rankings have influenced higher education, how efforts to measure homosexuality have shaped gay and lesbian politics and the commensurate practices necessary in order to transform air pollution into a commodity that is traded on futures markets.

[12] http://www.ons.gov.uk/ons/index.html (accessed on 14 August 2020).

guidance on acceptable techniques in these areas, aiming to understand and reduce error rather than to set a standard for 'perfect' measures, which may be unattainable. This is an extremely difficult area, and perfect techniques for error detecting are not available. Also, on this point, the ONS is developing further technical guidance (2007), working with subject experts. These ongoing works are indicative of how the subject to be addressed is extremely delicate and complicated.

Information framework

The interest in quality issues, such as *trustworthiness* and *provenance*, for instance, has increased among private and public organizations, as well as among newsrooms worldwide, as witnessed over the last 20 years by computer-assisted and data-driven journalistic techniques. The reasons for this feverish attention might be summarized in the following general but fundamental three points (Walczak, 2004):

> One, the exponential growth in the number of real and potential users of information, both at local and international level. This is partially due to the globalisation progress that fosters information access/ collection thanks to IT technologies. Two, improvement in the education level of, and as a result, better preparedness of citizens for individual use of statistical information related to, but not limited to, international affairs. Three, deeper and pervasive democratisation process in economic and social life resulting in awareness promoted within wide social spheres. The number of people who demand wide and free access to a varied range of information is constantly increasing. This is a vital aspect and has importance to the wider audience from an information quality point of view.

It is helpful to briefly consider a scenario in which the quality of each of the points mentioned above could not be guaranteed nor understood. This lack of clear understanding of quality can only lead to detrimental consequences: costly errors, confusion, impasse and missed opportunities, remaining at a generic level. Indeed, part of the difficulty lies in putting together the right conceptual framework that is necessary to evaluate and analyse quality in the journalistic workflow.

Regarding information quality, Luciano Floridi points out that despite a wealth of available results, these results seem to have had a limited impact because research in the area has failed to combine and cross-fertilize theory and practice. This paragraph intends to move away from this limitation by attempting to sketch a theoretical framework suitable for the purposes of news reporting by 'cross-fertilising' philosophical studies and some urgent quality issues that impact on society.

In fact, statistics, data analysis and information quality are becoming critical for human beings and organizations. Defining, manipulating, measuring and improving the quality of social data and information that are exchanged in our everyday life, in business, in the administrative processes of public administration and in newsrooms, is becoming a constantly growing worry not just for practitioners, but also for those working in academia.

Paraphrasing the book *Cognition in the Wild* (Hutchins, 1995), we consider quality issues 'in the wild' where the term 'wild' refers to human cognition in its cultural and political habitat 'whose particular character has consequences for error detection and correction' (1995, p. 78); the tension between the costs and benefits of error occurrences and constraints and how these processes inevitably affect a system's efficiency and individual learning. From the journalistic point of view, the ability to detect error is linked to the ability to assess the reliability of a source. From the statistician's point of view, this ability deals with what is known as 'threats to internal validity'. One significant constraint here appears to be open versus closed world assumptions, a factor that influences quality by posing itself as a 'semantic constraint'. Understanding these assumptions, in database management for journalistic purposes, for example, means having understood where the short line that divides truth from falsehood lies, and in so doing, distinguishing the signal from the noise.

Italian scholars Scannapieco, Missier and Batini (2005) expand this discussion further by saying that we can take into consideration the challenges and changes in the information quality paradigm when they are studied not only in the captivity of traditional database systems, but also in the information ecosystem – a kind of ecosystem produced by networks and semantic information extraction processes in our everyday lives. This ecosystem is also what we need to analyse when we attempt to understand the role of quality statistical data in shaping truthful and credible news.

Philosophical framework

From the information framework to the philosophical one is a short step. Overall, the issues of quality in general, and of information quality (Abdi & Valentin, 2007) in particular, appeared in the field of computer science in the 1990s, when a research group based at Massachusetts Institute of Technology (MIT) launched an initiative to develop more standard definitions in the field and the group became greatly influential and the community has thrived since then. The message that the MIT group wanted to convey is that quality of information is information that is fit for purpose, and this goes far beyond mere accuracy of information, an issue under constant scrutiny for those journalists committed to this cause. Since the MIT group elaborated the IQ measures as data management for business, they conceived data as a valuable and important product even if the consumers of that product are internal to the organization. It is now commonly accepted that IQ is a multidimensional concept with accuracy being only one dimension of quality.

In terms of quality dimensions we have two schools of thought: the MIT and the so-called 'Italian School'. Two different methodological approaches, diverse but complementary, are worth reviewing here; their results brought to light that academic approaches try to cover all aspects of quality, whereas practitioners focus on particular problems of their context, a kind of separation that leads to some interesting insights. The first methodological approach was called 'empirical' by Scannapieco and Batini (2006); the second was called 'ontological' by Wand and Wang (1996).

The first methodology consists of surveying IQ professionals, both academics and practitioners, about what they consider important quality dimensions and how they classify them. This empirical approach is based on initial work by Wand and Wang (1996) and, in line with the focus on information users, data consumers have also been interviewed (Scannapieco, Missier & Batini, 2005). The categorization made by R. Y. Wang at the MIT is one of the earliest and still the most influential categorization of quality dimensions. However, the aforementioned papers do not *define* quality dimensions such as objectivity, timeliness and so on; instead, they *categorize* them. Wang, for example, talks of having 'empirically derived' quality dimensions (Wang, 1998, p. 38). It can be said that the most important result, as an initial starting point, is that information consumers need more than merely accurate information.

The second methodology refers to an ontological approach and attempts to understand quality errors and how they are generated. Illari and Floridi (2015) comment that the assumptions are not always clear but the conclusions are interesting. The authors also suggest that future research should conduct testing to discover whether or not they enhance quality practice. The ontological approach seems to fit the purpose of journalism because it links the quality practice to error detection, and therefore it is a test for the reliability of a source.

Methodologically speaking, the first major area of developing quality is in unstructured data, particularly on *trust, provenance* and *reputation*. The questions are simple: Where do the data come from (provenance), are they any good (trust), and is their source any good (reputation)? To answer these questions and to approach quality issues, the Italian School developed the idea of the 'polygen' model, which dealt with the problem of heterogeneous sources, which seems particularly suitable for the purposes of journalism. *Provenance* is generally offered to the user by tagging data with where it comes from, and what has happened to it before it gets to the user. However, according to them, much more work is needed on how to model and measure the *trustworthiness* of data and the *reputation* of particular sources.

Indeed, ensuring the quality of statistical data has been a continuing concern for those in the information systems profession. It is commonly accepted that the principal role of an information system is to present views of the real world so that members of an organization can create products or make suitable decisions. According to Ken Orr, if those views do not substantially agree with the real world for any extended period of time, then the system is a poor one and, ultimately, 'like a delusional psychotic' (Orr, 1998, p. 25), the organization will begin to act irrationally. Orr supports the theory of the feedback control system in which data quality is the measure of the agreement between the data views presented by an information system and that same data in the real world. He thinks that the real concern about statistical data quality is not to necessarily ensure that the quality is perfect, but rather that the quality of the data in our information systems is accurate enough, timely enough and consistent enough for the organization to survive and make reasonable decisions. 'In conclusion,' Orr continues, 'the real difficulty with data quality is change. Data in our databases is static, but the real world keeps changing' (Orr, 1998, p. 26). In fact, real sense-data constitutes the raw material for the Information Age. However, unlike physical raw material, data is not consumed, and it can be reused repeatedly for various purposes, including for journalistic purposes.

Chengalur-Smith, Ballou and Pazer (1999) provide an example that seems to be suitable for the case of journalism driven by statistical analysis. They identify and discuss four dimensions of quality that can be found in Laudon's study of data problems in the US criminal justice system: *accuracy* could refer to recording facts about the positioning of a criminal case correctly; *completeness* in having all relevant information recorded; *consistency* to a uniform format for recording relevant information; and *timeliness* in recording the information immediately following the occurrence of an event.

Alongside the deepening of some theoretical issues of quality, it must be said that there are some very interesting developments in quality practice, as statistical information has come to pervade all human activities. The increasing availability of data and its use by multiple people and groups in science means that databases are increasingly crucial infrastructure for science. In this area the work of Sabina Leonelli at the University of Essex (2014), for example, is important to understand that nowadays quality information is vital to a well-functioning society, as well as also being hard to underestimate, especially in the field of journalism which is constantly challenged by the advancements of technology and emerging analytical skills.

Focusing on many possible dimensions and metrics by focusing on structured data, the Italian School individuates 13 methodologies for the assessment and improvement of data quality, in which there is a total of about 220 different dimensions. The most frequently cited dimensions are *accuracy, completeness, consistency, timeliness* and *currency*.

The 'Italian school' illuminates the influencing factors on quality, and briefly focuses on the open versus closed world assumptions, an issue also strongly debated among computer science and informatics practitioners and academics. Rather than explaining in detail what these assumptions state (that would require a separate article), we will use them here as metaphors to exemplify the approach journalists have when dealing with statistical databases.

Generally speaking, the closed world assumption (CWA) usually holds, in regard to databases, that any statement that is not known to be true is false. In knowledge bases, the open world assumption states that any statement that is not known cannot be predicated as either true or false. Accessing this CWA by understanding it, is in our view, one of the crucial factors that might influence the quality of the results, or the credibility dimension of news. Journalists, by unlocking these assumptions, can critically use the CWA as a basis for their investigations.

This issue strictly relates to the relationship between *data, information* and *truth*.. Some of the aforementioned quality dimensions pose the question of adherence to a certain representation of the real world. A critical question pertaining to philosophical disputes is whether quality pertains to facts of sense or rather to laws of logic, or else whether information quality is a matter of synthetic rather than analytic knowledge.

This issue seems to speak to the language of philosophy in particular about the two dogmas of empiricism against which Quine (1951) provided substantial arguments in favour of a holistic perspective. On the one hand, Quine rejected the distinction between truths independent from facts and truths grounded in facts; on the other hand, he contrasted reductionism as the theory according to which the meanings of statements come from some logical constructions of terms, exclusively referring to immediate experience.

This issue may also be related to the problem of knowledge of things by *acquaintance* (unstructured data) and by description (structured data) as stated by Bertrand Russell,

> We shall say that we have acquaintance with anything of which we are directly aware, without the intermediary of any process of inference or any knowledge of truths. (B. Russell, 1910, p. 86)

Hence, knowledge by description connects the truths (carried out by statistical data) with things with which we have acquaintance through our direct experience with the world (sense-data). It is evident that the question highlights one of the most controversial issues discussed in Western (also in Eastern) philosophy so far by posing the question of adherence to a certain representation of the real world. Russell analyses this issue by using the term *data* and particularly distinguishing *hard data* from *soft data*: 'the hardest of hard data are of two sorts: the particular facts of sense, and the general truths of logic' (1910, p. 88). At this point journalists should ask themselves to what extent quality dimensions may pertain to the domain of both hard and soft data. Therefore, the critical question is whether quality pertains to facts of sense or rather to laws of logic.

Besides, the main research questions also have a second goal, which is that of investigating whether philosophical research can help to clarify basic issues and influence factors of statistical data quality for journalistic purposes by bridging areas too often confined to technical perspectives in computer science and informatics. We are in favour of a more holistic perspective suitable for tackling what we described as a landscape 'in the wild', in which statistical information is published, processed and used with the purpose of creating credible and truthful news.

Quality frameworks and practices

Indeed, understanding information quality can be a crucial and pressing task, particularly from the viewpoint of journalism. When selecting information, journalists must concern themselves with the quality of the information available. At that stage, they act as if they were *Inforgs* in the *Infosphere* (Floridi, 2002), and they are also the actors of the Fourth Revolution (Floridi, 2014). They are not interested in just any information; they require the best information available for their purposes.

As noted by Patrick Wilson, a person wants 'to have what we can call the best textual means to his end' (1968, p. 21). This challenging passage translates not only into what makes information the best information available but also into the nature of information quality. According to Jens-Erik Mai (2016; 2013), the quality of information is something that exists or is developed in tandem with the meaning of information. Assuming that the matter in the hands of journalists is information, we therefore have to frame the concept of information quality.

It is evident that nowadays more and more people, especially journalists, are weighed down by information overload (or should we say 'information explosion'?),[13] and it also seems to be a fact that more information exists than ever before, so its quality is a central element. 'The most developed post-industrial societies live by information, and Information and Communication Technologies (ICTs) keep them oxygenated' (Illari & Floridi, 2014, p. 2), thus the better the quality of information exchanged the more likely it is that such societies will thrive. To address the topic in more detail and to contextualize it within the research questions, we will take two examples: the United States and the United Kingdom.

In the United States, the Information Quality Act, also known as the Data Quality Act, enacted in 2000[14] left 'undefined virtually every key concept in the text'. So, it required the Office of Management and Budget 'to promulgate guidance to agencies ensuring the quality, objectivity, utility, and integrity of information (including statistical information) disseminated by Federal agencies' (Congressional Report Service, 2004). Unsurprisingly, the guidelines have received much criticism and have been under review ever since (United States Government Accountability Office, 2006).

In the United Kingdom, some of the most important efforts in dealing with information quality issues have concerned the healthcare system. Already in 2001, the Kennedy Report[15] acknowledged that 'the assessment of the performance of clinicians and information for the benefit of patients depends on the collection, analysis and dissemination of data'. However, in 2004, the NHS Information Quality Assurance Consultation still highlighted that 'consideration of information and data quality are made more complex by the general agreement that there are a number of aspects to information/data quality but no clear agreement as to what these are'.

---

[13] The term *information explosion* seems to have appeared at about the start of the Kennedy administration in the early 1960s, when it was first used to describe the burgeoning number of articles being churned out by scientists around the world. Already by January 1966 *Newsweek* had produced a cover story, tied to the publication of a book by Marshall McLuhan, predicting the end of the information world as it had been. In the same year an internal CIA study, the Cunnigham Report, had flagged what it called 'More Is Better' attitudes. 'We were hypnotised by statistics and bits of information, particularly in the military and academia,' the Cunningham Report complained.

[14] It is usually called the *Information Quality Act*. See: http://www.whitehouse.gov/omb/inforeg_agency_info_quality_links (accessed on 14 August 2020).

[15] The report is written by Prof. Sir Ian Kennedy and is available at the following link: http://www.heartofengland.nhs.uk/wp-content/uploads/Kennedy-Report-Final.pdf (accessed on 14 August 2020).

Lacking a clear and precise understanding of IQ standards (such as *accessibility*, *accuracy*, *availability*, *completeness*, *currency*, *integrity*, *redundancy*, *reliability*, *timeliness*, *trustworthiness* and *usability*) caused costly errors and confusion. The first International Conference on Information Quality was organized in 1996. In 2006 the Association of Computing Machinery launched the new *Journal of Data on Information Quality*.

Information links

Drawing connections between journalism studies and information sciences, we can say that both are concerned with the production, organization, retrieval and use of information, and in this context information is thought of as being more or less equivalent to documents, or more precisely to the ideas, opinions, claims or facts represented or expressed in books, journals, newspapers, photos, films and webpages but also spreadsheets, graphs and figures. In other words, the kind of information studied is typically information created by people to communicate with other people about something. It could be intended to communicate, to argue, to inform, to convince or to state a particular idea. Whatever the circumstance, it is produced with the aim of creating meaning for the receiver of the information. In this sense information can be thought of as a vehicle in a communication process.

In order to gain insight and to be able to explain various phenomena in human communication, information creation and transformation, and the development of information systems, an overarching framework seems highly desirable, even necessary. Reviewing the literature in this context would take us far away from the research questions dealt with, so it is enough for the purposes of this chapter to cite Wei Hu and Junkang Feng (2004) who have found that all of these theories may be incorporated within a unique framework, which would help make sense of them, and make good use of them in *understanding* information and information flow. Semiotics and semantic information theories can be related and complementary to each other, especially in the context of the Information Source-Bearer-Receiver (S-B-R) framework.

Hu and Feng believe that such a framework should be formulated 'from the point of view of how information is created, carried and finally received' (2004, p. 3). Therefore they have created a framework consisting of Information Source, Information Bearer and Information Receiver, and the links between them. They call such an abstract model the 'S-B-R Framework'. However, how can we abstract this model for the purposes of journalism?

Particularly instructive is the 'fundamental equation' that Bertram Brooks formulated in 1980, which is written with the language of the mathematical logic, with the intent of developing a foundation that permitted "an objective rather than a subjective theory of knowledge" (1980a, p. 125) and in which 'information and knowledge are of the same kind' so that they can 'be measured in the same units' (1980b, p. 76). The following equation expresses in pseudo-mathematical language what he meant: **K [S] + ΔI = K [S + ΔS]**. In its very general way, the knowledge structure **K [S]** is changed to the new modified structure **K [S + ΔS]** by the information **ΔI**, the **ΔS** indicating the effect of the modification (1980a, p. 131).

Theoretically, if we were willing to test this equation in the broad area of journalism we would discover that this equation might be the secret to well-balanced journalism. But we are aware that it is not the goal of this research to test this formula even if, perhaps, this was exactly the hope of Walter Lippmann when he affirmed that 'only the discipline of a modernised logic can open the door to reality' (2012, p. 86).

Provocations apart, Ronald Day (2008) says that an understanding of such a formula can allow one to jump from information bits to information overload as if they were of the same kind. This approach and understanding of information is

A well-established tradition of library and information-science theory that understands ideas as being quasi-empirical objects – generated in the minds of authors – that are contained in documents and that are sought by and transferred to the minds of information seekers or users upon reading, viewing or listening. (p. 1644)

This thought is an important step to understanding the interplay between data, information and knowledge. Instead of conceptualizing data as (1) building blocks for information; (2) being of the same nature as information to allow for unified measurements; or (3) being different from information in order to establish information as what is true and verifiable. This concept can be viewed as a vehicle used in the production and exchange of meaning. Therefore, information is conceptualized as signs used in communication to produce and exchange meaning.

Paraphrasing Umberto Eco (1977), a sign is not only something that stands for something else, it is also something that can and must be interpreted. Charles Saunders Peirce (1966) developed a more elaborate conceptualization of the basic idea expressed by Eco, formulating the sign as a triadic relationship. According to J. Buchler, Peirce's editor:

A sign, or representamen, is something that stands to somebody for something in some respect or capacity. It addresses somebody, that is, creates in the mind of that person an equivalent sign, or perhaps a more developed sign. That sign which it creates I call the interpretant of the first sign. The sign stands for something, its object. It stands for that object, not in all respects, but in reference to a sort of idea, which I sometimes have called the ground of the representamen. (p. 99)

It is vital at this stage to understand the quality of information, because when that information is used to communicate and exchange ideas, it can be trusted. In the case of journalism practice, this represents the keystone upon which we (Cañizalez & Lugo, 2007) base journalistic values and their successful application. We agree with Mai, who suggests avoiding casting the notion of information quality among the 'pathologies of information' (under which lies the danger of inventing problems for which the only solution is 'the services of library/information professions') (J. E. Mai, 2013).

Specifically, the notion of IQ should be addressed in a broader context, and it needs to be tied to and build on Philosophy of Information, and therefore apply the outcomes to journalism practices. The notion of IQ, like that of quality journalism, goes undefined in its respective area of research. Scholars note that quality is an elusive and abstract concept and articulate a set of attributes that make up information quality.

Thomas Chesney (2006) in his analysis on Wikipedia's dimension of *credibility* noted that 'information with high quality is usually considered to have some or all of the following characteristics: Up-to-date, relevant, accurate, economic for the purpose at hand, on time and understandable to the person who needs it' (quoted in Mai, p. 681). Ofer Arazy and Rick Kopak (2011) asked students to evaluate information in terms of 'quality' (*accuracy, completeness, objectivity* and *representation*), and Soo Yeung Rieh (2002) based his research on previous cases in order to look for *goodness, usefulness, accuracy/validity, recency, perceived quality, actual quality, expected quality, authority* and *reliability*.

The list in Table 5.1 contains those concepts that have been associated with information quality and fits perfectly with the one list discussed in Table 3.1, Table 3.2 and Table 3.3. Each of these concepts has, of course, multiple meanings and interpretations.

Some argue that IQ is a subjective construct and that 'users of the information have to make judgments about its quality for themselves' (Rieh & Belkin, 1998, p. 53). At the same time the focus of much research is on 'quantifying', 'measurement' or the determination of a 'true quality control measure' for information quality. Others agree that information quality is a subjective construct (in the mind of the individual information user), but at the same time they believe that 'some dimensions may be less context-sensitive, relying more on intrinsic indicators that span across all tasks' (Mai, 2013, p. 31).

Table 5.1 Attributes of information quality.

accurate	correct	objective
appropriate	credible	true
authentic	current	trustworthy
authoritative	good	understandable
balanced	neutral	useful
believable	relevant	valid
comprehensive	reliable	

Between these views, Professor David Lankes (2008) at Syracuse University's School of Information Studies casts light on the notion of IQ, and his ideas fit with the purposes of journalism. He wants to move the understanding of the credibility of information from its current site in concepts of authority to a more dynamic position of reliability. Lankes understands the credibility of information is to be determined by the individual receiving the information and its mentalistic construct free from external influences such as the cultural or environmental context in which the information is received. David Lankes argues specifically that 'reliability and authority can be seen as opposite ends of a spectrum of credibility approaches' (p. 681). At one end of the spectrum we have authority where 'pre-existing agreements are in place and assumed: the conversation is over', and at the other end of the spectrum we have 'reliability [where] the conversation is open and ongoing' (p. 681). Interestingly, Lankes walks the line between defining credibility as an inherent property of information and developing an understanding of credibility that is solipsistic and divorced from social interactions and contexts, 'in an effort to overcome this challenging balancing act' (p. 668).

Hilligoss and Rieh (2008) suggest a unified framework to understand the user's assessment of credibility. They think the assessment can be divided into three levels: firstly, the conceptualization of credibility employed by the person (truthfulness, believability, trustworthiness, objectivity, reliability); secondly, the general rules of thumb employed; thirdly, the specific cues from source or content.

In the final discussion of the paper, they found that 'context emerged as an important factor that influences the three levels' (p. 1481). Given their focus on the individual user in the study, explains Mei (2013), the authors do not consider the contextual dimension in detail, and their framework focuses mostly on the aspect of credibility assessment. Reijo Savolainen (2011) further splits the balancing act into two components: quality and credibility – by restricting information quality to 'the message's information content' and information credibility to 'the qualities of the author of the message' (p. 1254).

The above is of great importance if applied to the journalistic workflow, as quality and credibility are the foundations of journalistic values. However, it is our view that information reliability, authority, trust and quality could be understood within the larger context of information literacy. When journalists seek information of high quality in the *Infosphere* they do so within an intricate web of information problems, information interactions and social-cultural contexts. By quoting Jack Andersen (2006), we understand how important information literacy is for journalism:

> Information literacy covers the ability to read society and its textu-
> ally and genre-mediated structures. Information literacy represents an
> understanding of society and its textual mediation. We might go as far
> as to say that information literacy implies a critique of society insofar as
> it includes a particular use and reading of particular information sources
> and use of particular forms of communication. (2006, p. 217)

One aspect of this understanding of information literacy is the ability to judge the quality of information. Such assessments will always be driven by the particular context, and within a particular understanding of the society in which the information is used. Translating this to journalism, this means that it is valid for the different types of journalistic cultures and related legal or political frameworks. At this stage a more sophisticated conceptual framework is needed for dealing with these notions and especially for establishing a better notion of information quality in journalism (Andersen, 2006); thus we shall now turn to the concept of Levels of Abstraction (LoAs).

Abstraction levels

Journalists should be extremely attentive to the concept of sources (Manning, 2000, 2008; Soley, 2008), to its decline and also to the role that such a concept plays within the epistemology of the journalistic discipline. Scholars like Paul Manning and Lawrence Soley (2008), to name just two, ask: What makes a source the source *par excellence*? What are the features of a subject that arouse journalistic curiosity?

To add to these questions we would like to cite the work by the Italian open source intelligence analyst Giovanni Nacci who can complement such questions with the following ones: Can these features be found in other LoAs? If so, what are the rules that differentiate the LoAs of a journalist from, for example, that of a historian?

To follow Nacci's analysis, the first similarity can be found in the idea of storytelling. In both cases the story must adhere to the facts and to the reality.

Yet if history performs its storytelling through the observation of inherent messages of either historical remains or sources from the past, journalism instead performs storytelling about 'contingency and daily life' comparable to what Umberto Eco defined as 'historiography of the instant'.[16]

Additionally, journalism also plays a role of mediation between the information source and its recipient. This function therefore has two main arguments: (1) the source (the information delivered by the source) and (2) the receiver, the reader as information user. In logical mathematical terms it can be said that the function is determined when the argument 'reader' is equal to zero (or rather, it is virtually and provocatively possible to do journalism without readers), whereas when there is no source, there is no mediation, therefore no journalism.

We suggest that this sort of mediation is to be interpreted as an 'incessant journalistic negotiation' that aims at highlighting how the interaction between the three systems is significant and seamless. If journalism is therefore a function that negotiates and mediates the informational interests of two classes of subject, we can talk of journalism as a *systemic interface* between the system that delivers the product 'information' (the sources) and the one that consumes and uses it (the reader). In other words, we talk about a LoA that interfaces, thanks to its transformation rules, two different LoAs.

The notion of interface is expected to possess a point of continuity and of unity between two entities or systems. In case this does not exist, the interface itself is a system of transformation and adaptation that transforms what a system delivers in input mode into something receivable by the other system. This means that the reader cannot tout court be called 'information user' (the original 'product', the raw material, the source); if so, the following things would fail: the necessity of mediator, of the interface, of the journalistic level of abstraction and, ultimately, that of the journalist. It would be much more appropriate to define the reader as the user of a mediation process that journalism triggers.

This view draws attention to the workflow, the method and the practices through which the mediation is carried out, or rather the modalities through which the interface between source and reader is achieved, and in so doing on quality, completeness and righteousness of the LoAs of the journalist. This level would indeed be achieved in order to meet certain requisites, such as *precision* – as advocated by Philip Meyer – *efficacy* and *objectivity* of the observation of the object 'source'. The pragmatic question is therefore: How is it possible to mediate and negotiate without affecting the source or the information that one aims to deliver?

---

[16] The quotation is commonly attributed to Umberto Eco. A precise reference is not available.

Journalism scholars Bill Kovach and Tom Rosenstiel, in *The Elements of Journalism*, seem to have an answer: 'the journalist is not objective, but his method can be. The key [is] in the discipline of the craft, not in the aim' (2001, p. 83). This deviation on the method and on the discipline anticipates the concept of 'verification'. According to the authors, journalism should rely on the discipline of verification because this is the only feature that distinguishes journalism from other forms of storytelling in which fantasy does not represent an obstacle. For example, in fiction and other arts, adherence to a factual reality is not a problem, and it can be avoided at any stage of storytelling. In journalism, the opposite case is seen. Kovach and Rosenstiel focus on the systematicity of how this concept is developed to transform storytelling into journalism (2001, p. 80). They note that 'in the end, the discipline of verification is what separates journalism from entertainment, propaganda, fiction, or art. Journalism alone is focused first on getting what happened down right' (2001, p. 79). We perceive between the lines that the authors consider journalism to be the only discipline that deals with the conventional 'truth', the only one which exists and is unamendable.

In other cases though, such as in those disciplines that deal with history, historiography or law, one behaves like an interpreter of remains and materials of the past, the historic truth, adopting an approximation partially conscious of a 'processual truth', based on documental proof. On these premises, the 'journalistic truth' is the only one able to approach the factual reality claiming to be a primary source of authentic reality. This discipline of verification consists of giving truth-value to sources and information. In so doing, journalists should comply with specific stages that are aimed at guaranteeing objectivity in the evaluation.

The principles below are valid not only if applied to the journalistic workflow but also to the intelligence cycle:

A more conscious discipline of verification is the best antidote to the old journalism of verification being overrun by a new journalism of assertion, and it would provide citizens with a basis for relying on journalistic accounts [...] We began to see a core set of concepts that form the foundation of the discipline of verification. Never add anything that was not there. Never deceive the audience. Be transparent about your methods and motives. Rely on your own original reporting. Exercise humility. (Kovach & Rosenstiel, 2001, p. 89)

However, the discipline of verification does not abstract from a comparison between an information body and the factual reality that was generated (Dover, Goodman & Hillebrand, 2013).

Giovanni Nacci again provides an example that might be useful here: if we are working in an office three levels below ground and a colleague tells us that it is snowing outside, it would be better for us go out and verify the claim, if we want to give a truth-value to that information. If it is snowing (or it has snowed, the source can indeed have a different chrono-reference) the information given has (or had) a truth-value. On the basis of these outcomes the source can be considered reliable (giving it a reliability-value) not only because of its adherence to the factual reality, but also because of its significance. If in August our colleague keeps telling us each hour that it is not snowing outside, even if the information given is true, this will not add any higher reliability-value. This means that for information to be considered information it should renew the body of knowledge of the receiving system.

In this example, the information given has been verified on the basis of the five senses of the information user, whose perception renewed the state of his body of knowledge. Unfortunately, such directedness is not often possible. Supposing that we have been prevented from verifying directly the information about the snowfall, we could have used other methods: perhaps using CCTV or a thermometer or making a call to a friend. These 'sensors', or sources, are no more than agents of information that expand our ability to perceive and interact with another agent of information (perhaps another colleague located at level-2) with a guest system. The journalist, or his LoAs, verifies the information in the same way, seeking within a system other agents of information that can validate the information given by his/her source.

It is therefore feasible to claim that the first property observable is: S is a source if and only if its reliability can be verified. Therefore, because it is possible to verify only one source through the discipline of verification, one can assume a second property, which is: S is a source if and only if it delivers information which can be verified. As previously noted, it is almost impossible to verify certain types of information through direct experience, and in the specific case of the reader/information user this can never be verified. Moreover, colleagues, CCTV and sensors can consciously or unconsciously deceive or show true (or false) information that might not correspond to the factual reality.

This double relationship between source/information and factual reality significantly increases the variability of interpretation, so a continued/continuous verification of sources (and of the information) is made indispensable. This verification is actually triggered through a certain number of agents of information that validate the source itself. At least in principle this improves the reliability not only of the verified source but also of the entire system of verification.

At this stage, the key words are 'reliability', 'network of agents of information' and 'network of sources'. We can therefore express the concept in this way: S is a source if and only if it delivers information whose truth-value Vs can be verified by a sufficient number of sources Sx so that it possesses a certain grade of reliability Rx, and that is within the network of sources N.

The above is a description of a methodology of validation and verification of the sources as strongly advocated by Kovack and Rosenstiel, who elaborated on the concept of objectivity that is the end result of a consistent method of information testing in a way that personal and cultural biases would not interfere with the accuracy of news reporting.

They implicitly support the third pillar/concept described earlier concerning the discipline of verification, namely: 'be transparent about your methods and motives' (2001, p. 82), which can be read as transparency of the LoAs.

However, if we want to go into detail with specific regard to the LoAs of the journalist, we have to highlight the peculiar strategic relationship between source, news and the intimate and intrinsic structure of the source itself. Some argue that the very concept of source is at the core of the epistemology of journalism (Franklin & Carson, 2010; J. Lewis, Williams, & Franklin, 2008; Sanders, 2010). Many authors have pointed this out starting with Gaye Tuchman (1972, 1978) because it lies at the basis of the news. One can also argue that there is a growing need for classifying the sources into a formal scheme so that the features, relations and, above all, the usability are enhanced. Sergio Lepri (2010) defines the concept of 'journalistic source' as follows:

> Those people and those documents that deliver information about circumstances [which are] objects of news reporting when the journalist is in position of being a direct witness' (Lepri, Accornero & Cultrera, 2010, p. 280)

An analysis of this definition reveals an interesting distinction. In a given circumstance (an event or a fact) two cases can be observed: (1) the journalist is a direct witness and therefore he/she can be present physically at the time and place of the circumstance with his/her perceptual skills; and (2) the journalist is not a direct witness. We can thus argue that the source is verified in the case of (2) even if it is legitimate to consider the hypothesis that journalist and sources are the same.

Lepri's definition illustrates two types of sources, later validated by Adam Penenberg (2010): *human source* and *documentary source*. This means that the information delivered can be respectively verbal or textual. However, the most important feature for a source to be considered a journalistic source is that it should not only be/provide information about 'circumstances' but also be information about circumstances worth being reported and therefore an object of news.

At this stage, if we have to establish which properties transform any object into a specific source, we should affirm that a source can be whatever thing delivers information about news. As a result of this reasoning, the question would be: Journalistically speaking, what differentiates news from information about a circumstance? We believe that the answer lies in one of the many definitions that define US journalistic practices 'news is what newspapermen make it', therefore news is what a journalist determines to be news. This definition sounds good as it is, but if a journalist decides what 'information about circumstances' becomes news, then he/she also decides what the source is. The logical conclusion that can be drawn is that: a source is whatever thing a journalist decides to be a source. This statement leads to one of the last questions: What are the elements with which a journalist confers newsworthiness to a given circumstance, to an event or to information?

Sergio Lepri (2005) again suggests a set of parameters to follow with regard to the newsworthiness of facts. More precisely he divided the parameters into two groups. In the first group: (1) the object; (2) the subject; and (3) the circumstances. In the second group we can find: (1) source; (2) information mean; (3) competition; and (4) the journalist. The first group is focused on the socio-informational effects and their impact on the information user. The second group is concerned with an evaluation of the ontology of news and that of the source.

In order to summarize these points, and for the purposes of the LoAs of a journalist, we can say that something is a journalistic source if it is informative (that the information delivered about facts can potentially become news; unpublished – the information delivered updates the user's body of knowledge; relevant – the information delivered about facts has socio-informational relevance; engaging – the information delivered has the purposes of emotionally engaging the user; authoritative – it possesses a proved authority; honest – correct and loyal in drawing explicit relations to specific lobbies; referenced – the information delivered about facts is also validated by competitors; comprehensible – in terms of the various degrees of understanding of journalists.

It is worth noting that John Merrill (1974) put together the discipline of verification and the awareness of the origin of information (Duffy & Freeman, 2011). He argued particularly that 'the discipline of verification is what distinguishes journalism from other forms of communication' (Merrill, 1997, p. 38). At this point another question still remains unanswered: Can a robust discipline of verification disclose and remove lies and disinformation?

More specifically, can a discipline of journalistic verification detect statistical fallacies, numerical lies or simple innumeracy?

The irrelevance of truth

In 2013 Paul Craig Roberts published *Why Disinformation Works. In America "Truth Has no Relevance. Only Agendas Are Important"*, which helped to define two important concepts: that of disinformation and that of lies. Disinformation can be extremely dangerous. It can directly cause serious emotional, financial and even physical harm if people are misled about important topics, such as medical treatments, investment opportunities or political candidates. In addition to this, and perhaps more importantly, it can cause damage indirectly by eroding trust and therefore inhibiting our ability to effectively share information with each other.

Inaccurate information or *misinformation* is a lucrative business as highlighted by the Center for Media, Data and Society at Central European University, Budapest, Hungary. It can mislead people whether it results from an honest mistake, negligence, unconscious bias or (as in the case of disinformation) intentional deception. Disinformation comes from someone who is actively engaged in an attempt to mislead. This threat to the quality of information has become much more prevalent in recent years. New information technologies are making it easier for people to create and disseminate inaccurate and misleading information. For instance, Darrel Huff, Joel Best and Mark Monmonier, despite the titles of their books, are not willing to deliver instruction manuals for liars. They are intended to help all of us to avoid being misled by showing us the various ways that people might try to mislead. Don Fallis, professor of philosophy and computer science at Northeastern University is clear in this regard:

> Disinformation is a type of information. More specifically, disinformation is information that is intentionally misleading. That is, it is information that (just as the source of the information intended) is likely to cause people to hold false beliefs. The most notable type of disinformation is the lie. According to the traditional philosophical analysis, a lie is a false statement that the speaker believes to be false and that is intended to mislead. (2014, p. 231)

The philosopher of science James H. Fetzer (2004a, 2004b) equates disinformation with lying by claimining that disinformation 'should be viewed more or less on a par with acts of lying. Indeed, the parallel with lying appears to be fairly precise' (2004, 231). Lies are not the only type of disinformation and

Fallis criticizes Fetzer's analysis as unlike lies, disinformation does not have to be a statement. Fetzer's analysis incorrectly rules out what we might call visual disinformation. He continues that unlike lies, disinformation does not have to be false. Fetzer's analysis incorrectly rules out what we might call true disinformation. Several philosophers have pointed out that even accurate information can be intentionally misleading. Finally, unlike lies, disinformation does not have to be intended to mislead. Fetzer's analysis incorrectly rules out what we might call side-effect disinformation.

While most philosophers agree that a lie must be intended to create a false belief, they disagree about what that false belief must be about. For instance, many philosophers claim that a liar must intend to mislead someone about the *accuracy* of what we actually say. In contrast, some philosophers claim that a liar only needs to intend to mislead about *his believing* what he says.

Other philosophers like Luciano Floridi (2004) go even further and claim that a liar just has to intend to mislead someone about something. So, in addition to (1) the accuracy of what he says and (2) his believing what he says, there may be other things that a liar might intend to mislead others about. As far as information articulation and production are concerned, Luciano Floridi points out that 'the process of information is defective' (2004, p. 101) in many other ways. So, we have to conclude that the flow of information is manipulated both in principle and by a third party. As a matter of fact, the most obvious example of manipulating the flow of information is *censorship*. This sort of manipulation can take place at various stages of the communication process, as seen in Table 5.2 below.

In addition to manipulating the flow of information between other parties, one can hide his/her own information from others in order to keep them

Table 5.2 Examples of definition for 'disinformation'.

Disseminate misleading information.
Example: disinformation.
Restrict information access.
Example: censorship.
Biased information access.
Example: search engine personalization.
Hide information.
   – Mask (e.g. steganography → cryptography)
   – Repackage
   – Dazzle
   – Decoy
Make access to information difficult.

in the dark as in the case of propaganda (Bellamy & Taylor, 1998; Miller, 2004) and spin-doctoring (Hollins & Bacon, 2010; Kristensen, 2006; Miller & Dinan, 2007), for example. With *masking* (or *camouflage*), the person or the thing to be hidden is not intended to be seen at all.

By contrast, with *repackaging*, the person or the thing to be hidden is made to look like something else – this is relevant for the argument, as the issue of 'statistical repackaging' can be the most arduous problem journalists can face when dealing with numbers. In this regard, Joel Best memorably describes the production of 'mutant statistics', whereby the meaning of numbers is 'stretched, twisted, distorted, or mangled' (2012, p. 62). Steganography is the study of how to mask information. It is one step beyond cryptography. Not only does it keep other people from deciphering a message, but it also keeps other people from even knowing that there is a message. Finally, *dazzling* is quite common in the context of information. The work by Cristiano Castelfranchi at the University of Siena in Italy refers to this technique as 'obfuscation', mostly known by intelligence officers as 'information pollution' (Castelfranchi, Falcone, & Pezzulo, 2003; Castelfranchi & Poggi, 1994; Castelfranchi & Tan, 2001).

To sum up, an awareness of the diverse ways in which people might try to mislead us is highly advisable because it can theoretically help us to avoid being misled by disinformation, which represents a serious threat to information quality. Also, a better understanding of the essence of disinformation, together with a robust discipline of journalistic verification, can facilitate research on techniques to discover different methods of detection.[17]

---

[17] 'Fact-checking' can be considered one of them.

Chapter 6

JOURNALISM MEETS STATISTICS IN REAL LIFE

Our central question, so far, has asked about the nature of the engagement between journalists and statistical data in the pursuit of quality. In so doing, we would want also to know if the quality statistics automatically lead to quality journalism. If so, we ought to know if the information quality then translates into quality journalism. Does the nature of a statistic's source affect the news reporting? What is the purpose of statistics in news reporting? Do journalists emphasize a certain type of statistics? What statistics sources do journalists use most often? And, how does the audience engage with statistically driven stories?

To answer these and other questions, we used a mixed-method approach, in which we have triangulated qualitative and quantitative methods as this 'is major research approach' (Johnson, Onwuegbuzie & Turner, 2007). The importance of such a triangulation is the validity of the results that can lead to a more balanced and detailed answer to the research questions by also comparing and contrasting different accounts of the same situation (Turner & Turner, 2009). The aim was to develop a 'practical theory' that would help to rationalize the issue under scrutiny (Altrichter, 2010; Altrichter, Posch & Somekh, 1993). We included content analysis, semi-structured interview, close reading and focus groups, which allowed us to carry out a multilevel assessment of the data. The overall mixed method used in this research should be understood in a broader 'cross-sectional design' (F. L. Cook et al., 1983; Johnston & Brady, 2002), which allows a combination of quantitative and qualitative research.

Therefore, this chapter presents the analysis of the data collected followed by a discussion of the research findings that resulted from each method. It provides a detailed account of the findings, in the hope that these results will elucidate the uses of statistics in articulating the five quality dimensions in news reporting.

Overall, our findings suggest that journalists tend to use statistical information as a tool to fulfil their deontological expectations of producing quality journalism. However, as it became clear from the interviews, one of the underlying motivations seems to also be the need to achieve credibility and authority, which entails a certain degree of building up the ability to persuade by means of trust. In other words, while journalists tend to make normative claims about the use of statistics to improve the 'quality' of their outputs, the same data suggests that statistics also play a role in fulfilling aspirations around credibility and influence. This aspirational aim was further challenged by the audience's attitude towards statistical information in the news. Even though this study is not primarily concerned with audience studies, the focus-group data highlighted that there is a problem of 'public trust' in numbers, particularly around the way they are published and conveyed through news media.

The importance of these findings lies in the fact that this apprehension towards statistical information can eventually result in a broken 'social contract' (a non-written agreement between journalists and their readers). This informal contract, made explicit since the early twentieth century, has awarded journalists the ability to 'speak' in the name of the public, and a degree of legal protection, in exchange for responsibility for truth and trustfulness. This is achieved by making sure that they adhere to explicit codes of practice and/or legal regulations (as in the case of broadcast news media in the United Kingdom).

Therefore, the incorporation of numbers into their stories seems to be directed at fulfilling some of the requisites of this contract, as they catalyze 'quality' in terms of transparency, reliability and context to the stories. This contract – in most Western countries – has been formulated around practices associated with the notion of objectivity, including fairness, balance and detachment. Consequently, the use of statistics is seen by many journalists as helping to underpin these practices and achieve the core notion.

The findings also suggest that journalists engage with numbers in a reactive manner, rather than a proactive one, by letting the statistics set the agenda. This could be interpreted both as a way of fulfilling the aspiration of objectivity and a manifestation of the journalists' inability to intervene with these numbers beyond a descriptive level.

Certainly, statistical reports are believed to be truthful in principle since numbers are treated, as Alain Desrosières (2002) would say, as 'social facts' by journalists. Consequently, these numbers are presented without critical thinking and without a theoretical framework that would allow a more comprehensive interpretation of the statistics in the news stories. Paradoxically, this lack of critical thinking – which is not carried out because of a lack of skills and apprehensions about possible subjectivity – has a negative effect on the delivery of quality, as numbers are often presented in a stand-alone format without context and often without critical elaboration. The content analysis confirms these findings, as it shows a serious lack of critical thinking around the numbers reported. Only on a few occasions were the statistical sources questioned or cross-referenced to others, as often happens with more traditional news sources.

The interview data brings to light the underlying dynamics behind the content analysis data. They suggest that journalists work under the constraints of limited educational backgrounds and struggle with the challenges imposed by diminishing resources in their working environment, which tends to compromise normative aspirations around ethical values in the newsrooms. Most importantly, the understanding of the meaning of 'quality', according to the interviews, is very vague, and it seems not to be fully integrated into the daily journalistic routine. Nevertheless, there is a wish to convey a 'completeness of information' and to achieve quality as a goal, even though this is neither properly defined nor fully embraced in practice.

We want to highlight another set of findings around time and time constraints, as this is often one of the reasons cited as preventing journalists from achieving 'quality' in their work. As several authors have pointed out (A. Bell, 2000; Phillips, 2012; Reich & Godler, 2014; Starkman, 2010), journalists struggle with deadlines and timely access to information, and this often has a negative impact on their ability to work effectively with data (Borges-Rey, 2016; Coddington, 2015; Seth C. Lewis, 2015). Our findings suggest that this is not necessarily the case. This consideration is related to the timeliness dimension, which refers to the reportage of up-to-date and timely statistics within three months of their release. The data also suggests that, on many occasions, the statistics used by journalists had been available for some time, but that this has made no difference in relation to the ability of the journalists to process them.

Content analysis

We present here the results in the form of graphs and tables, which were used to identify the frequencies, percentages and correlations of most of the 26 collection points, divided into five dimensions, as previously explained. Our data was evaluated using SPSS Statistics (Version 23) and covers topics such as crime and health in the *Guardian* and the *Observer*, the Times and the *Sunday Times*, the *Daily Mail* and *Mail on Sunday*, the *Daily Mirror* and the *Sunday Mirror* between 2013 and 2016.

Test-retest reliability has been applied to guarantee consistency over time. The content analysis has examined, in quantitative terms, how journalists engage with the five quality dimensions in the articulation of statistical information. From the results, two of the main findings are worth mentioning here

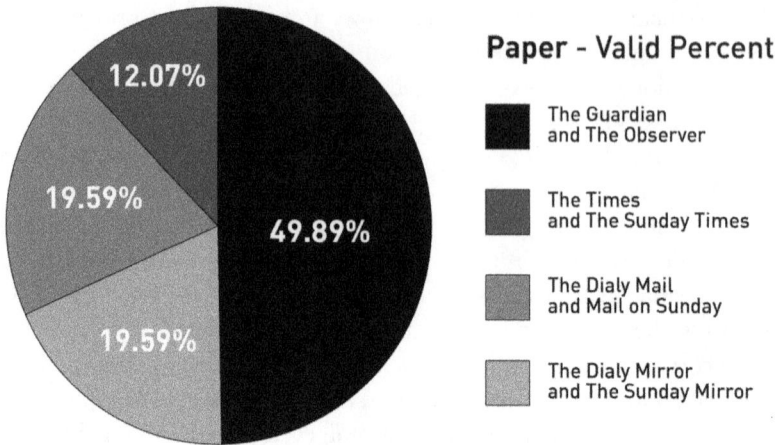

Figure 6.1 Sample of newspapers analysed and subdivided by title.

as an introduction: (1) there is an over-reliance on official statistics, which poses serious questions about the nature of the journalist-source relationship in terms of the quality dimension of Accessibility; and (2) there is a lack of critical thinking about statistical reports, which seems to drive journalists to omit information in relation to the quality dimensions of Accuracy and Timeliness.

Of the 439 articles containing data, 219 (constituting 49.89 per cent of the total) were published by the *Guardian* and the *Observer*, followed by the *Daily Mail* and *Mail on Sunday* with 86 articles (19.59 per cent). The third position is occupied by the *Times* and the *Sunday Times*, with a slightly lower number of articles than the *Mail* (81, or 18.45 per cent). The *Daily Mirror* and the *Sunday Mirror* come last, with only 53 articles, or 12.07 per cent of the total. These results suggest that the *Guardian* and the *Observer* make use of statistics in a much more extensive way compared to the other newspapers analysed, showing their clear inclination towards using numbers (Figure 6.1).

Table 6.1 shows that there is no remarkable difference in the use of statistics in the coverage of crime and health news overall. The number of articles per topic is well distributed across the newspapers.

A general overview of the data shows a substantial homogeneity in the use of statistics over the four-year period 2013–16, with 222 articles about medicine and health and 217 about crime, law and corrections. The procedure through which the newspapers were indexed might explain, however, the preponderance of statistics in the sample. From a different perspective, the picture seems to change when looking at each newspaper individually, as shown in Table 6.2.

Table 6.1 Newspapers divided by topic.

Topic		Frequency	Per cent	Valid per cent	Cumulative per cent
Valid	Medicine and health	222	50.6	50.6	50.6
	Crime, law and corrections	217	49.4	49.4	100.0
	Total	439	100.0	100.0	

Table 6.2 Cross-tabulation of paper with topic.

		Topic		Total
		Medicine and health	Crime, law and corrections	
Paper	The *Guardian* and the *Observer*	101	118	219
	The *Times* and the *Sunday Times*	46	35	81
	The *Daily Mail* and *Mail on Sunday*	50	36	86
	The *Daily Mirror* and the *Sunday Mirror*	25	28	53
Total		222	217	439

On closer examination, it can be said that statistics in medicine and health are used more in the *Times* and the *Sunday Times* (46 articles, compared to 35 on crime) as well as in the *Daily Mail* and *Mail on Sunday* (50 articles, compared to 36 on crime), whereas the statistics for crime-related issues are used more in the *Guardian* and the *Observer* (118 articles, compared to 101 on medicine and health) and in the *Daily Mirror* and the *Sunday Mirror* (28 articles, compared to 25 on crime), but in the last two newspapers there is little difference in the coverage of the two topics. This difference, despite being small, might say something about the editorial preferences of the newspapers. Such preferences can be understood through the newspapers' willingness to appear 'scientific' to their readers, as if the reporting of numbers only – seen as part of a scientific process in the pursuit of what Philip Meyer called 'precision journalism'– would easily lead to ethical validity, transparency, impartiality and, ultimately, quality.

Regarding this use of statistics, the American Press Institute claims that 'the statistics establish the appropriateness of the example, the credibility of the owner as a source on local business activity, and telegraph to readers that the story involved a higher level of reportorial effort'. The use of statistics also seems to be part of an ethical procedure that allows journalists to acquire more credibility and authority. But, as the results of the content analysis show, this does not automatically lead to neutral and unbiased information. In other words, statistical information does not translate automatically into quality journalism.

This 'higher level of reportorial effort' that can be translated into the umbrella term of quality is articulated in the five dimensions of Relevance, Accuracy, Timeliness, Interpretability and Accessibility. All these dimensions mark the threshold in the achievement of quality. Wherever possible, we have to look at each dimension on two levels: to see how journalists use statistics to successfully achieve each dimension and how statistics help to successfully achieve such dimensions.

One first dimension is that of relevance. Journalists use the concept of relevance to engage their readers and make them feel part of the story: 'the first challenge is finding the information that people need to live their lives. The second is to make it meaningful, relevant and engaging. Engagement really falls under the journalist's commitment to the citizenry' (Rosenstiel & Kovach, 2001, p. 189). Relevance is one of the criteria that journalists look for when assessing potential news: 'it considers stories about issues, groups and nations perceived to be relevant to the audience' (Harcup & O'neill, 2001, p. 263).

A news item is deemed relevant when it is meaningful to the readers. It can be summarized in a sentence: 'people care most about things that affect them' (American Press Institute). To be meaningful, statistics should also be relevant: 'statistics should be germane to the democratic debate […] in ways that are relevant to the democratic process and cycle' because '[statistics] inform decisions right across society and those decisions affect the lives of us all' (Bumpstead, Alldritt, & Authority, 2011, pp. 1–2).

As we argued previously in this work Relevance is a threshold of quality. But in order to analyse whether this threshold has been fully achieved or not, we made use of a concept which stems from the idea of relevance: the human interest (Figenschou & Thorbjørnsrud, 2015). In journalism theory, human interest is sometimes described as 'getting the story behind the story' or 'putting a human face on the news' (Lynch, Kent, & Carlson, 1967, p. 675). Indeed, human-interest journalism takes a closer, more personal look at the news. In its essence, 'human interest is the universal element in the news' (Hughes, 1940, p. 37). This dimension is evaluated here by cross-tabulating the variable of *humans with other variables of *paper, *topic, *category and lastly *genre. This is because we assumed that the human-interest aspect of the use of statistics has some degree of correlation with (1) the newspaper, (2) the topic, (3) the category journalists deal with and (4) the genre of the article (Figure 6.2, Table 6.3).

Humans - Paper Crosstabulation Count

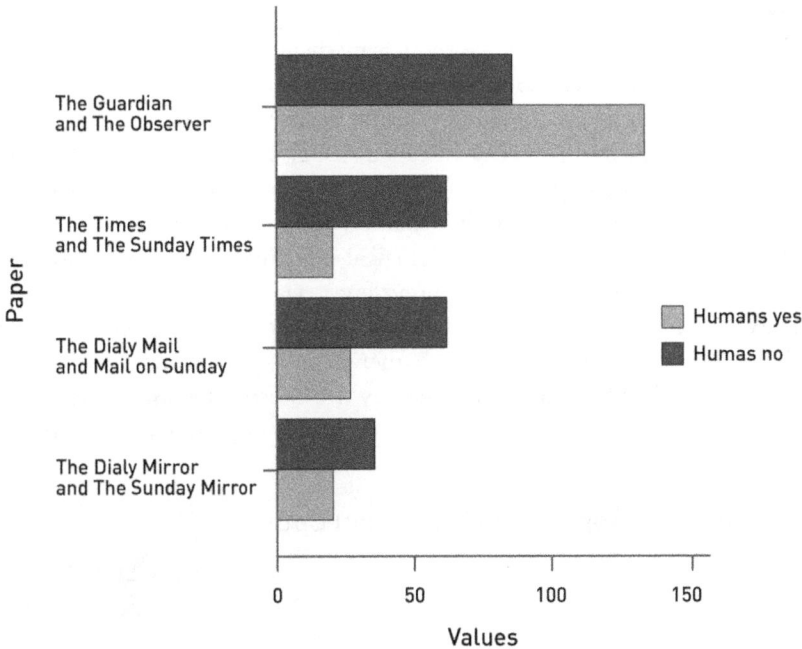

Figure 6.2 Cross-tabulation of newspapers with the human-interest variable.

Table 6.3 Cross-tabulation of the variables *paper and *humans.

		Paper				Total
		The *Guardian* and the *Observer*	The *Times* and the *Sunday Times*	The *Daily Mail* and *Mail on Sunday*	The *Daily Mirror* and the *Sunday Mirror*	
Humans	Yes	134	20	26	18	198
	No	85	61	60	35	241
Total		219	81	86	53	439

To the question: *Do the statistics involve any human-interest issue?* the answer is generally no. According to the data, the *Guardian* and the *Observer* emerge with 134 articles (out of 219) that integrate statistically driven arguments with human-interest issues in the editorial line. The statistics used in the other newspapers only occasionally involve statistics with the purpose of conveying human-interest stories. Division by topic will help to understand this result better.

The bar chart (Figure 6.3) shows that medicine and health stories are the most represented under the variable of human interest. Taking into account previous research in the area, these results seem to confirm the results of a study by Entwistle and Hancock-Beaulieu (1992), who noted clear differences between quality and popular press coverage of health, noting that 'the quality press provides more satisfactory information about health issues' (1992, p. 22). In that study, for example, epidemiological information, such as morbidity/ mortality rates and incidence of prevalence, was given in 26 per cent of quality articles mentioning diseases, but in only 13 per cent of popular articles.

The study shows that public health (mental and sexual health), sex offences, diseases and disorders, and epidemiology are those categories where statistics are used to address the human-interest criterion. Referring to quality

Humans - Topic Crosstabulation Count

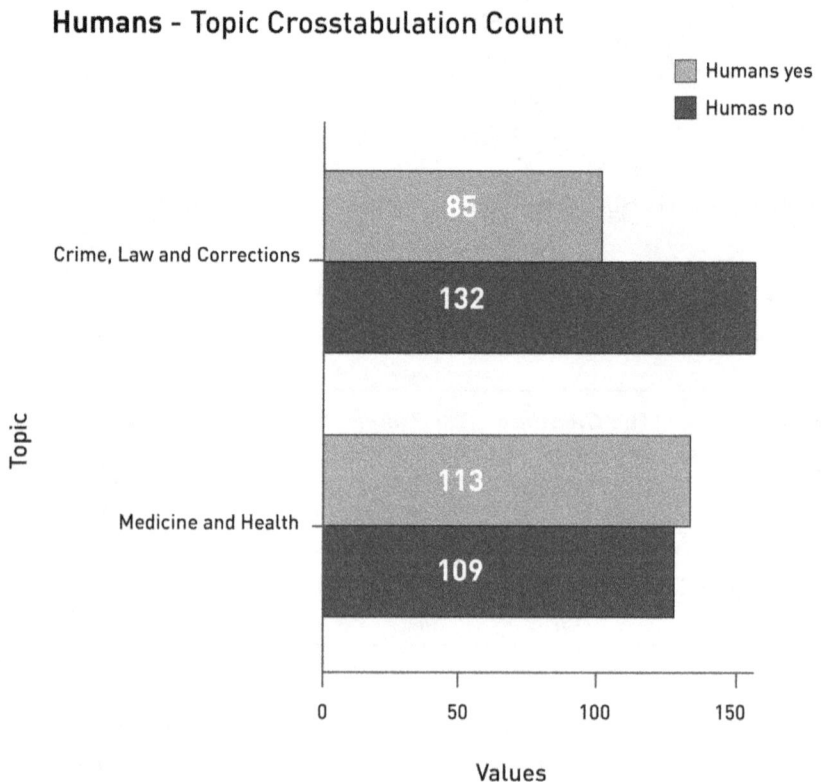

Figure 6.3 Cross-tabulation of topic with the human-interest variable.

journalism, Robert G. Picard (2011) reports that on the specific subject of medicine and health coverage, the literature is scarce. However, recent work by Daniel C. Hallin remains a cornerstone study in the area, especially when he refers to the forms of 'biocommunicability' as manifested in healthcare reporting (Briggs & Hallin, 2007, 2016; Hallin & Briggs, 2015). Pietro Ghezzi at Sussex Medical School has also recently conducted leading research in the United Kingdom on evaluating quality health news online (Chumber, Huber & Ghezzi, 2015; Maki, Evans & Ghezzi, 2015; Yaqub & Ghezzi, 2015).

In one case, Weitkamp (2003) examines the coverage of health in five United Kingdom national newspapers and confirms earlier reports (like that of Hansen, 1994) that within the branch of science reporting, medicine and health-related topics tended to dominate newspaper reports, accounting for more than 50 per cent, whereas the next most popular, biology-related topics, accounted for less than 20 per cent. Weitkamp also explains that this may reflect the need to make news stories *relevant* to the readers. An explanation reflected on this first dimension where statistics are used to make news stories sound relevant and to address human-interest issues in stories. A closer analysis of the categories into which the two main topics are subdivided shows the following numbers: public health (mental and sexual health) with 42 articles, sex offences with 29, diseases and disorders with 10 and, lastly epidemiology with 10. These numbers represent 25.74 per cent of the total articles.

Contrary to the aforementioned study by Entwistle and Hancock-Beaulieu (1992), which showed that quality newspapers covered causes more often than treatments, and that in popular newspapers, the responsibility for health is placed with the individual, our own findings suggest that health statistics are articulated in ways to be *relevant* to the readers. Examples of this occur in the *Daily Mail*, in the *Daily Mirror* and in the *Times*, which focus more on the victims of treatments or diseases, while the *Guardian* makes use of statistics particularly to inform about newly released medical reports or about healthcare policies. In other words, the *Daily Mail* and the *Times* give more space to stories where the statistics substantiate the main argument, whereas the *Guardian* places the statistics at the centre of the story, becoming its main element (Figure 6.4).

To make a story relevant, an appropriate writing style is one of the skills required (Mencher & Shilton, 1997). To further this point, writing about statistics, and with statistics, is one of the main concerns not only for journalist educators and journalistic organizations (see, for example, *Working with Numbers and Statistics: A Handbook for Journalists* by Charles Livingston and Paul Voakes, and *Understanding Statistics: A Journalist's Guide* by the Knight Center for Journalism in the Americas) but also for statistical agencies (see, for example, *National Statistician's Guidance* from the UK Statistics Authority and *Making Data Meaningful* by the United Nations). To assess this specific aspect, we found it

Humans - Category Crosstabulation Count

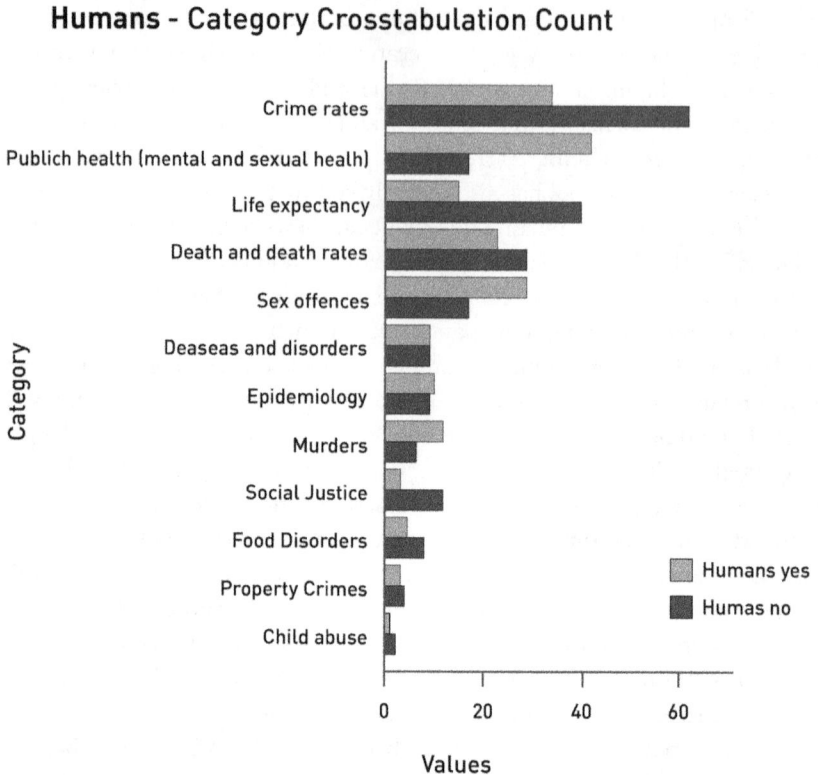

Figure 6.4 Cross-tabulation of the human interest with the category variable.

particularly useful to examine the genre of the article as a variable by cross-tabulating *humans with *genre. The results are shown in the pie charts that follow (Figure 6.5).

The data suggests that beat reportage and hard news do not contain, in more than half of the articles, human-interest issues. Beat reportage (58.33 per cent with 'no' human interest) is about 'informing the readers' and is also 'the regular coverage of a topic or a governmental agency' (Mencher & Shilton, 1997, p. 22). Similarly, hard news (55.59 per cent with 'no' human interest) is up-to-the-minute news related to politics or economics.

Again, when we asked: *Do the statistics involve any human-interest issues?* in the specific case of *genre, feature stories appear to be better represented, with 71.43 per cent human-interest stories. This looks coherent with the use of numbers in the journalistic practice, as we will see in the interviews later in the chapter, where the data analysis and its interpretation of data can take hours

Humans - Genre Crosstabulation Count

Humans yes
Humas no

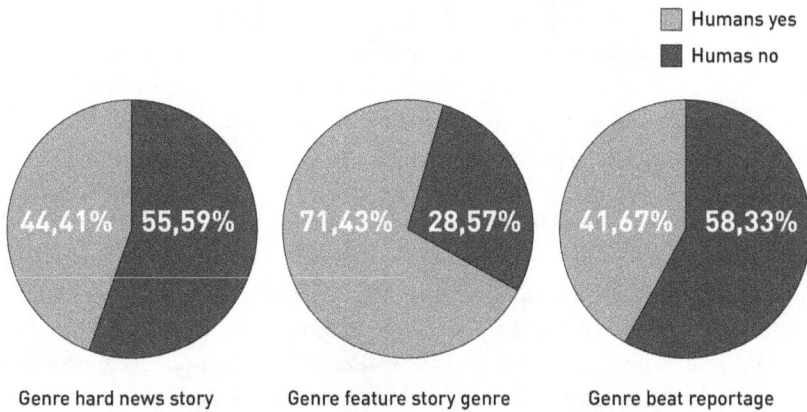

| 44,41% | 55,59% | | 71,43% | 28,57% | | 41,67% | 58,33% |

Genre hard news story   Genre feature story genre   Genre beat reportage

Figure 6.5 Cross-tabulation of the variable *humans and *genre by percentage.

Table 6.4 Length of the articles analysed divided by length.

		Frequency	Per cent	Valid Per cent	Cumulative Per cent
Valid	Long story	228	51.9	51.9	51.9
	Short story	211	48.1	48.1	100.0
	Total	439	100.0	100.0	

or even days to be finalized, impacting, in this way, on the speed of the news production cycle (Rosenberg & Feldman, 2008).

Statistics seem to be, therefore, mostly used by journalists to produce feature articles. This means that articles that make use of statistics are often written in feature style, which allows journalists to write a long story containing expert opinions and offering not only the big picture of an event, but also telling the reader what happened in detail: 'feature writing is often seen by the aspiring journalist as a release from the structural and stylistic restrictions of hard news by allowing much more creativity of thought and opinions' (Rudin & Ibbotson, 2002, p. 58). In fact, this is confirmed by the data in Table 6.4, which shows that over half of the news items (almost 52 per cent) containing statistics had more than 500 words, the minimum length to consider a story a 'feature' story.

A second dimension relates to accuracy and to evaluate it, we made use of two key concepts in journalism: verification and criticality or critical thinking (Ruminski & Hanks, 1995, p. 4). Journalists should be able to verify (verification) and question their sources as part of the journalistic ritual (Shapiro, Brin, Bédard-Brûlé, & Mychajlowycz, 2013, p. 657) and demonstrate this investigation with a high level of critical thinking (criticality) (Browne & Keeley, 2007), which translates into an accurate level of argumentative skills (accuracy), leading to support, or refute, a statistical or scientific source (Dunwoody, 1982, p. 196). According to Bill Kovach and Tom Rosenstiel, journalism is considered to be 'a discipline of verification' because 'in the end, the discipline of verification is what separates journalism from entertainment' (2001, p. 79). The question *Is there any mention of missing/partial statistics?* helped us to see whether journalists verified or not the statistical source upon which their stories were based. In particular, this contributed to evaluate whether the journalist had actively interrogated the source rather than passively accepting what had already been written. The binary answers yes/no clarified the data in relation to Accuracy, conceived as a quality threshold.

According to the pie chart (Figure 6.6), there is no evidence that journalists in almost 99 per cent of the articles questioned the sources of the statistics used. This is an interesting finding, given the fact that among the five quality dimensions, Accuracy is the most important indicator of 'a strong ethical commitment [...] towards [...] truthfulness' (Keeble, 2008, p. 13). This is not fully achieved here. The *Reuters Handbook of Journalism* says that 'accuracy is at the heart of what we do' (MacDowall, 1992, p. 32), while Paul Bradshaw, a journalist and expert in data analysis, claims that 'accuracy can influence how

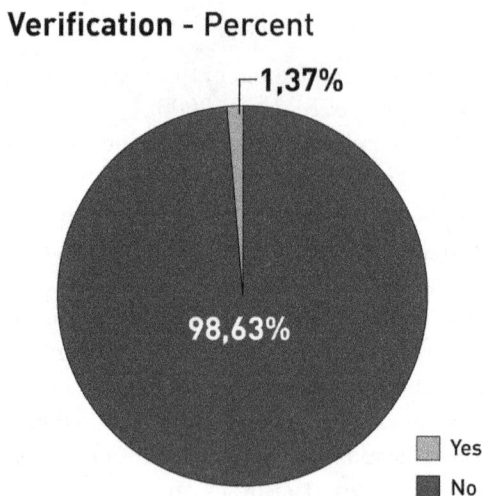

Figure 6.6 Percentage of *verification variable.

we analyse data stories or our publication of data itself' (2013a). Accuracy is therefore an essential dimension in the assessment of quality.

On the one hand, journalists do not verify the statistics themselves and, on the other, they do not use statistics to verify or cross-reference. This cross-verification as a constituent of a 'mediated knowledge' (Godler & Reich, 2017) can also be a strategy of communication (Hansen & Paul, 2015), a good sign of critical thinking in the delivery of quality information. It seems, however, not to be fully integrated into the journalistic practice.

Furthermore, inspired by a wealth of research regarding differences between the genders in performance in mathematics (Hyde, Fennema & Lamon, 1990; Lindberg, Hyde, Petersen & Linn, 2010; Spencer, Steele & Quinn, 1999), we wanted to see which gender tended not to mention any missing or partial statistics. There is also a need to explore this in terms of percentages, whether the problem was due to the gender of the journalist or not. Results show that males tended not to report any type of verification (260 articles), with 59 per cent of the total articles (Figure 6.7).

As already explained before, we have split the concept of Accuracy into factual, practical and scholarly criticism (Richards, 2003). Factual, or empirical, criticism is an objection raised about facts due to something wrong with the evidence of the known experience relevant to it (Collett, 1989). Generally,

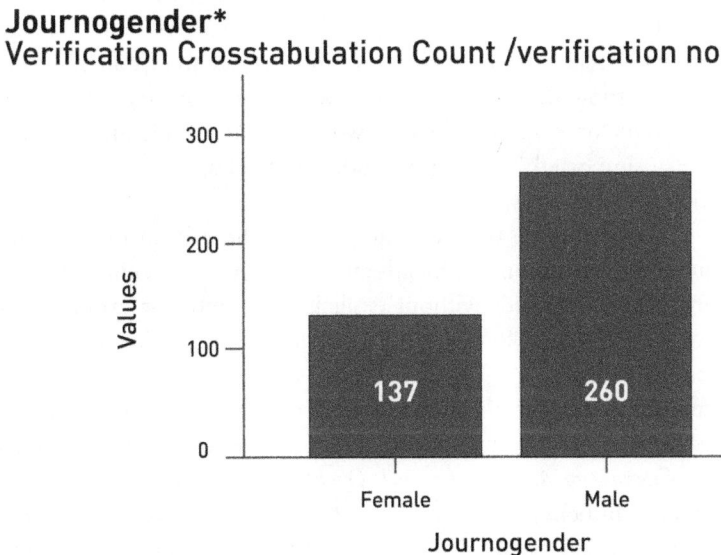

Journogender*
Verification Crosstabulation Count /verification no

Figure 6.7 Cross-tabulation between the *journogender and *verification variables.

Table 6.5 Cross-tabulation of the variables *topic and *criticality2.

Count		Criticality2				Total
		Factual	Practical	Scholarly	No criticism	
Topic	Crime, law and corrections	2	4	5	206	217
	Medicine and health	6	4	5	207	222
Total		8	8	10	413	439

the presentation of facts is deemed biased, and important relevant facts are missing. Practical criticism (Craig, 1984; Feighery, 2011) is an objection or appraisal that refers to relevant practical experience – in this case related to the practical application of statistics in the everyday life of citizens. Among the three types of criticism, scholarly criticism is perhaps the most important in journalism (Klaehn, 2003). A scholarly critic digs deeply into a problem, is very argumentative and tries to be as neutral as possible.

By analysing *evaluation2 and *criticality2 separately, we could observe whether journalists are critically engaged with the statistical sources or not. Hence, by cross-tabulating the variables *topic and *criticality2, we wanted to see what type of criticism (factual, practical, scholarly or none) was used by journalists with respect to the topics of crime and health (Table 6.5).

The results show that there is an overwhelming majority; 94 per cent of articles contain 'no criticism' in the two topics of health and crime. This result is also supported by using two other variables, such as *source1 with *evaluation2.

From the table (Table 6.6), we can see that there is an over-reliance or, better put, an over-citation of official statistics, with 61 per cent of the articles publishing official statistics without explicit verification or critical thinking. The percentage reaches 92 per cent if we include 'non-official' and 'unknown' sources in the count.

These results have serious implications in the context of delivering quality. In this regard, it is relevant to remember the report *Citation Statistics: On the Use of Citations in Assessing Research Quality*, commissioned in 2008 by the International Mathematical Union (Schatz et al.), whose results can be summarized in two main points: 1) the sole reliance on citation data provides, at best, an incomplete and often shallow understanding of research; numbers are not inherently superior to sound judgements; 2) while numbers appear to

Table 6.6 Cross-tabulation of the variables *source1 and *evaluation2.

Count		Evaluation2			Total
		Positive	Negative	No comments	
Source1	Unknown	2	3	59	64
	Non-official statistics	4	4	76	84
	Official statistics	13	9	269	291
Total		19	16	404	439

be 'objective', their objectivity can be illusory. Because this subjectivity is less obvious for citations, those who use citation data (journalists) are less likely to understand their limitations.

As for the news reporting of statistics and citation of statistical reports, we see that in more than half of the articles (61 per cent) analysed the 'objectivity' of official reports is not questioned. Here, the often controversial journalist-source relationship, well known in Journalism Studies, is vividly brought to light. The journalist-source relationship has been described by academics such as Herbert Gans (1980) as 'part dance and part tug-of-war' (p. 45), while Jerry Palmer (2000) calls it a transaction in which both 'journalists and sources have motives which lead them to interpret events in particular ways' (p. 67).

In the present study, sources are often statistical reports, government scientific studies and the opinions of expert statisticians who are considered scientists by the scientific community. The book *Scientists and Journalists* (1986), though old, is still valid because it highlights risks and benefits of the role of scientist-as-source within the production of news. Among the risks, the book highlights the over-citation of government scientific reports because they are believed to have high credibility and authority, and therefore there is no need for them to be reviewed critically by journalists. As Tony Harcup (2006) puts it: 'If a contributor's view is contrary to majority scientific or professional opinion, the demands of accuracy may require us to make this clear' (p. 174). The findings indicate that this clarification does not happen, and when dealing with the dimension of Accuracy, this can hugely impact on the delivery of quality.

The third quality dimension refers to the 'Timeliness' with which journalists make use of statistical reports. Official statistical reports are generally released publicly in the form of a bulletin, every three months, by the Office of National Statistics (www.ons.gov.uk). It is important here to remind ourselves that the issue of time of release and publication of statistics in the public domain has been contested over the years by the authorities and journalists alike (Jairo

Lugo-Ocando & Faria Brandão, 2016). Moreover, the UK Statistics Authority has recently ended pre-release access to official statistics.[1]

The reason for this change was explained by journalist Ben Chu, who wrote, 'the move brings to an end a practice that has long been criticised by experts as serving no legitimate governmental function and running the perennial risk of market-sensitive data leaking' (Chu, 2017). Timeliness in relation to statistics in the news remains a sensitive area, and one which is constantly revisited by those dealing with numbers, particularly around crime (Altheide, 1997; Blanes & Kirchmaier, 2017; Chibnall, 2013; Sheley & Ashkins, 1981). Therefore, it is crucial at this stage to evaluate whether the three-month time limit after release is satisfied or not.

We cross-tabulated the variables *paper and *timeliness1 to see whether a statistical report had been used by the journalists within the period of three months. The results are shown in Figure 6.8. The results reveal that the *Daily Mirror* and the *Guardian*, with their Sunday editions, make use of statistics that are over three months old, as does the *Daily Mail*. What is interesting, however, is the high rate of the unknown age of statistics, which covers a significant proportion of articles (a total of 53.5 per cent) that do not mention the year or date of the statistics' release. The highest score in this regard is the *Times* and the *Sunday Times* with 51.8 per cent of articles that do not contain any time reference.

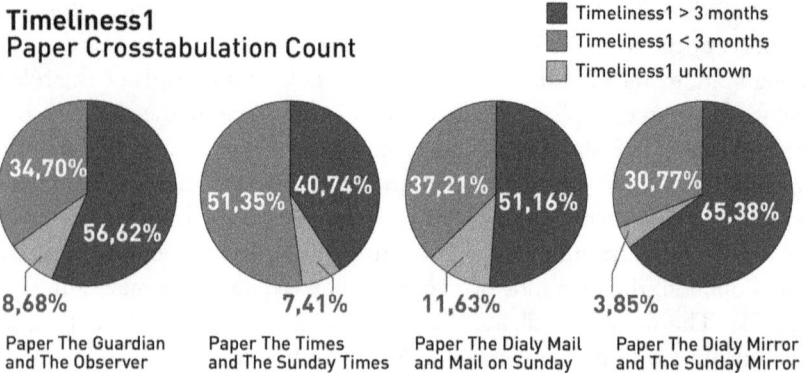

Figure 6.8 Cross-tabulation of the two variables of *timeliness1 and *paper.

---

[1] www.ukstatisticsauthority.gov.uk contains the downloadable official letter from John Pullinger, National Statistician, to Sir David Norgrove, Chair of the UK Statistics Authority.

Table 6.7 Cross-tabulation of the variables *topic and *timeliness1.

Count		>3 months	<3 months	Unknown	Total
		Timeliness1			**Total**
Topic	Crime, law and corrections	112	20	84	217
	Medicine and health	123	17	82	222
Total		235	37	166	439

This translates into a lack of transparency for readers, although possible explanations can be found in the use of numbers as contextual references or just to substantiate a claim. If the latter is the case, then one can reiterate the claim that journalists not only use these numbers to enhance quality in their stories, but also to give credibility (as they expect that numbers will have this effect).

By cross-tabulating *topic and *timeliness1, the situation does not differ much, with slightly more than 53 per cent of articles lacking timeliness in the reporting of dates and years of statistics, whether for health or crime stories (Table 6.7).

In terms of quality, this lack of transparency in relation to Timeliness might negatively affect the credibility of the story by compromising the overall 'completeness of information' delivered to the readers. This is because 'time plays an important part in any newsgathering operation both in terms of getting the story and in terms of when the event became newsworthy. An event must be topical within the period of publication' (Frost, 2015, p. 25). Delivering such completeness means that journalists have a responsibility to report an important matter in a timely fashion, and that it is crucial that they allow their audiences to know which period these statistics refer to, given the fact that they are a snapshot of a set of events.

'Interpretability' is the fourth dimension, and it refers to the use of statistics as a tool that can help reporters and audiences elucidate more comprehensively the meaning of a given story and, at the same time, help reporters scrutinize the same story better. Therefore, to be effective and to enhance civic engagement with the news, the statistics in the story should be easily interpretable by the readers. By means of statistics journalists are able 'to turn moral claims into empirical claims' (Ettema & Glasser, 1998, p. 78). By facilitating interpretation, statistics should therefore allow greater civic engagement and interaction with the story. Statistics that provide additional rationales and explanations to specific events have, therefore, a crucial role in enhancing

Statsclaim Percent

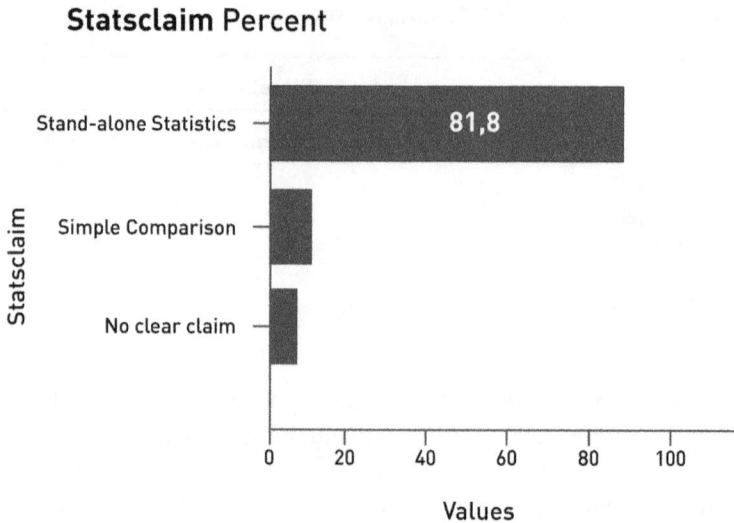

Figure 6.9 Percentage of the variable *statsclaim.

quality in the news. To put it succinctly, a set of statistics that can contribute, for example, to contextualizing a specific event in the wider perspective of public policy, or that allow audiences to understand how the event will affect them, is in fact adding quality to the news.

In order to evaluate this quality dimension, we firstly focused on the two most commonly used statistical narrative tools: stand-alone statistics and statistical comparisons (Abelson, 2012). The first refers to statistics that are isolated, stand-alone figures, while the second makes comparisons between observations and, in this case, statistical reports or expert opinions. In the second, statistical comparisons are, by definition, able to clarify the meaning of specific news stories. The majority of the articles used stand-alone statistics (almost 82 per cent) followed by a simple comparison. Both stand-alone and comparison statistics should make the story interpretable. In the context of this study, Interpretability means a good verbalization of the technical vocabulary and terminology typical of statistics and mathematics.

As Figure 6.9 shows, almost 82 per cent of the articles used stand-alone statistics as a preferred way of verbalizing data-driven stories, and therefore it is unlikely that these statistics somehow make these topics easier to understand. The ability to interpret the meaning refers mainly to the verbalization of statistics, which is a key point in making a statistical claim easily interpretable to readers.

However, following what Morrow and Weston (2015) illustrated in their chapter entitled *Statistics Need a Critical Eye*, the verbalization of statistics is understood here as only a part of a wider context of defending arguments with statistics. To go deeper into the analysis, this result should be corroborated by the scrutiny of the type of statistics that are used in the articles, whether descriptive or inferential, and in which topic they are used most. This is because each type of statistics makes a distinctive contribution to the way journalists and audiences make sense of the outside world.

In the case of crime, for example, many authors have discussed the contributions that both descriptive and inferential statistics make in relation to the way the public constructs social reality around deviation (Lugo-Ocando, 2017). Therefore, analysing the type of statistics is an important step in assessing the quality dimension of Interpretability. Indeed, being able to make a distinction of descriptive or inferential statistics is essential in 'comparative reasoning' (Pfannkuch, Regan, Wild & Horton, 2010) and, we argue, also in the news reporting of statistics, which involves a considerable degree of reasoning skills (Dunwoody & Griffin, 2013; Knowlton & Reader, 2009).

Figure 6.10 shows that descriptive statistics are used preferentially for crime stories (156) whereas inferential statistics are used for health stories (86). This result agrees with the literature in the area (Osborne & Wernicke, 2003), which sees descriptive statistics as the primary statistical tool of the crime analyst and of the crime reporter too (Lugo-Ocando, 2017). Descriptive statistics involve summarizing data into a format that provides a 'descriptive' picture of an event or a series of events. Other descriptive techniques in crime reporting are measures of variability and measures that define the relationship (association) between two or more data elements. Descriptive statistics are also used for medicine and health topics, but slightly less often (136). Compared to descriptive statistics, inferential statistics are used less in general (147, compared to 292). The topic where journalists use inferential statistics most is, however, medicine and health (86). This is not a popular statistical method in healthcare, as some literature in the area suggests (Allison et al., 2000; Fowler, Jarvis & Chevannes, 2013), mainly because inferential statistics are compiled by a process of inductive reasoning based on the mathematical theory of probability and knowledge, and among doctors and nurses there seems to be very little knowledge of this type.

These data could be explained by a reliance of journalists on official public health and crime reports. Indeed, while news values around health tend to overwhelmingly refer to the probability of someone being affected by a specific condition (or being cured by a treatment), crime reporting tends to focus instead on wider trends reported to officials by the different police bodies.

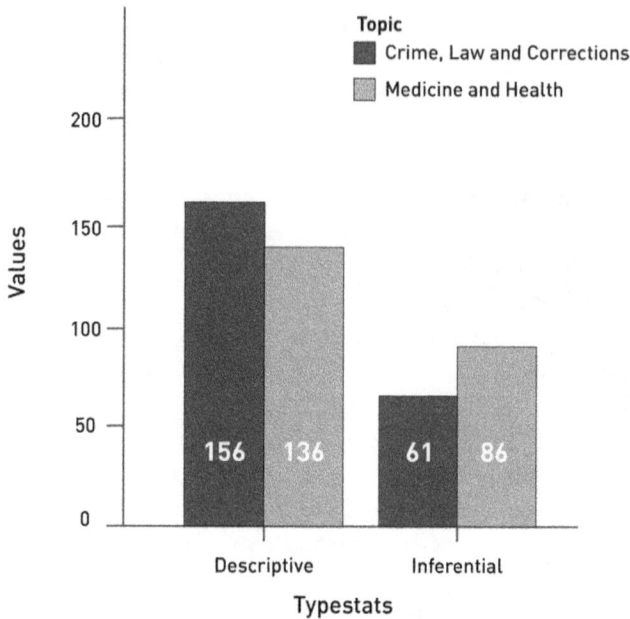

Figure 6.10 Cross-tabulation of the variables *topic and *typestats.

While to a reporter it seems perfectly acceptable to use inferential statistics when referring to a health issue, he/she might not be so open to referring to survey-based information when dealing with crime. A recent study by Hayat, Powell, Johnson and Cadwell (2017) shows that P-values and confidence intervals (results from the use of inferential statistics) appear in more than 76 per cent of public health reports that were analysed. Similarly, inferential statistics are not journalists' preferred method, and only seem to be applied to health issues when necessary.

Overall, these findings suggest that journalists' choice of which statistics to use influences their ability to interpret the meaning of each story. It also seems that, in terms of enhancing quality, these choices make little difference, and reporters do not seem to link these choices to the need to improve the verbalization of statistics or to develop the contextualization. In this sense, one can argue that practice does not match aspirational expectations around quality.

It is precisely because journalists rely so much upon the official sources that they have limited opportunity to make their own choices around which statistics to use. Hence, crime reporters will be more likely to use stand-alone statistics and use inferential or descriptive statistics depending on the news beat they cover. This is because that is the information they receive from official sources, a practice that is, in the end, detrimental to quality, as we have seen here.

Another crucial dimension of quality is to know whether the use of statistics helps to make the information more transparent and, consequently, reliable (accuracy). This Accessibility cannot be understood in terms of interpretability (as examined above) but instead needs to be seen in relation to transparency. In other words, the normative expectation is that the use of statistics should contribute to the ability of journalists to make the stories more accurate.

To analyse this dimension, we have examined the number of statistical sources that were cited in each article as a way of evaluating, in quantitative terms, whether journalists were giving the same type of scrutiny to statistics as they did to other sources (where they often cross-referenced more than one source). Our assumption was that the greater the number of sources, the more accessible the story was, as it would present not only a greater diversity of statistical views, but also these statistical views would cross-check each other (this, of course, is a general assumption). In the context of an assessment of 'completeness of information', quantifying how many sources are cited inside a newspaper article is important.

Citing more sources has its advantages and disadvantages. One of the advantages is that of showing a degree of completeness by comparing and contrasting different sources 'because otherwise you would have been hooked into competing anecdotes' (Ettema & Glasser, 1998, p. 78). There is, however, a drawback to this advantage, as it is up to the journalist to manage the multiple sources coherently by 'testing the information against known facts or other sources' (Frost, 2015, p. 69).

In response to this, as Figure 6.10 suggests, most of the articles across the four UK newspapers relied on one source only. Some might argue that this is perhaps better than having none, but we disagree. We suggest instead that by having only one statistical source, the story, if anything, might become even less accurate, as it depends on only one source that is provided in most cases by government officials. This in turn can affect the transparency of the story, as there is no cross-examination of the validity of these numbers. In other words, one single statistic can also mean one single version of the story, obscuring the journalists' ability to challenge official accounts. Figure 6.11 shows that

Source3* - Paper Crosstabulation Count

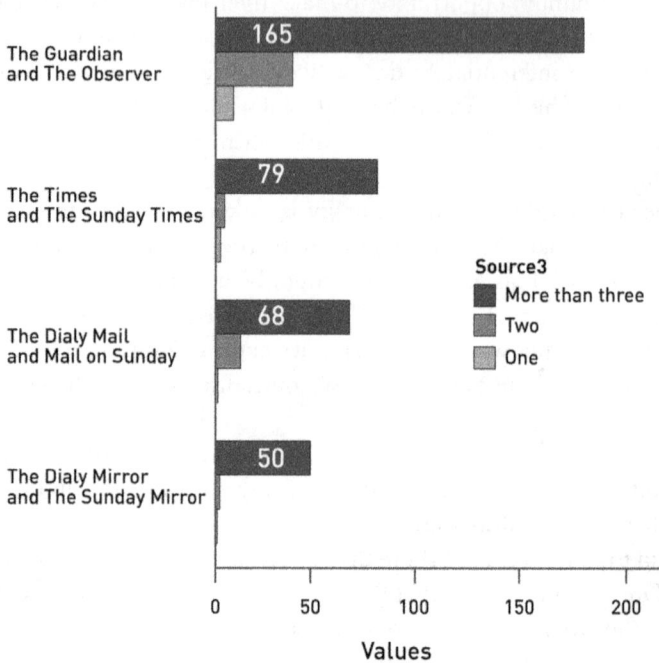

Figure 6.11 Cross-tabulation of the two variables *source3 and *paper.

journalists make use of one source only in the two topics studied here: 81 per cent in health and 84 per cent in crime stories. Other significant data show a 54.7 per cent citation of government reports, followed by 23 per cent where sources are not mentioned, as highlighted in the pie chart (Figure 6.12).

Again, similarly to the Accuracy dimension, the journalist-source relation-ship appears to be crucial in this quality dimension, especially as far as the *not mentioned* sources are concerned, which account for 23 per cent of the total articles analysed. This means that where only source was used, one quarter of the journalists did not mention where the statistics came from. In those cases, for reasons that are not possible to identify through content analysis alone, the journalist failed to identify the source. This is an important finding that brings to light a previously unseen journalistic deficit in relation to the reporting of statistics. However, journalists' 'bad habit' of not citing primary sources is well known in the academic literature (Ewart, Cokley & Coats, 2004; Franklin & Carlson, 2010).

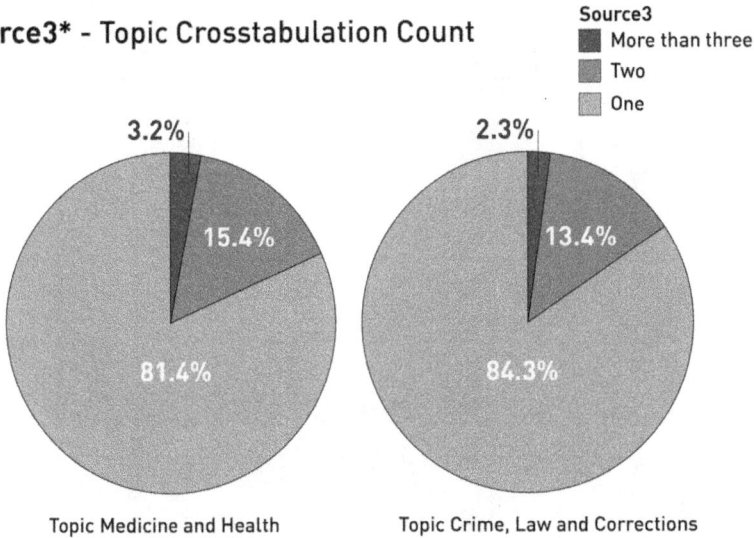

Figure 6.12 Cross-tabulation of *source3 and *topic by percentage.

Ben Goldacre warned readers of *The Guardian* with an article in 2011 entitled *Why Don't Journalists Link to Primary Sources?* Also, the online Reuters Handbook of Journalism clearly states that: 'our reputation for accuracy and freedom from bias rests on the credibility of our sourcing. [...] A named source is always preferable to an unnamed source'. In addition, if we consider the overlapping of duties and the Levels of Abstraction between a journalist and a historian, Martin Conboy (2013) says that journalists should not rely on one source only 'to understand a phenomenon or a social trend, but on many, so that they can construct their own interpretations about the present or the past by means of comparison among sources by sifting information contained in many sources, by listening to many voices' (Howell & Prevenier, 2001, p. 69). In general, by identifying the sources, journalists bring transparency and accessibility to the information: 'Unfortunately, virtually all news sources, by their very nature, provide information that is distorted, either because of pressure of time or resources or because of a deliberate desire to deceive. This is why it is so important to check one source against each other' (Frost, 2015, p. 69) (Table 6.8).

The selection of sources is very problematic, as the literature regarding this issue has shown (Franklin & Carlson, 2010). Sometimes journalists choose a source based on their familiarity (Xie & Joo, 2009), while others do so based on their own area of expertise (Allgaier, 2011). Journalists have

Table 6.8 Cross-tabulation of the variables *paper with *source2.

			Paper				Total
			The Guardian and the Observer	The Times and the Sunday Times	The Daily Mail and Mail on Sunday	The Daily Mirror and the Sunday Mirror	
Source2	Government reports	Count	112	43	59	26	240
		% within source2	46.7%	17.9%	24.6%	10.8%	100.0%
		% within paper	51.1%	53.1%	68.6%	49.1%	54.7%
		% of total	25.5%	9.8%	13.4%	5.9%	54.7%
	International organizations (UN standard)	Count	15	4	1	2	22
		% within source2	68.2%	18.2%	4.5%	9.1%	100.0%
		% within paper	6.8%	4.9%	1.2%	3.8%	5.0%
		% of total	3.4%	0.9%	0.2%	0.5%	5.0%
	NGOs	Count	13	1	1	1	16
		% within source2	81.3%	6.3%	6.3%	6.3%	100.0%
		% within paper	5.9%	1.2%	1.2%	1.9%	3.6%
		% of total	3.0%	0.2%	0.2%	0.2%	3.6%
	Academic independent	Count	10	2	4	2	18
		% within source2	55.6%	11.1%	22.2%	11.1%	100.0%
		% within paper	4.6%	2.5%	4.7%	3.8%	4.1%
		% of total	2.3%	0.5%	0.9%	0.5%	4.1%
	Private organizations	Count	25	2	6	9	42
		% within source2	59.5%	4.8%	14.3%	21.4%	100.0%
		% within paper	11.4%	2.5%	7.0%	17.0%	9.6%
		% of total	5.7%	0.5%	1.4%	2.1%	9.6%

Not mentioned	Count	44	29	15	13	101
	% within source2	43.6%	28.7%	14.9%	12.9%	100.0%
	% within paper	20.1%	35.8%	17.4%	24.5%	23.0%
	% of total	10.0%	6.6%	3.4%	3.0%	23.0%
Total	Count	219	81	86	53	439
	% within source2	49.9%	18.5%	19.6%	12.1%	100.0%
	% within paper	100.0%	100.0%	100.0%	100.0%	100.0%
	% of total	49.9%	18.5%	19.6%	12.1%	100.0%

even, in a reportage crisis, come to rely on familiar sources (Meer, Verhoeven, Beentjes, & Vliegenthart, 2017). The issue has been further problematized in recent years by what J. Lewis et al. (2008) highlighted as the increasing reliance on pre-packaged information released from those 'information subsidies' on public relations input (referred to as 'information foraging providers' in paragraph 3.4).

Therefore, to see whether there was a correspondence between newspapers and the type of source-information subsidies (government statistics or non-official statistics), we decided to perform a correspondence analysis (CA) to explore possible relations among the two categorical variables of *source2 and *paper. We produced a biplot (Figure 6.13), which offers a visual display of each of the values in the dataset plotted with their axes. This provides a global view of the trends within the data.

The distance between any row points or column points in Figure 6.13 gives an idea of their similarity (or dissimilarity). Also, distances between row and

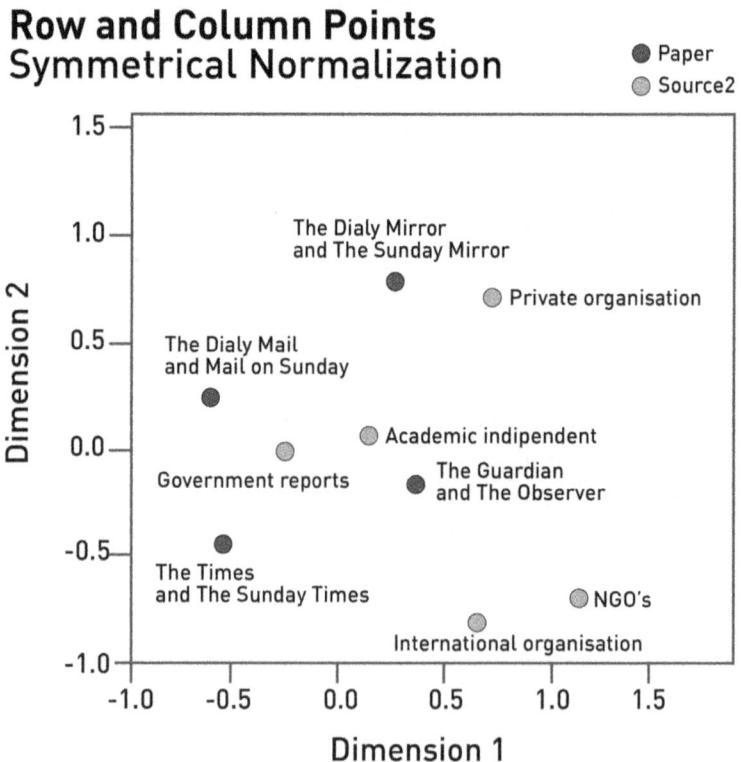

Figure 6.13 Biplot (exploratory graph) obtained from variables *paper and *source2.

column points can be interpreted differently. It is worth noting that the *Daily Mirror* and the *Sunday Mirror* are close to private organizations and the *Guardian* and the *Observer* are close to independent academic reports and slightly less close to government reports. This means that there is a relationship or correspondence (not necessarily an over-reliance) between the *Daily Mirror* and private organizations and the *Guardian* and academic reports.

A general consideration based on the CA leads to results indicating that journalists need non-official statistics in these newspapers. Nowadays there is an increasing amount of information, produced by non-official organizations, where the quality standards vary greatly. In their routine, journalists include the production, for example, of specialized statistics: 'Official sources cannot be universally accepted as the best choice only because they have been produced by public institutions' (UN Statistical Division, Committee for the Coordination of Statistical Activities, CCSA 2016). Also, when reporting issues from or about countries that are politically sensitive and relatively 'young' in terms of existing statistical standards, official or government statistics may not always reach quality standards (Mort, 2006).

In conclusion, Accessibility, as a threshold of quality, suggests two forms of interpretation. One relates to the use that journalists make of statistics in order to present more accessible information and make sure that statistics (official and non-official) are accessible enough for readers to be able to check for validity and reliability. The second relates to the accessibility of statistics themselves by those journalists skilled enough at 'scraping' the data (Bradshaw, 2013b).

Through the lenses of the five dimensions chosen at the beginning of the study as a threshold for quality, we observed that journalists engage with numbers in a reactive rather than a proactive way, passively reporting statistics without critical engagement. This attitude towards numbers vividly brings to light some journalistic shortfalls in terms of credibility and authority.

This pentagonal approach to quality enabled me to also assess the nature of this lack of critical engagement and explore how journalists can engage with statistics to successfully incorporate every single dimension and to analyse how statistics help to achieve such dimensions (Figure 6.14). A full discussion of the findings will follow the close-reading rhetorical. For each single quality dimension, below is a summary in five points.

First dimension: in this dimension, statistics should be used to make stories *relevant* to the readers, by adding human interest as a way of contextualizing isolated events in the wider societal context. In this sense, the findings show that newspapers have different strategies when using statistics to 'humanise' their stories. In the *Daily Mail*, the *Daily Mirror* and the *Times*, statistics appear to be at the centre of the stories as the core of the argument. In the *Guardian*,

Figure 6.14 The pentagonal approach to the concept of quality.

statistics are instead used to substantiate the story and to make the particular news story part of a wider societal problem. Indeed, there are different ways to articulate the dimension of Relevance to deliver quality, and this is in accordance with the news values of the newsrooms. The data indicates that certain types of statistics are relevant in health news while crime news tends to use others. Contrary to our initial expectations, the overall results suggest, however, that Relevance, understood through the human-interest criterion, is not used to achieve quality.

Second dimension: as the literature in the area of journalism suggests, Accuracy should play a pivotal role in news production for every journalist, with no exception. However, in terms of verification and critical thinking, this quality dimension contains surprising results. The data suggests that an overwhelming 98.63 per cent (see Figure 6.6) of statistical reports are neither verified nor questioned. This means that journalists rely exclusively on

official data without any critical engagement, regardless of the topic. This attitude clashes with the deontological duty of verifying the sources, which is one
of the globally accepted ethical norms that keeps the journalistic profession
cohesive across cultures. Statistics are supposed to increase the accuracy of
news, but without proper verification or cross-referencing with other statistical
sources, the achievement of accuracy to deliver quality remains at a merely
theoretical level.

Third dimension: in relation to the third dimension, Timeliness, the results
show that statistics often come from statistical reports more than three months
old, especially in the case of medicine and health. This contradicts common
assumptions and claims that journalists do not have enough time to evaluate
and give sufficient consideration to numbers. The results also suggest that
journalists do not cite the year of the statistical report in almost 40 per cent of
the articles, which, as already suggested, might be because statistical information is used to substantiate stories or underpin assertions made by journalists.
The reasons will be explored later in this book.

Fourth dimension: as discussed here, Interpretability means a good verbalization of the technical vocabulary and terminology typical of statistics and
mathematics. This quality dimension is concerned with the ability to make
data easily interpretable, and also to use the data to make the story more
accessible or understandable. Almost 82 per cent of the articles used stand-
alone statistics as the preferred way to verbalize data-driven stories, suggesting
that this quality dimension is not achieved either.

Fifth dimension: this dimension was examined by looking at the numbers of sources used in each story and their nature. The analysis showed
an over-reliance on official statistics and government reports. This can be
explained by the way journalists tend to approach and engage with news
sources in general. Thus, the way journalists relate and engage with their
sources appear to be crucial under this quality dimension. The findings show
that 25 per cent of the articles analysed had not identified the source. This
suggests that the attempt to make information more accessible by incorporating statistics is a procedure that does not necessarily translate into quality
(Figure 6.14).

The results from the content and close-reading analysis were used to
develop the interviews, which offer an explanatory framework as to why
journalists do what they do. The semi-structured interviews aimed to explain
the findings from this analysis and answer the question of how statistical information is used to articulate and legitimate quality. Furthermore, the interviews
allowed us to underpin the dynamics behind the journalistic uses of statistics
and how journalists understood the meaning of quality within the journalistic
workflow. To do this, we collected the data from fourteen ($n=14$) journalists

from the *Guardian*, the *Times*, the *Financial Times*, the *Telegraph*, *Trinity Mirror* and freelancers. This section presents the results of these interviews, which can be summarized in three key findings.

The first key finding is concerned with an understanding of the concept of quality that generally appears to be scarce among the interviewees. Journalists lack a definition of what quality is in its broadest sense; therefore, they tend not to incorporate this concept into their daily routine. Rather, they are aware of one or more dimensions that could lead to quality, such as that of verification or accuracy, for example. But quality is conceived as a value to aspire to – it is understood as a path that can lead to a more perfect way to be a journalist, a sort of attitude of perfectionism that can easily be threatened by internal and external factors in a day-to-day work routine.

The second key finding highlights two main internal issues that can prevent journalists from attaining quality: statistical innumeracy and statistical accessibility. In the first case, the educational background of the journalists, and lack of mathematical training and statistical reasoning, is a major stumbling block that can hinder journalistic speed, negatively impacting on the news production cycle. In addition to this, the lack of easy access to statistical reports can prevent journalists from delivering news in a timely fashion.

The third key finding evidences an external factor: the politics of numbers. Journalists see statistics as a political tool and therefore as biased at source. However, even if they are aware of this political bias, they tend to prefer the safest route and make use of official and government statistics without being critically engaged with them.

The problematic sense-making

The content analysis showed that there is no single case where the five quality dimensions are comprehensively addressed. There can be an emphasis on one or more dimensions at the same time, but the data did not suggest that quality, as it is interpreted in this study, is fully achieved. In seeking to know what the causes are, we contacted journalists who routinely deal with data and statistics to understand how they use numbers when writing a story. We wanted to evaluate their quality awareness, that is, a very basic understanding of what quality and its dimensions are and what they mean for them when applied to the journalistic daily routine.

The importance of this assessment lies at the historical level. Theodore Porter has argued that because of numbers' longstanding association with rationality and objectivity, quantification can be a useful 'strategy for overcoming distrust' (Porter, 1996, p. 22), especially in professional fields that are susceptible to external criticism.

At a time when the notion of 'datafication' of society (Baack, 2015; John Walker, 2014) is replacing the idea of 'quantification' (Crosby, 1997; Wootton, 2015), becoming more and more pervasive, we might expect the standards of journalistic evidence to become increasingly quantitative and statistically driven. But it seems not to be the case. Distrust in government is even more evident nowadays than before (see Jamie Grierson, 'Britons' Trust in Government, Media and Business Falls,' the *Guardian*, 16 January 2017).

As Tim Berners-Lee puts it in *The Data Journalism Handbook*, 'it used to be that you would get stories by chatting to people in bars, and it still might be that you'll do it that way sometimes. But now it's also going to be about poring over data and equipping yourself with the tools to analyse it and picking out what's interesting' (Gray, Chambers & Bounegru, 2012, p. 12). Through the interviews, we will follow what Berners-Lee suggests and try to determine whether journalists equip themselves with these important quantitative tools.

To begin with, among the 14 journalists interviewed, only 2 were critical (#INT09; #INT13) of the concept of quality. Three (#INT01; #INT04; and #INT07) remained silent on the issue of quality. The others, however, could identify and capture single dimensions that constitute the concept of quality, as a pre-determined set of five dimensions.

> To be honest I never happened to think about this idea of quality. The first thing that comes up in my mind is the sense of being loyal to my readers. I mean I have no rights to cheat on the information I provide. I should be as accurate as I can be. And for what concerns statistics I should make use of my skills at their best in order to perform the data analysis. Make sure that the numbers are accurate. (#INT09)

> Quality is simply a myth. We need to be down to earth. I don't see quality as a tangible and achievable concept as a whole. It is abstract and journalists do not deal with abstractions and theories. We have deadlines and we need to come up with results that is a story, no matter what. (#INT10)

The quotes above reflect, from the beginning, two big problems with quality and its definition/s. On the one hand, journalists do not think specifically about the idea of quality as they are much more concerned with the idea of 'loyalty' to their readers and 'accuracy' when dealing with statistics. It is interesting that #INT09 tends to rely on his own data analysis skills without seeking the help of professional statisticians. This leads to the second-quality dimension used for the content analysis: Accuracy. The data gathered contradict, in fact, what #INT09 said: almost 99 per cent of journalists do not mention any partial or missing statistics in their stories. This means that, from our own perspective as a researcher, there is no evidence as to whether journalists critically question the statistical source they use or not.

On the other hand, the very idea of quality seems to be a hindrance to the speed of journalistic routine. #INT10 suggests that deadlines are often seen as something to fulfil 'no matter what'. This can be related to the third of the quality dimensions: Timeliness. According to this journalist, the speed and routine in newsrooms do not allow journalists to use fresh datasets. This validates the 53.5 per cent of data (from the content analysis, see Figure 6.8) older than three months and, perhaps most surprisingly, the 38 per cent where no reference to time is mentioned at all. This can be explained by the limitations journalists have experienced since June 2017 in accessing pre-released statistical reports, and the answer might also explain the gap between the normative claims of quality and the pursuit of trust and credibility. Other journalists provided more explanation when asked about quality:

> I think quality goes together with verification. Being journalists, we have the duty to verify our sources and use government statistics because they are official. Yes, I would say that official sources are of quality and we can use them with no fear. (#INT02)

> Quality is not only about delivering a good story, a story that is credible. Yes, I think statistics can enhance this credibility. Statistics are the cause and the effect. The cause because a statistical analysis can trigger a good credible story. The effect because they are the means through which you can show the evidence of what you are talking about. (#INT14)

By these means, 'verification' and 'credibility' represent the drivers through which an achievement of quality would therefore be possible. Verification of statistical sources would be the key to delivering quality, and credibility would be the ultimate goal. However, as we have seen with the content analysis, verification of sources failed in almost 99 per cent of the articles analysed (see Figure 6.5). #INT02 mentions that official sources automatically mean quality, and journalists use them without asking questions.

We perceive a contradiction here. If verification is central to quality, the usage of sources, whether they are official or non-official, should be accompanied by a good degree of scepticism and critical thinking, and we should not blindly trust them as the phrase 'with no fear' would suggest. In fact, this is confirmed by the content analysis that shows under the variables *criticality2 and *evaluation2 that the overwhelming majority of articles do not contain any type of criticism, or comments regarding the statistical sources.

#INT14 argues that statistics enhance the story's credibility and that quality is not just a credible story. According to him, statistics themselves are the means to deliver credibility because they are used to support hard facts and show the evidence of journalistic claims. He talks also about two specific quality dimensions: Accessibility and Interpretability conceived as 'the evidence of what you are talking about'. The above consideration is supported by recent literature that shows how statistical information tends to reinforce the institutional perspectives typically found in news coverage (Wahl-Jorgensen, Berry, Garcia-Blanco, Bennett & Cable, 2016).

Another journalist pointed out the balance that a kind of journalism that uses statistics should achieve.

> Quality journalism has a meaning if it is used in the public interest. It is well researched journalism and non-sensationalised. It is an intelligent way of making journalism. I personally use data as just another source of news – I use statistics to interpret data and construct well researched, non-sensationalised, meaningful stories and deliver quality. (#INT08)

In this case, quality conveys an idea of impartiality and balance and, most importantly, journalists link the idea of quality to public service (Ettema & Glasser, 1998). This point has been recently corroborated by Stephen Cushion when he says, 'when scrutiny is applied, it is often through the lens of impartiality rather than an attempt at objectivity' (2016, p. 2). According to #INT08, balance represents the smartest way to achieve quality journalism. She stresses the fact that statistics are 'just another source'. Rather than talking about what makes statistics official or non-official, this journalist says that statistics are to be considered a good source for 'well-researched and non-sensationalised' journalism. Indeed, the risk here is that statistics could be 'entertaining' by publishing sensationalized numbers with odd correlations (Gallagher, 2014) rather than 'informative' (Livingston & Voakes, 2005). This point is further clarified by another journalist,

> There are criteria to follow. If journalism doesn't meet these criteria it's little more than sensationalistic fluff. Some of the best articles I've read, or programs I've listened to, take one seemingly unintelligible and complicated concept and break it down piecemeal through the lens of a relatable character. Quality journalism is telling the truth by telling – nonfiction – stories. (#INT11)

This journalist acknowledges the existence of certain criteria, similar to Harcup and O'neill (2001) and their criteria about what is news. When asked to rationalize such criteria, only one journalist, however, was willing to go into detail, as described below (numbers in square brackets are to simplify the reading). As someone who contributes to a journalism project that tries to put an emphasis on data quality reporting over data quantity, the characteristics that embody quality journalism are:

[1] All facts and data should be verifiable. 'Number of people with diabetes up to 60% in the last decade' is not particularly verifiable. 'NHS spokesperson told reporters at a press conference that diabetes is up to 60% in the last decade' is verifiable. If you attribute something to someone, it should be appearing in your notes (or on audio) and this should be available to reviewers who actually review it to verify that what you wrote matches your notes. Datasets work in a similar way. They should be available both to the journalists who are dealing with that and to the readers, who might want to get access.

[2] It must be neutral. Lots of material that is passed off as neutral fundamentally is not. And when people do meet up with neutral, fact-based information, this type of neutral journalism often leads to accusations of bias because they are unable to understand what neutral means. People should be able to draw their own opinions from the facts alone and here from simple statistics.

[3] The topic is newsworthy. The newsworthiness should be measured by answering all the key questions: who, what, where, when, why, how? Same for statistics. And it should be current, reporting on an event that took place in the past 48 hours. In the case of statistical releases, they shouldn't be older than 1 year. Otherwise news ceases to be news. Though facts do not cease to be facts.

[4] It needs to be written for an international audience, explaining why this matters. Putting context in for an international audience is important. Also, putting in the key facts matters. I have read sport reporting where I got to the end and had zero idea what sport was being discussed.

[5] It needs to comply with a style guide and be reasonably well written. (#INT09)

The above quotation touches on some of the five quality dimensions: (1) relates to Accessibility; (2) to Accuracy; (3) to Relevance and Timeliness; and both (4) and (5) to Interpretability. In summary, according to #INT09, quality journalism should: (1) follow five criteria to be successful; and (2) privilege the quality of data over the quantity.

If point (1) corroborates the main assumption of this study, point (2) touches on a very long-debated issue of data overload (Nordenson, 2008; Whitney, 1981). Implicitly, it brings to light that quality criteria, or quality dimensions, can be conceived as an effective means of counteracting and making sense of such an abundance of data. To prevent such quantity of data from deteriorating their quality, another journalist points out the attention on (1) the time factor and (2) the expertise that makes quality news and can impact on overall data management:

In my opinion, quality is expertise plus time. I regard all kinds of people as experts, if one has no formal education or can't even read but has a lot of hands-on experience with ducks, this person will probably be a duck expert. Sure, it might take a while to understand this kind of expertise because it has taken a path wildly different from what most people in the media profession have taken, namely schooling. That's expertise, but it takes expertise of expression to publish this expertise and it will take time to reflect on one's opinion. If this is done properly, quality will be produced. Transparency should never replace objectivity, it's a condition of objectivity. Transparency without objectivity is by itself not a bad thing but should only serve as a flag warning an opinion is biased or without expertise at best. Since objectivity is an ideal and something which can never be fully reached, every article that is published as objective should be transparent. That's why scientific research references are the very building blocks of its argument. In most quality journalism, we assume objectivity and I believe it's what they strive for as well, but I would like to see their resources more prominently. More scientific if you like. (#INT07)

Journalist #INT07 makes a link between 'transparency' and 'objectivity'; cardinal points for those who conceive the journalistic profession under the lens of the Social Sciences, as it was for Philip Meyer. The point made by #INT07 is useful to understand two points. On the one hand, expertise is a key factor to produce quality. Expertise, as such, requires time to be assessed, and this is a pre-condition in the achievement of quality. On the other hand, the time factor sounds secondary in relation to expertise, and time can be practically used to evaluate expertise. This takes us back to the quality dimension of Timeliness.

In the content analysis we have seen that journalists make use of statistics that are more than three months old. Therefore, they have enough time to perform an appropriate data analysis over that time period. From the qualitative point of view, however, there is no explanation or justification of how they maximize their time. A reliance on expert opinions would explain a deferential attitude, which is the opposite of the kind of journalistic attitude that claims to be 'scientific'. The true scientific attitude is that of being sceptical even towards expert opinions (Gannon, 2004), in line with what Richard Feyman is believed to have said: 'science is the organised scepticism in the reliability of expert opinions'.

In the literature review we also referred to the Philosophy of Information (PI), and this approach is also very much concerned with evidence gathering and expert opinion. In this regard, PI sees the evidence produced by expert opinion as information about the person's experience of the given topic. There is some exchange of information that occurs between individuals who apply methods to generate evidence and individuals that evaluate the generation of evidence (Baumgaertner & Floridi, 2016). This 'exchange of information' happens between journalists and statisticians or data experts. Again, this is confirmed by the content analysis that shows that 55 per cent of the articles make use of official reports and report expert interviews.

To paraphrase Kovach and Rosenstiel, objectivity calls for journalists to develop a consistent method of testing statistical information so that personal and educational bias does not undermine the transparency of their work. If this is good in theory, it is not in practice. The next journalist contradicts what the two authors have just said to be the basic 'elements' of journalism and introduces what is the second key finding of the interviews: statistical innumeracy. #INT10 focuses on numeracy and its importance for finding stories that are relevant and informative:

> Journalism that not only scratches the surface, but gives a broad context. Well written, good graphics and maps, hard topics explained clearly, relevant in the longer run. If you're comfortable with numbers, you can dig deeper and find stories that otherwise would stay untold. And you can always look at a dataset from another angle: for example, what happens if you take a larger or smaller window of a time series? And a lot of reporting sticks to the average. But what about the median? Why not draw a chart that shows all the variation? To me, these are elements of a high numeracy quality journalism. (#INT10)

According to #INT10, statistical numeracy should be part of the sense-making of quality. It is a skill that enables journalists to write deeper stories by looking at data from different perspectives. Again, the content analysis showed that, regarding the quality dimension of Accessibility, journalists should be able to make statistics accessible. Failing to know how to treat data and publish it in an accessible manner because of lack of statistical training would negatively impact on the overall quality. This point about mathematical numeracy can be further developed by explaining key finding 2.

So far, the interviews have shown the problematic sense-making of quality through each dimension. There is a need to consider the first of the two main interferences to quality journalism by examining the difficulties journalists experience in managing numbers, as #INT07, #INT08 and #INT11 succinctly highlight:

> Many journalists have no mathematical qualifications and don't know what to do with numbers. (#INT07)

> Without a doubt: statistical knowledge is lacking. It is still very underdeveloped in journalism. (#INT08)

> The main disadvantage is lack of understanding of statistics. It is sometimes time consuming, you need a lot of skills (data gathering, cleaning, analysing, visualising, reporting). (#INT11)

Statistical innumeracy is the first internal interference to the achievement of quality. This seems to show that the use of numbers in news reporting is still not fully understood by journalists. On the one hand, literature in the area also highlights the lack of statistical training, which remains underdeveloped (Nguyen & Lugo-Ocando, 2016), and on the other, journalists complain about how the data analysis process would increase the journalist's workload. In the era of speed-driven journalism, performing statistical analysis would therefore be time consuming (Juntunen, 2010).

> Not everything can be measured and converted to data. Some argue that if you can't measure it, it doesn't exist. But new phenomena may be hard to count, things fall between the cracks of different categories, phenomena that are currently too small to measure (but one day will be important). Sometimes this means that no secondary data is available and you have to collect the numbers on your own. But often quantitative data is just not the right format. Sometimes you need a good narration to tell a story. (#INT03)

#INT03 elucidates what happens when dealing with statistical data. There are internal difficulties that pose a threat to quality. For example, secondary data are often not available, and often not in compatible formats. Also, a story needs to be narrated by means of a clear verbalization of mathematical terminology. This is specifically related to the quality dimensions of Accessibility, the use of statistics to make information more accessible, and Interpretability, the use of narrative tools to improve a story.

Balancing accessibility and interpretability is crucial to the delivery of information quality (Howard, Lubbe & Klopper, 2011), especially in journalism. There is also the assumption that numbers through science can explain everything in the world (Santos, 2013; Weinberg, 2004), but the traditional way of talking to people cannot be entirely replaced by figures (Ettema & Glasser, 1998), and statistics themselves cannot explain everything (Reinhart, 2015), as #INT12 observes:

> Statistics can't explain everything; and it's no substitute for talking to people. Numbers can tell you that criminals are very likely to commit further crimes where you live, but they don't explain why that might be the case. (#INT12)

At this stage, it is important to understand how journalists engage with statistics when dealing with crime and health stories. Newspapers adopt different approaches when reporting crime and health statistics. #INT14 and #INT9 offer an insight into the challenges they experience:

> Crime statistics is a mess. Since there is no officiality, journalists can twist it at their pleasure. Health statistics are different, another world. In that case, my experience tells me that it's the methodology used that give validity, but again, only a bunch of journalists can detect whether a methodology is correct or not. (#INT14)

> The main challenge is making statistics-led stories accessible to the public. This is crucial for medical journalism. Sometimes you know something is important such as NHS trust mortality rates. The challenge then becomes how to write the story in a way that is both accurate and accessible to the public who will probably not have much of a statistical background. (#INT09)

We observe here two urgent issues in the articulation of crime and health statistics: methodology and accessibility. Methodology – how data are gathered and collected – seems to be neglected by most journalists who deal with crime, maybe because their educational background does not allow them to spot fallacies, or because there is no homogeneity in how statistics are collected, especially in the area of crime. For this reason, they should be equipped with more stringent investigative tools. In the journalistic practice, the methodology of seeking evidence can be found mostly in investigative journalism techniques at the crossroads with some open-source intelligence methods. In the case of crime statistics, the cause might lie in the huge problems that crime statistics have in relation to their categorization and collection. According to a 2006 independent review commissioned by the UK secretary of state of the Home Department: 'crime statistics have long been recognised as having a number of weaknesses. [...] A number of attempts have been made over the last years to address these problems, but they largely remain'. Also, as far as health statistics are concerned, a recent study by Yavchitz et al. (2012) confirmed that half of medical reporting is subject to spin, which casts serious doubts on the reliability of mainstream medical and health journalism.

Accessibility is also at the centre of concerns for those who deal with health statistics (Kendrick, 2014). In the case of health statistics, however, this should be translated into transparent risk communication (Gigerenzer, Gaissmaier, Kurz-Milcke, Schwartz & Woloshin, 2007). Almost 85 per cent of the articles on both crime and health topics have shown that journalists use only one source – the most accessible one. Lack of accessibility to a wealth of varied sources is not the only problem. #INT06 considers other difficulties, for example, the lack of clarity of numerical terminology contained in certain non-official sources.

> There are lots of traps you can fall into when analysing data, such as confusing percentage points with percentages, not understanding confidence intervals and not considering data suppression for small numbers. If you make any of these mistakes your story is likely to be less accurate and therefore of lower quality. (#INT06)

> Inferential statistics make the story sound more authoritative and, if you wish, scientific. Where descriptive statistics are for everybody with a minimum of mathematical skills. (#INT14)

The last quote can be seen through the lens of the content analysis data in the quality dimension of Interpretability. We made a distinction between descriptive and inferential statistics; descriptive statistics are used most for crime stories and inferential statistics in health news. Regardless of the preference for one method or the other, a constant effort to appear 'scientific' is noticeable. In the pursuit of this scientific value lies the risk that scientists themselves pursue their own goals, and these goals often involve raising money for their research. In doing so, they sometimes formulate their findings in a way that can mislead journalists into believing a study to be more significant than it is (A. Bell, 2016; Dunwoody, 2014). There is, however, another interference that is voiced even more strongly by the journalists interviewed, and that is the political interference of statistics, which is addressed as key finding 3.

The third interference to quality is external and it comes from those statistics that are biased or deemed to be biased for political reasons. The interrelation between numbers and politics is not only a historical affair (S. M. Stigler, 1986), but a lively and timely matter that influences our daily lives. This urgent and growing concern has been widely addressed in recent work by Lorenzo Fioramonti (2013, 2014) who exposed the hidden agenda underpinning the use of statistics. The following analysis shows that among journalists there is also a very tangible concern about the use of statistics for political ends,

> There are thousands of companies, pressure groups and political parties out there trying to influence the news agenda with numbers. It seems obvious that news organisations should have at least one person helping journalists get the numbers right. (#INT13)

> Official data is politicised. The Government has an interest in presenting numbers in a way that suits it, and even non-partisan organisations often present their data in a way that reflects the news agenda. For example, the ONS publishes a section on gender differences in pay when it publishes its annual pay survey. (#INT02)

The viewpoints of the two journalists regarding this 'politicised' data are exemplificative and confirm what the writer Tim Harford illustrated in his article 'How Politicians Poisoned Statistics' published in the *Financial Times* in April 2016, which centres on the basic argument that in politics we are witnessing a rise in 'statistical bullshit', or misleading statistics.

To make things worse, when we asked about differences between official and non-official statistics, we often perceived a hesitation. This would explain the over-reliance on government reports, as the content analysis showed. This also explains the dichotomy of the proactive/reactive approach to numerical information. A proactive approach would help to eliminate problems before they even have the chance to occur; its opposite, the reactive approach, is based on responding after something has happened. When journalists cannot recognize the difference between official and non-official, they tend to react and use data released by well-known national government bodies.

Other journalists have changed their opinion regarding government statistics and have become more proactive, rather than reactive, as in the case of #INT13. It is interesting to note a shift in the opinions, now being more sceptical than ever, mainly due to recent political occurrences, such as the Brexit referendum and the US presidential elections:

Before Brexit and Trump I would've said statistics is not politicised. But today there is a lot more criticism of experts and the numbers they use to explain and convince. 'Lies, damn, lies and statistics'. So, statistics are used a lot in politics, but in a marketing way: to prove one's own point and to convince, not to explain the truth. A lot of the time data used is cherry picked and used, charts are misleading. (#INT13)

This puts forward the belief that the government uses data from third party bodies for marketing purposes. Therefore, by selling a product, which in this case is the statistical report, numbers are used to convince and persuade people about the product's quality by means of 'branding'. Generally, the position of journalists is well summarized in the following statement,

In the main I don't think the figures released by the ONS and other government departments are politicised at source. But yes, data can be interpreted in different ways. This means that different political sides can spin statistics to fit their agenda. This was particularly apparent during the EU referendum campaign. (#INT09)

For the question of how statistics are used to deliver quality, this represents a crucial point. Even though there is a good awareness of what quality means and of the risks concerning the political bias, journalists seem to prefer to play safe and make use of official statistics. Within the newsroom, subjective decisions are made, journalists use the data they want, and they tend to support this data by means of expertise and officiality. In this way, they wish to protect the quality they want to convey from external interferences.

The interviews expand the findings and our views of the topic. Despite a high level of quality awareness, and despite the fact that journalists clearly identify what the drivers that lead to quality journalism are, two main problems can still damage this predisposition or ambition towards quality. One issue is related to a gap between the data releases and their comprehension by journalists, which entails two other problems, the validation process of such data and an over-reliance on official government data. The second main issue is training; considering that only two of the journalists interviewed have a mathematical background, it became clear from the analysis that the lack of statistical training would negatively impact on the adherence to all five quality dimensions. Also, given the problems of accessing and validating the data, the traditional mechanism of verification and validation used in other journalistic fields is not performed by journalists when dealing with numerical information.

Why do they do it?

Overall, this research found three main interferences that prevent journalists from attaining quality in the news: (1) the low level of understanding of what quality is; (2) statistical innumeracy, mainly caused by a lack of mathematical training together with statistical accessibility and its limitations; and (3) the political side of numbers that is perceived as a potential interference to the transparency of the journalistic workflow.

It is important to remember here that the National Council for the Training of Journalists in places such as the United Kingdom, where our fieldwork took place, often claims that 'maintaining quality' should be at the centre of the journalistic profession. Journalists, however, have a low level of quality awareness, and there is a gap between what they understand as 'quality' and what they do to maintain it during the data manipulation process. This gap clearly impacts on the articulation of quality statistics in news reporting.

Despite statistical agencies claiming to be free from political interferences, as for the Office of National Statistics in the United Kingdom, according to the personal experience of a former government statistician and now informer, Jacob Ryten (2012), there are at least three types of interferences 'which can be found in just about every country with a long enough history of official statistics' (2012, p. 9): (1) to 'muzzle' (prevent or delay publication of statistics ready to be published); (2) to handcuff (prevent regular surveys from taking place); and (3) to takeover (government officials occupy the physical space of the statistical agency; according to Ryten there are examples of this in the Latin American region).

The first interference to quality raises concerns over the journalists' ability to properly describe what role quality plays in both the journalistic workflow and in the data manipulation process. Therefore, there are reasonable doubts regarding how they write their stories and use the data to achieve quality. Quality seems, therefore, far away from the journalistic practice of data analysis in newsrooms. This perhaps sounds quite drastic, but it has also been noticed by Jarmo Raivio (2010) in the Reuters Oxford report entitled *Quality Journalism: The View from the Trenches*. In this report, Raivio concluded that 'quality journalism' seems to be a highly elastic concept, maybe 'to the point of not being very meaningful at all' (p. 74). However, in the present study such quality illiteracy goes in tandem with that of statistical illiteracy. In fact, this leads to the second interference, statistical literacy, which is crucial in the articulation of quality statistical information. If the importance of the uses of statistics in newsrooms is shared among the journalists interviewed, the lack of training is even more apparent.

Most journalists have never done any scientific or statistical training and often have never been asked to have knowledge in quantitative methods, even in Logic and Argumentation or Probability. In this respect, we agree with Johanna Vehkoo (2011) in her Reuters Oxford report entitled *What Is Quality Journalism and How It Can Be Saved*, where she came to the conclusion that journalists must specialize: 'journalists will have a set of skills that allows them to be truly platform-agnostic in their work' (p. 73). According to Vehkoo, journalists should be experts able to create a following, perhaps even a community, around their stories. This point has already been addressed by Barbie Zelizer (1993), who points out that journalists represent the interpretive community.

Journalists are members of a professional collective, as we have mentioned, that offers an interpretation of key social and political trends, in this case using the interpretative tools of statistical analysis. In addition to this, expert authority and statistical accessibility bring forward the controversial issue that involves official statistics and its credibility: there is no practical way of verifying if such statistics are right or wrong, and this leads to the conclusion that we either believe what the official agency tells us or we do not, but proper verification seems beyond anyone's capabilities, especially in the time constraints of the journalistic workflow. The case of official crime statistics is exemplificative, as they are an inaccurate reflection of our everyday experience of crime (MacDonald, 2002) and efforts have been made by the UK Statistical Authority (2010) to overcome such limitations.

The third and last interference to quality, as the findings describe, is represented by the political side of statistics and its impact on the five dimensions. This point has its historical roots in what Max Weber (Mommsen, 1974; Weber, 1946) prophesized as a rational bureaucratic legal society. Our Western society has indeed become a bureaucratized society where Michel Foucault (Espeland & Stevens, 2008; Sauder & Espeland, 2009) identified the 'quantificatory episteme', which is the 'science' of quantifying the human experience (Frängsmyr, Heilbron & Rider, 1990) and of turning raw information and data into knowledge. In recent history 'nothing was left untouched by the statisticians' argues Ian Hacking (1982, p. 280), who links the rise of statistical thinking to the Foucauldian concepts of Biopower, Biopolitics and Regimes of truth.

Doing journalism in an era of data abundance poses questions of growing significance, because it involves 'some of the most fundamental aspects of news and its production', and questions around 'what such changes actually mean for news, democracy and public life' (Seth C. Lewis, 2015, p. 321). The maintenance of quality and its dimensions are subjected to these changes and struggle between figures of arithmetic and figures of speech (Poovey, 1993), between the needs of politics and the needs of journalists (Meehan, 2000; Prewitt, 1986). Under these constraints, journalists perform statistical analysis and report numbers in a way that might resemble a form of standardized and predictable 'McJournalism' (Franklin, 2003): 'while market theorists claim diversity and quality as the essential products of competition, the reality is McJournalism and McPapers with similar stories' (Keeble, 2008, p. 161). Consequently, the public tends to receive information that is not always up to quality standards, and this makes newsrooms and governments an object of suspicion, fostering in this way feelings of anxiety and mistrust (Tateno & Yokoyama, 2013), for example, in the cases of risk communication (Renn & Levine, 1991), crime (Heilbrun, Wolbransky, Shah & Kelly, 2010) and health issues (Bennett, 2010).

Focus groups and audiences

Using focus groups allowed us to understand better the end-users of statistics, and how the news cycle shapes readers' views and attitudes towards statistical information. We did this by asking: How does the audience engage with statistically driven stories? The focus groups were organised in Leeds and Manchester and involved 22 ($n=22$) participants. Participants read four ($n=4$) articles that contained anecdotal and official data related to crime and health news.

We will summarize the data analysis in one major area, which is the key finding of this methodology. This is followed by an expanded description of participants' narratives about their views on the use of statistics in news reporting. Excerpts from focus group discussions and words used by participants are integrated into this narrative to provide a greater understanding and appreciation of the ways in which statistics are experienced, understood and talked about by participants.

The findings suggest that quality articulated in five dimensions fails to be transmitted through news reporting. Readers are particularly sceptical about three main areas: (1) authority, where statistical expertise, the 'branded statistics', is seen by the participants as part of a hidden process that aims to manipulate public opinion; (2) accessibility, mainly related to ways of obtaining full access to public statistics; and (3) accuracy, which involves the methods of data collection, which are often unclear. Throughout the four focus groups, the prevailing attitude was that of scepticism towards what was reported through statistics, undermining in this way any effort in the pursuit of quality from the journalists.

Authority, accessibility, accuracy

Focus-group participants were asked to discuss the numerical information as presented in the articles, to give their own definitions of quality and, wherever possible, to summarize their understandings of the statistics contained in the four articles. We found that nearly all the participants could not define or grasp the concept of quality. Hesitation and silence were the common 'answer' to questions about quality. A few individuals, three at most, expressed their views on quality as, for example, 'too complicated to define'. The attitude was extremely critical, ranging from simple doubts to rejection of the concept: 'talking of quality in numbers is like talking about honesty with politicians, I don't believe in it, I don't believe it is possible'.

On the one hand, the silence we witnessed seems to speak volumes about how the readers were not aware enough of quality to discuss its multiple definitions and the implications that these could have on the public discourse of statistics and their values in democratic life. On the other hand, the feeling of 'hostility', or 'suspicion', is not exclusively towards the concept of quality itself – it goes beyond involving the concept of public trust.

In this regard, the effort of the UK government to improve the public's trust in statistics has been admirable. *Statistics: A Matter of Trust*, a consultation document released in 1998 by the Labour government aimed at finding 'modern' ways to improve public perception of statistics by claiming that 'reliable official statistics are a cornerstone of democracy'. The following year, the report *Building Trust in Statistics* was released, with a clear statement that 'official statistics need to be of assured quality and be compiled and presented in a way which is free from political interference'. Since then, the last accessible report in 2014 was published with the title: *Public Trust in Government Statistics: A Review of the Operation of the Statistics and Registration Service Act 2007, Session 2013–14.* These three government documents are perhaps the most significant in casting some light on the various strategies to improve trust in the government. Despite such efforts, there are still tangible problems in 'communicating with statistics', as another government report highlighted in 2013.

What we call the three A's of distrust are in fact areas where readers experience a lack of confidence. Based on the qualitative data collected from the focus groups, we identified the following three areas: (1) authority: readers are sceptical, specifically about the nexus of expertise-authority-competence; (2) accessibility: readers are sceptical and concerned about full public access to statistics; and (3) accuracy: readers are sceptical about the methodology of data collection by journalists. These are clear signs of distrust in statistics.

We argue that this lack of confidence in the statistical data, as published in the news media, might lie in what Theodor Porter would call the 'engagement-detachment' game that is played by the readers. Indeed, during one focus group, two participants offered an exchange of opinions that is representative of a willingness to be engaged with statistics (a willingness to listen) and at the same time a reluctance to accept them as truth (a willingness to suspect):

P4:   Statistics have fallen into disrepute, partly because they are often manipulated by those who have an agenda. I have seen it claimed that, statistically, very few people die because of Islamic terrorism when compared to other forms of terror. When I actually looked into the statistical evidence for these claims it was utterly bogus, since it failed to recognise so many examples as being religiously motivated.

P3:   The same in health, like the example of the article we are reading today. But people who do that probably aren't deliberately trying to mislead, they are only seeing the data that suits their preconceptions. (#FG1)

These participants acknowledge that there is an obstacle that prevents them from trusting numbers: statistics seem to be miscommunicated by those who have a political agenda. Also, they feel manipulated by those who want to use them to fit their *preconceptions*, or already established assumptions. These statements are indicative of a general but consistent attitude toward numbers in news.

An explanation might be found in history, in the evolution of the concept of *public reason* whose concern 'is the very basis of our collectively binding decisions […] it envelops all the different elements of a constitutional democracy […] in which we ought to stand to one another as citizens' (Larmore, 2003, p. 368). The journalism-statistics-public relationship reason is even stronger in the United Kingdom because 'contemporary public life in Britain would be unthinkable without the use of statistics and statistical reasoning. Numbers dominate political discussion' (Crook & O'Hara, 2011, p. 22). But this relationship entails what we have previously called an 'engagement-detachment' game, as P5 of #FG1 suggests when he says: 'people are not numbers and democracy is not a number'.

Throughout the sessions, participants were asked to expand on this feeling that was described with words such as 'anxiety', 'frustration' and 'tension'. Two participants summed up such a feeling as follows:

P5:   People are not numbers and democracy is not a number. Numbers impose a rigid, mechanistic system upon us which is deeply unpleasant. And why should you trust something you cannot understand that has been thrust on you by experts, many of whom are being paid money to support certain ideas? (#FG1)

P4:   The problem is that most people don't understand statistics. People fear what they don't understand. In an age where everyone is clever, telling them they don't understand something is the biggest insult. It taps into people's fears and insecurities. Greedy politicians are just capitalising on it. (#FG2)

Because the use of statistics looks rigid and imposing, it is perceived as 'deeply unpleasant', a kind of feeling known in the scientific literature as 'math anxiety', often described as 'a feeling of tension, apprehension, or fear that interferes with math performance' (Ashcraft, 2002, p. 181). In addition, participant P4 criticizes the fact that readers are forced to believe in something that has been previously elaborated by experts who seem to be paid to drive public opinion in certain directions. The expertise-authority-competence nexus, when dealing with statistical reporting, is criticized even further. This is what it is considered to be the first of the three A's of distrust; authority, which encompasses a strong degree of scepticism towards expert opinions somehow related to the political sphere.

Politics and 'greedy politicians' are often blamed for making money and taking advantage by also 'throwing facts number-based on gullible readers'. Politics is seen as a major threat to the supposed neutrality of statistics. Again, interviewee P6 insists on a sort of connivance between journalists and politicians, whereas the debate between P1 and P2 in #FG3 highlights a problem of expertise:

P6:   You all are correct. But there is no separation between politicians and journalists who have become very intertwined. In some cases, joined at the hip with a new class of journalist politician, like Johnson and Gove. And so low have standards of journalism become that politicians' views of journalists are often well known. With opinion and statistics selected to continuously present those same fixed political views. (#FG3)

P1:   I think this article is taken from *The Guardian* and statistics are there only to be abused. Such as in the repeated stories about the pay gap. It's been at the forefront of making false assertions via bad stats for years, with the pattern being too strong to be simply down to ignorance. Look at their 'the web we want' data, for example. Stories are not randomly assigned to people of various colours or genders, meaning that you cannot make any assumptions about whether colour or gender affects the amount of abuse received, yet this paper did that, repeatedly. I can't take any opinion about statistical integrity, or usefulness, or quality, seriously if it's made on *The Guardian*.

P2:   There is no such thing as bad stats just bad analysis, I think. (#FG3)

The *Guardian* is not a credible source of statistical information, according to this reader. The word '*abuse*' certainly denotes a strong position but at the same time, his argument denotes a good knowledge of scientific, mathematical issues: 'citizens encounter statistics in multiple life contexts: as readers, listeners, viewers, workers, or actors in community activities, civic duties or political events' (Roten, 2006, p. 243).

When asked to define quality, P1 in #FG3 juxtaposed the concept of quality with that of '*usefulness*' and most importantly that of '*integrity*'. The Organisation for Economic Co-Operation and Development (OECD) says that integrity refers to 'values and related practices that maintain confidence in the eyes of users in the agency producing statistics and ultimately in the statistical product'. Integrity is, however, only a driver that can lead to quality. This means that when participants are asked to define the concept of quality, they make use of related concepts. When they look at the negative sides of the use of statistics, they can easily recognize when quality is lacking, regardless of the newspaper's business model (Meyer & Kim, 2003). Their attitude does not seem to change, even when asked to specifically comment on health statistics and crime statistics in the news.

P1:   By reading this article about health I can only say that NHS statistics are particularly misleading. If a patient is an arranged emergency admission they will pass through casualty to an assessment area and then possibly to a ward. One patient, three attendances. That's how the government can get away with claiming emergency services are overwhelmed. They are not, they are simply underfunded and the attendances triple counted. Unless independently collected never trust NHS statistics. (#FG3)

Without going into the details of the NHS's system of emergency admission, the view of this participant is clear: health statistics are misleading. He also recommends that statistics should be '*independently collected*' in order to be trusted. For example, the concept of integrity is paramount in medical statistics to prevent poor-quality research (Altman, 2002).

The concept of integrity is a good point and makes a distinction regarding the sources by indirectly revealing that non-official sources might have a higher level of accuracy because they are perceived as independent. Despite this hint of positivity, there is an obstacle that prevents statistics from attaining quality and that is accuracy. Accuracy is in fact the second A of distrust, part of the key findings explained in this section. The literature in this regard is extensive and has spanned, over the years, both health (Gigerenzer et al., 2007; Sainsbury & Jenkins, 1982) and crime (McDevitt et al., 2003; Price, 1966). Another participant pointed the finger at the marketing side of statistics, which brings us back to what the journalists said during their interviews, and to the literature review (section 3.4):

P1:   One thing is for sure, commercialisation is at the forefront of data analytics, big data and statistical release, finding ways to milk the populace of hard-earned funds, this is not for the good of society but for the good of corporations. It has come to the stage where an apple is bad for you (unless fully organic), because it has pesticides in its very make up... we are nearing a point of no return.

P2:   I agree. Statistics themselves have been commercialised to the point of tedium. (#FG3)

Together with political ends, commercial ends represent another obstacle to building trust in statistics: 'many national statistical institutes (NSIs) now have marketing sections that do indeed mimic many of the functions of the retail sector, although the extent to which the activity truly is marketing is debatable' (Blakemore, 1999).

This lays the groundwork for the third A of distrust: Accessibility. This is in fact the reason behind the decision of the Office of National Statistics to end the practice of allowing access to the pre-release before the official release. Traders might exploit leaked UK statistics to make money (Chapman, 2017). This important aspect also came to light in another focus group session, where the sale of statistics was seen as an impediment to the delivery of an honest and truthful depiction of society.

P2:   Well if governments and newspapers told the truth in the first place, we might not have been here to talk in this focus group... Also, context needs to be given, always. Personally, I think that's the way they like it as actually statistics can reveal a lot.

P1:   But what is truth, man?

P3:   It is totally dependent on the question asked.

P1:   The thing that actually happened and its context or at least its source given if not seen first-hand. I meant indirectly that statistics are an amazing tool to ferret out truths, but seem to be maligned because of misuse by the few. (#FG2)

This exchange says a lot about trust in government. In this regard, Uri Friedman from the *Atlantic* reported in 'From Trump to Brexit: Trust in Government Is Collapsing around the World' that an international survey by the PR firm Edelman showed how people tend to trust business more than government because 'business at least gets stuff done'.

It is obvious that statistics, in their two-sided feature, do not have a good reputation among the participants, as some comments contain a high dose of scepticism and suspicion. In another session, one participant gave a very mindful explanation, by pointing out that this negative attitude could be softened if only a sampling method strategy were used:

P1:   I think that a good article as a good piece of research can create good statistics, if good sampling methods are used, and if the researcher or the journalist is able to ensure their own performances don't influence the results too much. But statistics can never represent the absolute truth. Also, I think the problem is more about how people try to use statistics to win arguments, and how they portray their chosen statistics as if they were proof that they are right. If statistics were used with a little more intellectual modesty, and with more honesty about the limits being used, there might be less hostility towards them. (#FG2)

Again, the participant's claim is that statistics 'can never represent the truth' and P1's argument centres on three main issues: (1) how people try to use statistics to win arguments; (2) how they portray their chosen statistics; and (3) how to be sure that journalistic performance does not influence the results. Misuse of statistics is a tangible concern among all participants because they do not see how they are produced, as the two following quotes succinctly illustrate:

P3:   It's not the statistics. It's how they are used and by whom.
P4:   ...and for what purpose.
P5:   Yes, but the person who prepares the statistics has some responsibility for trying to ensure that they are as unambiguous as possible.
P1:   ...and how they are compiled. (#FG1)
P2:   Well I am a quantitative researcher and I can say that we are quite modest about what our data are telling us. Our findings then get reported on by laymen such as journalists and politicians, and by the time they reach the public, they are reported as ironclad 'facts' whatever that means. This is not an issue of statistics, and, of course, by no means reduces the validity of the point you are making in your comment.

P3:   I am on the same page. I mean most researchers clearly define very strict limitations on how their findings may be interpreted. (#FG3)

The usage of statistics implies an interpretation first, and then those numbers are put into a frame and disseminated in the public sphere to be 'invoked and disputed as a critical part of public debate' (Crook & O'Hara, 2012, p. 264). Statistics can be considered part of the democratic value of a nation. According to Bumpstead and Alldritt (2011) from the UK Statistics Authority, 'in a democracy, decision-making is ultimately made by the people, therefore statistics cannot only be the bookkeeping of the state. They must be understood and used by the many' (p. 4). One of the issues raised, however, is the vocabulary and the verbalization used which is not easy to understand:

P1:   It annoys me when mainstream media report an average of some value as if that were sufficient. They seldom, if ever, indicate how the sample was chosen, what the whole population is, when the sample was collected and most importantly what the variance was, or the trend.

P2:   Indeed 'average' seems to be the most misused word in statistics as in the two articles we have just read. It is not typical. Or most common, or the middle of a range of variables even though most journalists seem to think that it is.

P3:   Perhaps that is why it is referred to as the 'mean' value?! (#FG1)

When layman journalists perform data analysis, they must be sure that results are not biased and the methodology of collecting statistics is clear. This would depend on the skills journalists have acquired by direct training. But many journalists suffer from a 'blind spot' for numbers (Nguyen & Lugo-Ocando, 2016). This view was further developed in another focus group session:

P1:   The saying attributed to Disraeli stems from a misunderstanding of statistics, and should read 'there are lies, damned lies, and misused statistics'. The problem lies not in the statistics themselves but the cherry-picking of them for political ends.

P2:   Oh, that is so true. Genuine statistics are cherry picked for political gain, whilst disregarding other data that does not promote the cause. The data remains true but can also be very misleading. (#FG2)

'Cherry-picking' is one of the methodological concerns that could influence the outcomes of the data analysis. We have already addressed this issue by mentioning Marcia Bates (1989), who compared the actions of someone searching for information to those of someone picking berries, but the political interference is a constant worry and genuine statistics are cherry-picked for political gain.

P4:   You are right. Most of the polls were conducted over the phone or face to face, and people are likely to please the interviewer. Even though they are said to be representative of the country's population. In the UK, most polls were conducted online, which is a method more likely for people to be honest in their answers. The flip side is that, even though about 90% of the UK population have access to the Internet, most polls were not representative of the whole universe, leaving out segments with limited access to the Internet. (#FG3)

A failure or a 'betrayal' of public trust in numbers has created an echo of suspicion and a high level of judgment that was tangible across the four focus group sessions, which took place during these two turbulent political moments in the United Kingdom and the United States. The Brexit referendum and the US presidential elections did not foster a positive attitude among the public towards numerical information.

As far as public trust in official statistics is concerned, even experts do not agree with each other. Ian Simpson from the Royal Statistical Society writes that any change in trust in official statistics can be seen through a comparison between questions asked in 2014 and those asked in 2016:

So, did we find any drop in trust in official statistics in 2016? The answer is no. Indeed, we found some evidence of small increases in positive attitudes towards official statistics. Despite Gove's comments about experts, there continues to be a widespread belief that official statistics are important for understanding Britain (92% of those giving an opinion agreed) and that statistics produced by ONS are free from political interference (70% of those giving an opinion). Both these figures have remained stable over the past couple of years. (Simpson, 2016, p. 5)

This opinion is, however, challenged by what Jamie Grierson has written for the *Guardian* in an article entitled 'Britons' Trust in Government, Media and Business Falls Sharply': 'The annual trust barometer survey by PR firm Edelman has for the first time published a separate UK-specific supplement, which showed a sharp drop in levels of trust in the last 12 months. Trust in the British government, which was already low at 36% at the start of last year, fell to 26% by the start of 2017, the survey showed.' This quote helps to explain what we mean by the 'echo of suspicion':

P2:   Ahaha. Leave a bunch of monkeys in a room with a typewriter, sooner or later you'll get Shakespeare. Leave a bunch of politicians in a room with objectivity sooner or later they'll find an argument against it.

P3:   However, the probability of a universe full of monkeys typing a complete work such as Shakespeare's Hamlet is so tiny that the chance of it occurring during a period hundreds of thousands of orders of magnitude longer than the age of the universe is extremely low…

P2:   So, statistics are useful. For finding out about monkeys.

P1:   I tend toward the belief that what you'll likelier get is a broken typewriter. (#FG2)

The image of monkeys with a typewriter is used here to metaphorically explain that even non-expert people can perform statistical analysis and sooner or later get the numbers right. Most importantly though, this last quote underlines, with a quite vivid image, a distrust towards the uses of statistics in news reporting.

The analysis of the focus group transcriptions reveals one prevailing attitude in the articulation of statistics in news reporting: a constant scepticism about their portrayal of social reality and their scope, mainly for political or commercial ends. Together with this attitude there is also a noticeably low understanding of what quality means in its broadest sense and what role it has in the sense-making of statistics. We observed three main areas where trust in statistics is lacking, called the three A's of distrust: authority, accessibility and accuracy.

Authority is part of the expertise-authority-competence nexus and is seen by the participants as manipulative of public opinion. Accessibility is related to the full access to public statistics, often problematic because they are filtered for marketing purposes. Lastly, accuracy relates to the methodology of data collection and its integrity, which is often not transparent enough for a public understanding of statistics. In summary, the delivery of quality is hugely compromised when the moment comes to assess the audience's point of view. Statistics do not help to achieve quality and journalists do not seem able to guarantee 'completeness of information'.

Q-sort analysis

This section only analyses the Q-sort data to support the focus group data and is not intended as an independent and comprehensive method. It aims only to corroborate the focus group analysis with more insight about participants' viewpoints in the context of the four articles read during the focus group sessions. By doing so, this analysis will ask: *How does the audience engage with statistically driven stories?*

In addition to the main qualitative data from the focus groups, the Q-sort evaluates the individuality of the 22 (*n*=22) participants who were invited to fill out a pre-arranged, forced-choice frequency distribution grid designed for use with a set of 30 items. The grid contains spaces or ranking positions ranging from -5 (strongly disagree) to +5 (strongly agree). By evaluating the individuality of the participants, the Q-sort methodology can confirm, disprove or add more information to what has been discussed in the focus group sessions (Table 6.9).

Table 6.10 shows the result of the analysis of the frequency distribution of 22 sorts that were filled in after having read the four articles. In brief, articles

Table 6.9 Q-sort details.

Number of sorts	22
Range	From -5 to 5
Depth	1 2 3 3 4 4 4 3 3 2 1

Table 6.10 Summary of the Q-sort test.

Items Listed by Ranking (>50% of Significance)		
1. The articles are easily comprehensible.	-5	strongly
18. I think the statistics in A support the overall argumentation (health).	-4	disagree
3. The data is easy to understand.	-3	
16. In general, I consider B-articles more reliable than A-articles.		
31. I think the statistics used in these articles can improve the information quality.	-2	
28. In B-articles, statistics are not appropriately represented.	-1	
11. In general, A-articles are more trustworthy than B-articles.		
15. I consider A-articles more reliable than B-articles.		
12. In general, B-articles are more trustworthy than A-articles.	0	neutral
27. In A-articles statistics are not appropriately represented.	1	strongly
24. I think the statistics in B-articles support the overall argumentation (crime).		agree
30. I do not think the statistics used in these articles can improve the information quality.	4	
5. There is no difference between A-articles and B-articles (health).	5	

with the letter A make use of official data whereas articles with the letter B make use of anecdotal data. The use of a flattened, or platykurtic, distribution offered a great opportunity to get a fine-grained discrimination at the extremes of the distribution, a strategy that allowed us to maximize the advantages of having participants with a good topic knowledge.

The data shows that participants did not find the statistics easily comprehensible at first glance (-5) and that the data used were not easy to interpret on careful reading (-3). Even though they thought statistics were presented in an appropriate way, the rank -1 would suggest that this presentation of statistics could be improved. It is interesting to notice, for the aim of this method, that more than half of the participants gave 0 to one of the most significant statements: 'B-articles are more trustworthy than A-articles'. This means that participants did not agree or disagree with the fact that anecdotal data are more trustworthy than official data (explained further later in this section). It is worth observing that when asked about the two different topics of crime and health, participants did not spot any difference in health articles ($+5$), whereas crime statistics with some officiality seem to support, quite well, the overall argument ($+4$). In general, more than half of the participants thought that statistics do not improve the quality of the information provided.

These results should be read within the context of the focus groups where the participants showed a high level of 'suspicion' towards the use of statistics in news reporting. In that circumstance the members of the focus groups were invited to share their own views with their fellow participants, but during the Q-sort they were forced to assess themselves and their convictions individually.

Therefore, the fact that statistics do not mean quality of information would confirm the critical and judgmental nature of their views. Furthermore, the fact that trustworthiness has a neutral position means that the participants were not able, in the end, to make a sound judgement between official and non-official statistics, and hence any decision-making was suspended.

Further discussion

In May 2013 the UK House of Commons released a report, entitled *Public Trust in Government Statistics*, whose main goal was that of implementing ways to improve the perception of the public about official statistics from the ONS and the Statistics Authority. However, by analysing the focus group sessions and the Q-sort tests contextualized with the recent literature, it seems that this goal has not yet been fulfilled.

The research question was: *How do readers interpret and understand quality statistics in news articles?* Indeed, the challenge here is not whether the readers are skilful enough to disprove statistical claims or spot mathematical mistakes, but whether they 'believed' the statistical information to be true or not, and the reasons behind their interpretative, often cynical, choice to disbelieve an 'article of faith' (J. G. Blumler, 1979), as the statistical information often aspires to be presented. The voice of the readers who attended the four focus groups has emerged as a suspicious reaction towards the numerical information. Suspicion was felt, in all sessions, towards all the aspects under evaluation, in particular in the articulation of the numerical information and how this is interpreted by the readers. Therefore, what Paul Ricoeur has called 'hermeneutics of suspicion' appears to be the best way to read the audience attitudes towards those newspapers that make use of numbers to legitimize their stories.

We argue that reader's voice has been channelled mainly through the theoretical lens of a hermeneutics of suspicion and particularly between a willingness to suspect and a willingness to listen, in what Theodor Porter would call an 'engagement-detachment' game. Applied to media studies, this theory has dealt with the role of the media in shaping consciousness, and consequently opinions, of the audience: 'the hermeneutics of suspicion can also be seen in the main traditions of research that have formed around specific understandings of the media and its impact on audiences' (Mathieu, 2015, p. 253).

This attitude to suspicion can be better understood through the active/passive role that audiences play when consuming media content. Generally speaking, the active audience is rational and selective, whereas the passive audience is gullible and vulnerable (Abiocca, 1988). The focus group data suggests that readers have an active role in judging and questioning what a newspaper article should or should not say, and how it does so. This active audience role also shows an individualistic and 'impervious to influence' approach towards the numerical information. To be precise, the active audience concept was theorized by the social psychologist Raymond Bauer, frequently cited among uses and gratifications theorists and critics (J. G. Blumler, 1979; Ruggiero, 2000). For them, the work of Bauer is a milestone in driving a 'paradigm shift' from an 'administrative' approach to a more receiver-oriented research perspective or, as Stuart Hall would describe it, to a more decoding perspective. We argue, however, that hermeneutics of suspicion is valid especially in the context of this study, not only because hermeneutics is the name for a way of dealing with texts, but also because Paul Ricour has said that all texts present us with the challenge of believing that the true meaning of the text emerges only through interpretation.

The qualitative analysis shows that the interpretation of numerical information, and what the purposes of such numbers are, happens under vigorous debates. The participants in the focus groups suspected that there were two main goals, perceived as a hidden agenda: political and commercial ends. Therefore, the statistical dissemination through news reporting has the clear objective of manipulation, according to the focus groups. They also acknowledged that statistics cannot always tell the truth. Even if it is not clear what the truth should be for them, it is clear that by crossing the focus group data with the Q-sort data that this situation of confusion, scepticism and suspicion against numbers might be caused by their inability to make sound decisions. Even highly educated people such as the members of the focus groups, who are equipped with a high level of skills in reading and text comprehension, are in trouble when the moment comes to make sound decisions based on numbers.

On the one hand, judgement skills are proved to be very analytical, mainly driven by an agnostic attitude towards numbers, often challenged as if it were an 'article of faith'. On the other hand, the use of numbers in news reporting does not help to improve any decision-making, but rather to deadlock it, with the consequence that any further progress cannot be made.

In conclusion, the hermeneutical act of interpreting numbers occurs between the readers and the statistics, where statistics is commonly defined as numerical facts assembled and clarified so as to present significant information. Hermeneutics is therefore the assembling and clarifying of facts so as to present meaningful information. Statistics, thus, is the hermeneutics of numbers, and the interpretation of quality statistics in news translates into a constant, multifaceted, often challenging, 'dialogue' between readers and numbers.

Our discussion here has examined the findings from the content analysis, close-reading analysis, interviews, focus groups and Q-sort analysis and aimed to examine how statistical information is articulated in news reporting through five quality dimensions through a triangulation of these methods. Within this research framework the articulation of statistics appears to be one of the means through which journalists aspire to deliver quality in the news.

Although this study suggests that there are internal and external interferences to quality, we can suggest that even an emphasis on only one of the five dimensions (such as Interpretability and Accessibility for example) or on different dimensions such as those of 'usefulness' or 'integrity' could represent an attempt at quality. Notwithstanding this reassuring approach, a contrary side is undeniable: a simple aspiration to quality is indeed not enough to gain the reader's trust and maintain it over time. Among the key findings, what this study also reveals is a big gap between what journalists think they do through the articulation of statistics and what is perceived by readers. This gap results in a kind of broken 'social contract' between journalists and their readers (Sjøvaag, 2010).

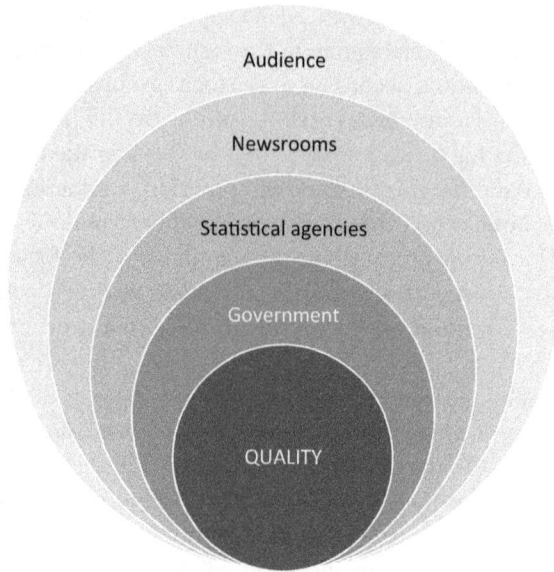

Figure 6.15 The 'quality ecosystem' with four levels of stratification.

Four levels of stratification emerge from the data analysis: (1) the governments that support (2) statistical agencies in their release of statistical reports to the (3) journalists who are in charge of making them available to the (4) readers. All four levels rotate around the need to achieve, maintain and transmit quality, as the Figure 6.15 illustrates.

This need for quality is at the centre of what we can call a 'quality ecosystem'. But the transmission and maintenance of such quality seems to undergo a change between the newsrooms and those readers who are actively engaged in questioning the numbers reported in the news. This change of perspective is mainly due to external and internal interferences that fail this aspiration to quality and affect how journalists engage with numbers. These considerations are supported by a body of research that suggests there is currently a miscommunication between the scientific community (the statisticians), the media and the public because of misrepresentation, miscommunication, inaccuracy and distortion of information.

While journalism and statistics can support a mutual 'construction of society' (Lincoln, 2014; Saetnan et al., 2010), what the findings reveal is that journalists articulate statistics as a means to make news objective and truthful in their aspiration to quality. However, because quality is not attainable in the short term, in the lengthy quality-making process of statistics, journalists often misrepresent numbers by failing to satisfy basic quality dimensions like, for example, Interpretability, which refers to the lack of clarity of expression and cohesion between statistical points contained in the articles, and Accessibility, which mainly refers to the methodology of data gathering that should be communicated to the readers.

From this perspective, a lack of mathematical training among journalists is one of the major problems impacting on the transmission of statistical quality. The failure to transmit quality statistics to audiences impacts on how readers react when exposed to statistical information.

Ultimately, this study points out that in our rational and technological society we need, more than ever before, a better educational background in scientific and mathematical language, even for journalists, as well as a basic knowledge of the branches of philosophy such as Logic and Argumentation that deals with Statistical and Probability thinking, as, for example, in the Philosophy of Information.

Chapter 7

THE IDEOLOGY OF
STATISTICS IN THE NEWS

Over the past years, governments and corporations have come to develop media strategies to 'manage' the dissemination of statistics within the public. As we have discussed in this book, this was part of a long history in using numbers to assert social control and that in the twentieth century took the form of cybernetics. In more recent times, this has meant enshrining statistics and data into daily life by means of the information and communication technologies to be used by individuals, couples, families and communities. In so doing, they have dedicated immense resources towards 'controlling' narratives and interpretations of statistics released in the public sphere.

Moreover, mediatization practices to shape the way these numbers go out into the public are now at the centre of the controversies and issues that journalism confronts. This 'mediatization of statistics communication' (Lugo-Ocando & Lawson, 2017) is one which is understood to be not a policy-making process directed by the media but overall a policy-process in which publicity-seeking activities and political decision-making become closely interlinked (Cater, 1965; T. Cook, 2005).

Statistics are far from being a neutral object in society and have their own politics and ideologies. They are also fundamental signifiers in the creation of social reality (Dorling & Simpson, 1999), displaying a politics of their own. Not that we ascribe agency to the output of a mathematical equation but that we see the equation itself as a human creation that has a history, a meaning and an intent. Over the years, as we have seen in this book, these numbers have gained a power of their own. From defining budgetary priorities to determining who can receive aid or buy a house, statistics and data, in more general terms, dominate human existence in many ways.

However, with the increasing presence of Big Data and controlling power of algorithms, we are entering into new uncharted territory, No longer is it just about the state or corporations controlling the production and analysis of statistics, but also about the active management of these numbers by means of mediated representation in the public domain. Recognized today as a process in which the logic of the media starts to permeate multiple social subsystems (Schrott, 2009, p. 42) including that of public engagement and use of all type of numeric data by those who normatively claim to bring truth to society.

The process of mediatization of statistics implies tailoring the presentation of these numbers in order to fit the media requirements. This is done in the search for public support and legitimation of the policies and actions that they aim at underpinning (Esser, 2013; Marcinkowski & Steiner, 2014). The enactment of authority in a policy-making process requires treating statistics as both a communicative achievement as much as a political one (Crozier, 2008; Hajer, 2009). It is because the use of statistics by journalists often happens within the framework of mediatized policy that we can argue that the incorporation of statistics into the news narrative and broader discoursive regimes signifies a new phase in reporting.

Data Journalism is not a practice nor a branch of core traditional mainstream news reporting but a set of ideologies around both statistics and quality. It is part long tradition to standardize journalism and takes whatever reminiscent remains from its humanistic roots and converts it into another human equation that is scientifically objective, given its mathematical nature. For more than one hundred years, journalism has presented itself to us in a diversity of forms. However, two stand out: that of a political institution and that of a social practice. In recent years, news reporting has been both, and as such it has been wonderfully schizophrenic, unable to define itself against being propaganda but never accepting that is only that simplistic distorted self-image only found in the mainstream news media or in Hollywood films.

The incorporation of data and statistics in journalism practice comes as a game-changer because it imposes particular professional standards that reflected a new professional ideology of truth that is mathematically based and that pushes aside alternative interpretations and forms to approach the world, giving preference to a particular paradigm of knowledge and truth. It also imposes new journalistic norms and values that bring back modernity upon existing forms of communicating news while channelling particular mainstream models that underpin overall hegemonic power and authorial control.

This book did not deal with this threat but has acknowledged it all along because it is key to understanding the way journalists engage and use data as part of today's efforts to construct social reality. Particularly, given what we know today, thanks to a robust body of research, about the way that data and statistics shape the epistemology of journalists doing their work. In this sense, several authors have argued that among the most influential knowledge-producing institutions in modern society, journalism has a distinct epistemology (Ettema & Glasser, 1984; Parasie, 2015; Seth C. Lewis & Westlund,

2015). That is, in terms of the mainstream organizational culture to produce news stories in which journalists operate as a collective professional body, they have their own way of knowing things. One that tends to be different from, let us say, novelists or historians.

To start with, journalists are part of a collective professional body and as much as they want to claim individuality and uniqueness in their work, they follow procedures and produce outcomes that respond to professional ideologies, as we already discussed. Consequently, they follow others in the way they gather information and then afterwards in articulating news stories. This means not only replicating overall routines but also reproducing cultural practices within the newsroom and sharing normative aspirations among colleagues (Ekström, 2002; Schlesinger, 1978). Even when the final cultural output is produced by one individual, which is never the case, the work of reporters is persistently collective. In relation to the use of data and statistics, our thesis is that in order to analyse the uses of statistics by journalists we should do so through five quality dimensions.

What is there

Across this book, we have tried to highlight and explore the dichotomy between the normative professional aspirations of journalism as a political institution in relation to the role of statistics in underpinning the quality of news. In so doing, we also assessed the way in which numbers and data are used to strengthen the authorial control of news reporters as storytellers and their ability to persuade audiences by means of numbers. To this end, our work has examined tensions and issues around the articulation of statistics and numbers in the practice of journalism and, in doing so, has also pinpointed a trust in news and, perhaps more important, in newsmakers as the central aspect of such tensions.

Although initially the concept of trust was not at the centre of the analysis, it gradually became so, not only in terms of the gap between journalists' reports and news audiences' perceptions, but also in relation to the ability of journalists to tell stories using data-driven argumentation and, ultimately, numbers. Trust, in fact, deserves far more attention in terms of its pivotal centrality in defining who controls the agendas and narratives that ultimately we take as truth.

Our aim was from the start to produce a body of knowledge that could help us improve overall our understanding of the use of statistics as a primary means for the construction of journalistic quality. We managed, albeit only partially and modestly, to do that given the complexity that we encountered along the way. However, what the findings did was to confirm overwhelmingly that the use journalists make of statistics plays a crucial role in the construction of both social reality and readers' reception of public affairs; however, as we saw, not because people trust journalists or the numbers they use to legitimize their news stories, but because of the mathematical character of truth since the Enlightenment.

The research findings also emphasized how journalists engage with numbers in their day-to-day practice, and how important they were in the process of storytelling. At the end, our analysis underpins that the link between the articulation of statistics and the ability to produce quality news is far more complex than originally assumed. The quest for 'quality' is central for most journalists, as it is part not only of the professional deontology but also because it helps them define their own identity as truth tellers. Journalists, with all their aspirations to be both historians and scientists, have been embracing the tool that they know the least but the one they know that they need the most: statistics. In order to understand the way they interact and later deploy this data, we explored the five quality dimensions, which we developed specifically for the study of the journalistic content.

In general terms, each dimension deals with different issues: (1) relevance – the degree to which a statistically driven story meets reader expectations in terms of content and coverage; (2) accuracy – how well sourced a story is and whether official and non-official statistics are used; (3) timeliness and punctuality – the time between the date of publication and the date to which the data refers, and the time between the actual publication and the planned publication of a statistic; (4) accessibility and clarity – the ease with which readers can access/read data, and the quality and sufficiency of metadata and accompanying advice; and (5) coherence – the degree to which data derived from different sources or methods, but that refers to the same topic, is similar.

The study found that while the concept of quality remains a theoretical aspiration among journalists, what they aim to attain is credibility and authority; statistics do not translate automatically into credible and authoritative news, mainly because of internal and external interferences, and numbers do not seem to fully support the main arguments when dealing with crime and health news. For example, the findings show that there are still some drawbacks in relation to the quality dimensions of Timeliness and Interpretability.

In relation to the dimension of Timeliness, the content analysis results show that statistics often come from statistical reports that are more than three months old. The results also suggest that journalists do not cite the year of the statistical report in almost 40 per cent of the articles. According to the journalists interviewed, time also represents an internal interference in the attainment of quality and therefore seems detrimental for the overall credibility.

Interpretability is understood as a good verbalization of the technical vocabulary and terminology typical of statistics and mathematics. This quality dimension is concerned with the ability of journalists to make data easily understandable, and to make the story more understandable for their readers. The content analysis data shows that almost 82 per cent of the articles made use of stand-alone statistics as the preferred way to verbalize data-driven stories. This was confirmed by the interviews, which showed that journalists, when needed to summarize and interpret the data, write the story in the easiest and quickest way possible.

More decisively following such findings, the study debunks the traditional claim that this tension is the result of time constraints and other types of pressure or interference, and instead confirms that, among the journalistic community, the lack of capabilities and skills is the main culprit for the misappropriation and misuse of statistics in the news. In fact, the research exposes a gap in mathematical education that eventually prevents journalists from attaining accuracy when reporting data. Thus one of the key tasks ahead is to generate better capabilities among journalists and their audiences in their ability to manage and interpret data (Halevy & McGregor, 2012; Kanari & Millar, 2004).

Having said that, these capabilities cannot be based exclusively upon instrumentalist needs to be accurate in the dissemination of statistics, but should focus on the critical interpretation of these numbers. The results showed here call for an urgent need for critical thinking when dealing with numbers as shown for the dimension of 'accuracy', where critical thinking was set as one of the criteria in the attainment of quality. These capabilities must combine a set of functions that are feasible to achieve for each journalist and that gives both the reporters and the public the ability to deconstruct and reconstruct the world around them.

Boosting these capabilities is urgent because this knowledge gap not only affects data collection and accuracy but also the ability to fulfil the potential of statistical data as a tool to enhance democratic citizenship. To be sure, as this research has showed, the current use of statistics in the news has led to an over-scepticism and even suspicion among readers, as the focus group data suggests. This is because many among the public seem to see through to the fact that these numbers are often not there to 'inform' but to 'convince', and in the context of their personal lives these numbers do not seem to be conveying the truth.

These perceptions might seem to be counter-intuitive, since the main goal of statistics is precisely to foster public reason by means of rationality, or rather mathematical rationality. Indeed modern societies operate today within a mathematical framework that validates truth through statistics and data (Restivo, 2013; Tait, 1986). However, it is precisely because society has been overloaded by information that it is so crucial for journalism to be able to present and dissect such information in a complete and critical manner, as much as it possibly can. Journalists therefore need to adhere to the deontological duty to guarantee a 'completeness of information', which can be understood ultimately as 'quality'.

Sociologists and scholars in mathematics agree that statistics make sense of the world we live in (Levitin, 2016) because statistical information offers a powerful insight into rational thinking. From Euclid to Gödel, these are the means through which a universal truth has been underpinned by mathematical thinking. Consequently, the appropriate use of such information is thus essential to draw conclusions and, most importantly, influence policy decision-making. Hence, it is vital that both journalists and the public learn to understand and engage with both statistics and the concept of quality, as many of the decisions we make in our daily lives are based on numbers and driven by the perception we have of quality. Within this framework, understanding the articulation of statistics inside the dynamics of journalistic practices, when dealing with quality, is crucial for the scope and the aims of this book.

Chapter 1 gave an overview of how statistics has historically developed as a vital part of what is called the Information Society. On the one side, statistics itself was known as 'political arithmetic' and therefore used for political aims. On the other side, the reportage of numbers was used for financial reasons and its roots can be seen in the old Italian city-states, known as maritime republics, where the accurate reportage of numbers was essential among merchant class members. All this happened at the dawn of the invention of journalism. The chapter also explored how the notion of quality came to be and was set against the concept of quantity.

In light of our findings it can be seen that even if the sociocultural landscape has changed from the past, some dynamics are still the same. Think, for example, about how politics still pervades the production of numbers and their dissemination. The communication of numbers still plays an important role for policy decision-makers and among those who work with information such as journalists. The interviews showed, for example, that even if technology changes at fast speed, the persuasive nature of numbers still remains the same as for the challenges to read and interpret such numbers.

Over the book we have had ample discussions on quality journalism and focused on the ambiguity and convergence of the concept among scholarly work. We focused on the problems of measuring the concept of quality for research and tried to link the concept of quality to that of objectivity, the latter seen as a means to overcome subjective approaches. We explored how scientific methods are used in the journalistic practice. Our findings show that the concept of quality journalism is still controversial among practitioners and that quality does not necessarily translate into objectivity. Journalists in general do not ignore the concept of quality, as it is set as a standard aspiration, but they have trouble in defining such a concept. According to them, credibility and to some extent authority is much more achievable when delivering a statistically driven story. Against the literature that almost unanimously sees quality journalism as a necessary goal for the practice of journalism, our results instead show a low level of awareness about quality among those journalists who routinely deal with data. Generally speaking, the concept is perceived as fragile and easily targeted by external and internal factors, such as educational background, that prevent its full attainment.

We have also tried to introduce some philosophical challenges, taking into account the branch of philosophy known as Logic. Adopting such a philosophical view to the issue allowed us to embrace a more critical and solid methodological approach to the topic under analysis, and we then applied it to journalistic performance, especially in relation to critical thinking, which entails a good degree of logical reasoning.

In addition, we adopted some philosophical views, mainly taken from the Philosophy of Information. This was of great help in laying the theoretical ground for the research methodology for what concerns the five dimensions of quality, the normative importance of the concept of quality in democratic life. Our findings underpinned our initial concerns with the problematic sense-making of quality through its five dimensions; the second involves statistical innumeracy and the educational background of journalists and statistical accessibility around the methods of data collection and interpretation for the purpose of storytelling; and the third has its main point on the political ends of official statistics and the issue of data manipulation. The focus group data identified three main issues linked together by a common feeling of scepticism. In this case the three A's of distrust were identified: Authority, Accessibility and Accuracy. *Authority* – readers are sceptical about the nexus of expertise-authority-competence; *Accessibility* – readers are concerned about full public access to statistics; and *Accuracy* – readers are sceptical about the methodology of data collection by journalists. These findings in sum have come to reinforce the notion that engagement with statistics and data to achieve quality is a problematic task at all levels and that current trends to improve professionalization by means of incorporating numbers is not necessarily the right pathway that has been promised by some.

Broader discussion

We hope that this book has helped to fill some of the gaps in the areas of both statistics in journalism and quality journalism. In addition, it has questioned the usage of statistical data as a normalizing and objectifying tool by looking at crime and health reporting. The research has brought attention to the existing links between statistical information and its uses and articulation in news stories. This included examining the role that statistics play in the production of daily news, particularly as tools in the construction of social reality, and how these numbers can be decontextualized and used to entertain rather than to inform the public. In addition to this, when we looked more closely at the relationship between quality and journalism we need to consider questions related not only to the broader notion of quality, as central to the discipline of journalism, but also to the association of statistics with the idea of scientific value, credibility and authority. It is the very idea that statistics are perceived of as bearers of quality, credibility and authority that is under scrutiny here, mainly because numbers are considered neutral and, most importantly, scientific (Benedictus, Miedema & Ferguson, 2016; Field, 2016).

Precisely at the intersection between this aspiration to be scientific and the use of statistical narratives to persuade – figures of speech and figures of arithmetic – lies the work of those journalists who are willing to apply the analysis of data to improve their stories. This willingness to use mathematical tools to write a story, to analyse the social reality and to make predictions wherever possible, is however challenged by one or more factors at the same time. This research has identified at least three types of interferences: 1) the sense-making of quality news is often understood differently at macro-level (every newsroom applies different deontological values) and at micro-level (every journalist deals with some personal ethical and educational issues); 2) an internal interference, which refers to the lack of statistical training that seems to slow down the data analysis work and consequently affects the understanding of how to get access to data and statistical reports; and 3) an external interference, which comes from government policy-making in terms of statistical data collection and methodology, perceived as biased at source and restrictive at end.

The above-mentioned findings seem to be the translation into practice of what Walter Lippmann theorized in his unfortunately little-cited April 1935 article, 'Elusive Curves' (Seyb, 2015) in which he sharply criticized those who try to understand future trends by employing statistics. The present findings show that little seemed to suggest that – at least on the surface – things have changed since Lippmann's time. In a more gradual sophistication of quantitative measurements (for example, the booming of Big Data), our society is again over-reliant on data and statistics more than ever to make decisions and to predict the future. On the same subject, it is worth reminding ourselves of philosopher Rene Guénon (2017 [1945]) who in his book, *The Reign of Quantity and the Signs of the Times*, foresaw this and warned that the decline of the West is intrinsically tied to the 'illusion of statistics' and its obsession with quantification.

Lippmann also observed that in journalists' pursuit of truth using statistics, they wear the clothes of analysts of reality, give the statistical curve an authority that it indeed does not deserve, an authority that could suspend reason and common sense to condescend the reputation and prestige of the otherwise known 'branded statistics', which can be identified in official statistics.

'The best statisticians', Lippmann cautioned, 'are very sceptical. They respect their tools but they never forgot that they are tools and not divining rods' (cited by Seyb, 2015). Again, according to Lippmann, statistical findings must be measured against the standards of 'common sense and knowledge' (cited by Seyb, 2015). A failure to do so would lead to a dangerous positivistic insistence, which could generate a misleading picture of the world that could thwart, rather than inform. Walter Lippmann triggered a still ongoing and controversial debate known today as the Bell Curve Debate (Herrnstein & Murray, 2010; Jacoby & Glauberman, 1995), which revolves around the notions of human intelligence and class structures. In this debate statistics are purposefully distorted to support the main argument that blacks' IQ scores are significantly lower than those of whites.

What the findings also show is that the 'positivistic insistence', mentioned by Lippmann, translates into an aspiration of journalists to be scientific, and therefore objectifying the reality they try to tell. Despite the appreciable aspiration to be scientific, this goal remains largely just an aspiration, with little avail upon quality. The content analysis evaluated the five quality dimensions that constitute the notion of quality, and the data indicated that all five quality dimensions are never fulfilled in just one single article, but rather these dimensions are used as an access point to this aspiration to quality. Through the lenses of the five dimensions, this study shows that there is no evidence that journalists engage critically with numbers even though they think they do. Three of the five dimensions are worth mentioning here: Accuracy, Timeliness and Accessibility.

Accuracy in news production is a keystone of the journalistic profession. However, we found that in many instances this concept fails to be adopted in practice, and the evidence suggests that only in very few cases did journalists verify or critically question their statistical sources. Instead, they seemed to engage with numbers in a reactive rather than proactive way. The fieldwork showed that contrary to the common claims around time pressures upon journalists, they do have enough time to process the information. This data shows that they have an average of three months' time to analyse the statistical data before using it in their stories. This suggests that journalistic routines bear little on the ability to engage and use statistics.

Finally, regarding the 'accessibility' dimension, the data indicates an over-reliance on official statistics and government reports. Journalists prefer walking the safest route and deal with those sources that they are familiar with. There is very little cross-referencing of sources and very little comparison with other statistical sources. Moreover, 25 per cent of the articles do not cite where the statistics come from. In addition, they do not cite the year of the statistical release in almost 40 per cent of the stories, a worrying habit that might impact on the 'completeness of information' that journalists are committed to deliver.

Overall, this attitude towards numbers is a symptom of some journalistic shortfalls in terms of credibility and authority. What the data from this research shows is that the adoption of social sciences tools into the journalistic routine can be problematic and, contrary to the common assumption, comes into play at the expense of the notion of 'precision'. Moreover, journalism as a political institution is moving into a territory in which the profession is far more about processing information and trying to make sense of it than using these facts to understand the outside world.

What many call today Data Journalism seems then as the last stage of a long journey to make journalism fulfil Lippmann's aspiration of converting it into a scientific activity, where objectivity was nothing but the facts. In this sense, this concept of 'precision' and of 'being precise' refers to the seminal work by Philip Meyer (2002, 2009) in this area. As explained earlier, Meyer took the key concepts and methods from the quantification approach to understanding social trends by merging journalism with social science methods. His point was driving journalism towards science where the term 'precision' refers to quantifiable facts measurable through statistical performance and data analysis. Nevertheless, the findings show that this approach is not so straightforward and 'precise' as it might seem, but rather presents grey areas like those of the quality dimensions addressed in this book.

Broadly speaking, precision journalism is seen both as a theory of news and as a set of observation techniques focused on data-driven reporting and analytical skills. Meyer's goal was that of turning journalists into social scientists. However, there are significant differences between social scientists and journalists. The former write scientific papers, the latter produce news stories. Journalists can borrow a great deal from social sciences to increase the quality, trustworthiness and authority of news reporting. However, as the study showed, even if it adopts a scientific aspiration, journalism is subject to internal and external interferences, which journalists are still not fully equipped to face.

In conclusion, it would seem plausible to interpret statistics in news as a legitimizing tool that most journalists use, but only in a few cases do they do so appropriately in accordance with the five quality dimensions model that we proposed here. This lack of capability to engage critically with statistics is at the cornerstone of the issues around quality in the news. There is in fact an enormous need for mathematical skills and statistical knowledge in the delivery of crime and health news, for example. As seen in the findings, these topics need a vast improvement of the understanding, usage and articulation of statistics – from the ways in which journalists select statistical data, to the methodology and the way they present it to the readers, to the education on statistics and ways in which readers consume statistical information.

Changes in information dissemination through data commoditization and services availability, and consumption modalities through technological developments, seem to have greatly impacted on journalistic performance. Nevertheless, that does not mean that it has made journalistic practices better in all cases as standardization has never brought about single and homogenous results.

Nevertheless, changes seem to have had a serious impact on the relevance of official statistics as trusted sources of information for society. Also, another good thing is that decentralized information of a variety of uncertified sources contributed to these changes in terms of quality and adherence to standard scientific statistical production methods. As Emanuele Baldacci, director of Methodology at *Eurostat*, puts it, 'the key issue is how to be authoritative and to develop quality knowledge in the new and changing information market' (2017, p. 5).

Scope for further research

We aspire that this research can be a step towards a better understanding of the articulation of statistics and quality information in the news. The study comprises a body of data that can pave the way to several future research possibilities that are already part of our own research agenda. We do not expect that others will give the same interpretation to our data but only that the discussion is open to other views and alternative interpretation to what for too long has been a constrained understanding of what numbers can do, and actually do, for news. In so doing, we attempted to produce some crucial information in the hope of promoting a better insight into how numbers are articulated by journalists inside their newsrooms.

Nevertheless, we are more than aware that future research needs to explore the ethical implications of the usage and manipulation of statistics by journalists and its relationship with quality and production and consumption practices around visualization and infographics. This, as well as understanding, betters the role of journalists in risk communication through the usage of numbers and assessing the whole question of news audiences and their understanding of statistics, of which we have only started to scratch the surface.

This research can be taken forward in the direction of 'information ethics' through a deep discussion of what 'data ethics' means in the practice of statistically driven journalism. The online dictionary for library and information science defines this as 'the branch of ethics that focuses on the relationship between the creation, organisation, dissemination, and use of information, and the ethical standards and moral codes governing human conduct in society' (Reitz, 2004). This area has been comprehensively explored both in theory (for example, the Philosophy of Information) and in practice, for example, the latest articles about the ethics in data-driven journalism (Seth C. Lewis & Westlund, 2015) and on the ethics of web-scraping (Virgillito & Polidoro, 2017), but it needs further development.

What is missing here is a critical discussion about the use of statistics for the public good through news media within the framework of the National Statistician's Data Ethics Advisory Committee (NSDEC). The NSDEC (2009) has advised the UK Statistics Authority that 'the access, use and sharing of public data, for research and statistical purposes, is ethical and for the public good'. It is thus necessary to conduct a deep reflection about the boundaries within which journalists can use numbers for the public good, and what this means when ethics leads to quality. Ethics and quality in fact share a common background and a common mission rooted in values and cultural contexts but often their meanings overlap in what can be called 'ethics of quality'.

A second issue relates to content engagement through data visualization. The literature on data visualization and infographics is well established, as is its history (Cairo, 2012). However, a focus on the risks and limitations of statistical visualizations in their relationship with the quality dimensions has yet to be addressed. Nor have the connections between visualization and scientific facts, or the level of readers' engagement through the quality dimensions by means of visualization. To push the argument further, it would be timely also to reflect on the role of immersive Virtual Reality in the communication of statistics through visualization on the one hand, and about the possibilities of multi-dimensional data analysis for the purpose of storytelling on the other. This issue poses urgent research questions about how journalists will engage both with VR and the communication of statistics; a point that could be linked to ethics and quality.

Thirdly, future research could build on the links between risk communication, statistics and journalism. There have been concerns about how journalists communicate statistics and risk, especially in the area of health (Bennett, 2010; Gigerenzer, 2008). Yet journalists and scientists often present risk and probabilities in ways that blur the intended message or the quality of the message. The translation of such a message to the readers is therefore a crucial task in terms of trust and authority. In particular, what needs to be addressed is how journalists make use of numbers by means of comparison between absolute and relative risk, for example, or between individual and population risk, and how they translate these into a story through a process of sense-making. Research of this kind could be done through textual and rhetorical analysis that could open new ways about how this area can be analysed through new approaches and methodologies.

Fourth, the question of news audiences and the way they engage and use statistics to make sense of the world should be addressed. As the most neglected area of journalism studies research, the issue of how people actually read and interpret statistics when consuming news is literally an unexplored area. This is a topical and crucial area we intend to engage with in the near future. Indeed, we plan to incorporate the above-mentioned issues into our own research agenda for the years that will follow. During the writing up, we have become increasingly aware of the urgency to produce knowledge around these topics. This urgency comes from the fact that rational and scientific knowledge is under threat, a phenomenon linked to the rise of anti-expertise sentiment and anti-intellectualism.

In the Post-Truth Era, where fake news is proliferating (Newman, Fletcher, Kalogeropoulos, Levy & Nielsen, 2017), today more than ever academics need to address a crucial topic that prevents liberal democracies taking any further steps towards qualitative growth: the relationship between experts and citizens. Indeed, there are forces that promote, and even pretend, that any opinion can be equally valid, and this could inevitably lead to unforeseeable consequences. Nichols writes that 'when the democracy is understood as an indefinite request of ungrounded opinions, everything becomes possible, including the very end of democracy' (Nichols, 2017). Nichols (1982) emphasizes the US perspective by also considering Alexis de Tocqueville, who had already explained that the distrust of intellectual authority is inherent in the egalitarian nature of overseas democracy. What has changed though, compared to the past, is not a reluctance to believe the official knowledge, but 'the emergence of a positive hostility towards that knowledge' (Nichols, 2017). In other words, the new element here is a shameless celebration of ignorance that could arguably be most prominently manifested in the rise of Donald J. Trump into power.

The rise of Trump has been underlined, from the very beginning, by a markedly anti-scientific position and contempt of experts, and it is our opinion that this position has also been widely echoed around the Brexit referendum. Alongside this crisis of expertise, we are experiencing a trust deficit in governments at a global level. The *Oxford Government Review* released in 2016 urges a reassessment of the policies aimed at building greater trust and improving perceptions of the government among citizens. For this report, trust is a fundamental element for the quality of governance, thus the concept of quality is recurrent here also in the field of government management.

Nichols (2017) lists several stories that display a fair and virtuous view of ignorance as a key ingredient in fuelling the lack of confidence in expertise, and the Internet plays a fundamental role in exacerbating the situation. In the list, there is also the so-called Google effect – that is, the illusion of becoming an expert with fast and superficial Internet searches. This inevitably involves journalism at large, and the consequent decline of the traditional ways of doing journalism. The profession of journalism has been hit by fierce online competition on business models that make slow and costly investigative work more and more rare and conversely foster clickbait (Chen, Conroy & Rubin, 2015) by disseminating fake news for the sole purpose of generating higher advertising revenue.

The pragmatic question therefore would be: Is the communication of statistics affected by this scenario? We think that the most original part of the book by Nichols is the one in which the experts are to be blamed for the erosion of confidence in themselves. Mistakes, lies, fraud, arrogance, cynicism, half-truths, loss of contact with the real politics and with academic and intellectual elites are part of such distrust, and statistics are also partly in question. All these factors create a whirlwind of irrationality that undermines one of the foundations on which democracy is founded: trust in certified knowledge. Hence, the question remains: Is the reportage of statistics a certified knowledge?

A significant number of scholars, experts and practitioners seem to think so. Data Journalism is now an entire branch of this profession and many journalism schools all over the world are incorporating it in their curriculum. A number of journals, plus a not less significant amount of publications, are now on display, underpinning what promises to be one of the greatest transformation of news reporting in the past 100 years. These promises see the potential not only in the ability to produce precise and accurate knowledge, but also in changing the epistemology itself of journalism and allowing it to produce knowledge that is truly objective and certain. The increasing ability to use data to articulate news can also bring about more effective manners to produce news, we are also promised. Hence, making these strands more appealing to news media owners and managers who see it as a way of surviving in a crunching market where old business models seem exhausted.

However, as we have discussed here, 'data' – either big or small – is also a socially constructed reality. It is not facts, as neither are the statistics behind it. Each number, including the binary ones, are just a fragment of the human imagination trying to control nature and other humans. These numbers have histories and ideologies and, as we have seen here, they reflect particular ideologies and worldviews. Data itself compares problematically to statistics as the former is even more closely associated to the market and what we individually and collective consume. Data is based on how we use material and immaterial media goods such a social media and our own mobile phones. Statistics, on the other hand, are a very discrete and intangible formulation of the state, and as such require the type of public scrutiny that has been traditionally associated with journalism. Data, on the other hand, is a growing testimony that we believe in the market to tell us the truth. Journalism, with its different traditions and epistemologies, oscillates between the state and the market as guarantor of truth. This oscillation is not new and dates back to the development of news reporting during the late nineteenth century and the first half of the twentieth century when journalism incorporated notions such as objectivity to its core norms and when newsmaking became the mainstream industrial operation that would come to dominate the public sphere in the subsequent years.

However, those years are over and many of the institutions that dealt with these tensions between the market and the state have been weakened by a relentless neoliberal agenda that has pushed for lesser taxation, which consequently seeks the reduction of the welfare state and erosion of the terms of equality provided by the justice system. One of the most affected areas, perhaps partly because few saw it as part of that welfare construct to provide political equality and social justice, was the ability of the mainstream media – either as public service broadcaster provision or by the unspoken social contract between journalists and society – to offer an element, not only of accountability to power, but also of social justice to those dispossessed of a political or economic voice.

This function of the news media and particularly journalism as a political institution has been profoundly eroded by a wave of scepticism and decline of public interest in public affairs together with changes in technology and the rise of powerful social media giants, which, by paying no taxes and stealing news content, have been able to disrupt and destroy the traditional political economy that sustains the mainstream news media ecology. These giants have become platforms that have facilitated the spread of lies and half-truths at speeds and distances never seen before. All this in the form of 'Fake News', which is 'symptomatic of the collapse of the old news order and the chaos of contemporary public communication' (Waisbord, 2018), which have come to erode mainstream journalism's normative claims to provide authoritative reportage of current events. The communication chaos – or cultural chaos as Mcnair (2006) called it – has also challenged some of the key normative arguments that journalism, as a political institution in Western democracy, made about itself. The past hierarchical order where news reporters exercised authorial control over truth is no longer there; neither is their ability to automatically and almost axiomatically count on the public's trust just because of their epistemological approach to truth by means of objective and factual reporting.

What we have been calling all along 'quality' in news reporting is nothing but a aesthetical construction that was developed in parallel across the globe, but that was claimed by US journalism in its historical accounts of news reporting as a universal practice. This aesthetical construction was based on particular deontological norms such as incorporating a type of news coverage based on objective and factual reporting as well as moral values and ethical principles which demanded to hear the arguments and see the facts from all sides and then report them in an impartial and balanced manner while providing an accurate account of the events.

This has been, at least in terms of normative claims, the epistemology of the journalistic quest for truth. One that has been accompanied by specific technics of presenting the news in particular formats (i.e. the 5WH and the Invert Pyramid) that were considered to be appropriate and a legitimate manner of claiming authorial control over what was reported. Behind these aesthetical formats was the attempt to pursue authorial power by means of credibility. In other words, this aesthetical construction was designed to anchor journalism on the trust of people by means of a process that guaranteed impartiality and objectivity, both from power and from individual subjectivity (Schudson, 1994; Ward, 2015).

Hence, 'trust', or the lack of it, is at the centre of this discussion. As some authors have reflected, news organizations and society at large face a paradox, if well a more sceptical citizen should always be welcome in a democratic ethos, no less is true of the fact that ordinary people are just 'not buying' what journalists say (Broersma, 2013). The erosion in public trust towards newsmakers and their news organizations is becoming increasingly detrimental to democracy itself and has opened the doors to all sort of populist movements that threaten the very existence of the freedoms that make news reporting possible in the West. To be sure, the citizens, as news audiences, have come to distrust governments and democracy itself, which seems to be entering into a deadly spiral. We have been here before, but even if history does not repeat itself it is appropriate to remind ourselves that these type of situations have led us in the past into political authoritarianism. Grounded scepticism is at the core of modern democracy and has been a central part of the progress that humankind has made in the past 300 years. However, it is something that can easily degenerate into the very same cynicism which makes people distrustful of others and lose hope in a better society.

Journalism faces this sense a duality: on the one hand, it plays an important role in the process of building of trust across society. However, journalism is not only a trust provider, it also relies on public trust itself in order to accomplish what it does.

On the other hand it serves the unwritten contract it has with the society of being a watchdog to power (Blöbaum, 2014). However, the loss of trust has not happened in a vacuum but as part of more structural societal changes that have been provoked by transformations also occurring in the realms of technology, economics and politics.

Regrettably, many in the industry and outsiders have failed to understand this and are placing all their hopes in a techno-deterministic and cybernetic understanding of what has been happening and needs to be done. One that seems to embrace the type of technocracy that those who pushed for cybernetics envisaged as the future of orderly society governed by numbers. For them, numbers and data can rescue journalism from its demise by making it so mathematically and scientifically objective that it could only produce unquestionable and universal 'factual truth'.

However, we should not forget that embracing this data-techno professional utopia can lead us to the danger of producing a type of journalism that would be unable to face authoritarian regimes and state/corporate control, which today stand in places such as the United States and China against democracy as we know it. In this sense, data-driven journalism has the great potential to use numbers and statistics to improve our world, and there is little doubt that in many cases it has fulfilled that potential. However, it can also help spread distrust and help particular regimes to maintain a firm grip over its own citizens. Statistics can also help enhance the role of watchdog and gatekeeper by means of numbers. Hence, understanding that journalism is as much about facts as it is about storytelling is key to all of this. Numbers, after all, are an abstract element in the process of creating social reality. Their supposed power to represent reality and provide truth is nothing more than a figment of our imagination to reduce uncertainty and try to make sense of a complex world. They have worked so far because they were auxiliary to our way of telling stories. However, now that they are encroaching into the core of journalism we face the risk of letting them tell us what the story really is. What happens next is not so easy, which is why we have put forward our own reflections on this matter.

EPILOGUE

While wrapping up this book, we witness the global crisis set in motion by the spread of the COVID-19 virus. According to the latest figures released in May 2020 by the European Centre for Disease Prevention and Control, there were almost 300,000 deaths worldwide at that time, and the consequences on the worldwide economy seemed probably huge and long lasting, although by then still unknown in detail. What was certain then and now was that many lives were shattered and whole communities disseminated by this crisis. Indeed, by the time it was officially declared a pandemic by the World Health Organization (WHO), it was already a full-scale destructive force that resembled – at least in the eyes of those in places such as Guayaquil, Ecuador, and in Bergamo, Italy – one of the Horsemen of the Apocalypse.

In response to these events, governments and political leaders engaged at different speeds in the implementation of emergency strategies that involved all sectors of their societies. The state of emergency forced them to undertake action, although only for some of these leaders the action and sense of urgency were in fact 'immediate'. This is because while some prioritized the health and lives of people, others instead believed that saving the economy was far more important. As these debates took place among elites, doctors, nurses, first responders and, overall, ordinary people such as postal workers, cleaners and rubbish collectors kept society afloat. The sheer number of ordinary people who suddenly became heroes but who until those days were often invisible to the public eye reminded us that society is not made by the few but by the many.

As the number of deaths climbed, fingers started to be pointed at culpables even before any peak was reached, perhaps looking to displace responsibilities. Some leaders spoke every day while others remained silent. During that leadership vacuum, fake news and the misrepresentation of numbers spread globally as fast as the pandemic did. The battle for the hearts and minds of the public soon became an information war or 'Infodemic', as described by the director-general of the WHO, Tedros Adhanom Ghebreyesus. He would go to point out in the Munich Security Conference on 15 February 2020 that 'we're not just fighting an epidemic; we're fighting an infodemic'. The WHO itself in one of its reports would go to add that

> The Infodemic is an over-abundance of information, some accurate and some not that makes it hard for people to find trustworthy sources and reliable guidance when they need it. It poses a serious problem for public health since people need this guidance to know what actions to take to protect themselves and others, and help mitigate the impact of a disease. In the context of the COVID-19 pandemic, the infodemic is exacerbated by the global scale of the emergency, and propagated by the interconnected way that information is disseminated and consumed through social media platforms and other channels. (WHO, 2020)

We ourselves are confident to assert that this Infodemic has quickly developed into what we can call a 'Datademic', where countries are competing – in an unhealthy manner, we would add – with each other on who has the lower number of deaths and whose ideological and power model is the best to face such a pandemic.

In Chile, to give an example, the then minister of health, Jaime Mañalich, would go on to admit that his government accounted those killed by COVID-19 as having recovered. The reason was, according to the minister, 'they are not a source of contagion for others and we include them as recovered. These are the people who have completed 14 days of diagnosis or who unfortunately have passed away' (La-Vanguardia, 2020). In other words, because the dead are 'no longer contagious' they can be counted as recovered.

All over the globe serious doubts emerged about the methods that certain countries use to measure the mortality rate or even register those affected by the virus, something that speaks loud and clear about the lack of harmonization on how data is collected among different countries. Harmonization of data (and lack of it) was indeed one of the central issues we only touched in this book, and it is a topic which reverberates across the challenges that journalists face when using numbers to bring about accountability to power, as suspicions around official numbers grow. This last is not only in reference to countries such as China and Russia, which were found to deliberately be hiding their real death tolls (BBC, 2020; Gershkovich, 2020; Watts, 2020) but also in regards to several Western liberal democracies, which seemed also to have given in into similar propaganda practices. Indeed, the London-based newspaper, the *Financial Times*, exposed that the coronavirus pandemic had already caused as many as 41,000 deaths in the United Kingdom, more than double the official figure released by ministers (Giles, 2020). Never before as today had society needed so much for journalists to properly verify and double-check numbers through quality criteria and bring about light to the shadows of lies.

Indeed, in that same country, statistics became crucial in changing the initial policy of the UK government, which initially opted for the Herd Immunity approach. The initial premise was in fact to disregard the advice of other European countries and the recommendations of the WHO in making people stay at home in order to flatten the curve of contagion. Instead, the Conservative government's intention was to allow people to continue life as normal while emphasizing upon protecting the elderly and vulnerable. In doing so, it was thought, the United Kingdom would 'reduce the peak of the epidemic, pull it down and broaden it', while allowing the economy to continue (FT, 2020).

Thankfully within days and under heavy pressure from the news media from all the political sides of the spectrum and experts that persistently quoted statistics publicly, the British government took a U-turn (although the cost of thousands of deaths that could have been prevented would be paid weeks later). Two particular statistical elements seemed to have had more prominence in the public imagination than others: 1) the news reporting of the soaring numbers of deaths in Italy and 2) the publication of the mathematical model designed by immunologists at Imperial College, London, which predicted an excess of 250,000 deaths if the government had continued its course of action (Kelly, 2020; van Elsland & O'Hare, 2020). However, only time would tell us in detail how much these numbers weighted upon that change of heart.

These current challenges remind us that statistics, numbers and data in the news are a powerful tool in shaping public discourse and underpinning argumentative persuasion within the rhetorical exercise of power (Desrosières, 2002; Fioramonti, 2014; Zuberi, 2001), particularly where quality and the best interest of the people may not be at the centre of the political agenda or at the heart of its elites. Hence, the urgent need to make sure that journalists can incorporate ethically, effectively and efficiently statistics into their daily work; this as to be able to face the challenges posed by an increasingly datafied society where good numbers do not necessarily translate into good news but where surely good journalism can always be counted on to make a difference. If our book can contribute somehow in achieving so, then we would know that it was worth writing these lines.

REFERENCES

Abdi, H., & Valentin, D. (2007). Multiple correspondence analysis. *Encyclopedia of Measurement and Statistics*, edited by NJ Salkin, Sage, USA.

Abelson, R. P. (2012). *Statistics as Principled Argument*: Psychology Press, Hove, United Kingdom

Abiocca, F. (1988). Opposing conceptions of the audience: The active and passive hemispheres of mass communication theory. *Annals of the International Communication Association, 11*(1), 51–80.

Abramson, J. (2010). Sustaining quality journalism. *Daedalus, 139*(2), 39–44.

Ackrill, J. L. (1988). *A New Aristotle Reader*. Princeton University Press, New Jersey, USA.

Adams, D. (2006). Journalism, citizens and blogging. In 2006 Communications Policy and Research Forum (pp. 1-24). Network Insight Institute.

Albers, R. (1992). Quality in television from the perspective of the professional programme maker. *Studies of Broadcasting, 28*(1992), 7–75.

Allan, S., & Thorsen, E. (2009). *Citizen Journalism: Global Perspectives* (Vol. 1). Peter Lang, Frankfurt am Main, Germany.

Allgaier, J. (2011). Who is having a voice? Journalists' selection of sources in a creationism controversy in the UK press. *Cultural Studies of Science Education, 6*(2), 445–467. doi:10.1007/s11422-011-9319-5.

Allison, J. J., Calhoun, J., Wall, T. C., Spettell, C. M., Fargason, J. C., Weissman, N. W., & Kiefe, C. I. (2000). Optimal reporting of health care process measures: inferential statistics as help or hindrance? *Managed Care Quarterly, 8*(4), 1–10.

Altheide, D. L. (1997). The news media, the problem frame, and the production of fear. *Sociological Quarterly, 38*(4), 647–68.

Altman, D. G. (2002). Poor-quality medical research: what can journals do? *JAMA, 287*(21), 2765–67.

Altrichter, H. (2010). Theory and evidence on governance: Conceptual and empirical strategies of research on governance in education. *European Educational Research Journal, 9*(2), 147–158. doi:10.2304/eerj.2010.9.2.147.

Altrichter, H., Posch, P., & Somekh, B. (1993). *Teachers Investigate Their Work: An Introduction to the Methods of Action Research*. Psychology Press, Hove, United Kingdom

Andersen, J. (2006). The public sphere and discursive activities: Information literacy as sociopolitical skills. *Journal of Documentation, 62*(2), 213–28.

Anderson, C. W. (2018). *Apostles of Certainty: Data Journalism and the Politics of Doubt*. Oxford: Oxford University Press.

Anderson, J. R. (2014). *Rules of the Mind*. Psychology Press, Hove, United Kingdom.

Anderson, M. (1992). The history of women and the history of statistics. *Journal of Women's History, 4*(1), 14–36.

Anderson, P. J., Williams, M., & Ogola, G. (2013). *The Future of Quality News Journalism: A Cross-Continental Analysis* (Vol. 7). Routledge, Oxford, United Kingdom

Anderson, R. L. (1970). Rhetoric and science journalism. *Quarterly Journal of Speech, 56*(4), 358–68.

Arazy, O., & Kopak, R. (2011). On the measurability of information quality. Journal of the American Society for Information Science and Technology, 62(1), 89-99.

Ashcraft, M. H. (2002). Math anxiety: Personal, educational, and cognitive consequences. *Current Directions in Psychological Science, 11*(5), 181–85. doi:10.1111/1467–8721.00196.

Authority, U. S. (2009). *Code of Practice for Official Statistics*. London: UK Statistics Authority.

Authority, U. S. (2010). Overcoming barriers to trust in crime statistics: England and Wales. *Monitoring Report, 5.*

Avakov, A. V. (2010). *Two Thousand Years of Economic Statistics: World Population, GDP and PPP.* Algora, New York, USA

Baack, S. (2015). Datafication and empowerment: How the open data movement re-articulates notions of democracy, participation, and journalism. *Big Data & Society, 2*(2), 2053951715594634.

Badiou, A. (2008). *Number and Numbers.* Polity, United Kingdom.

Badiou, A., & Sedofsky, L. (1994). Being by numbers. *Artforum International,* October, New York, USA.

Bardoel, J. (1996). Beyond journalism: A profession between information society and civil society. *European Journal of Communication, 11*(3), 283–302.

Bates, M. J. (1989). The design of browsing and berrypicking techniques for the online search interface. Online review, 13(5), 407-424.

Batini, C., & Scannapieco, M. (2006). Data quality. Data-centric Systems and Applications.

Baumgaertner, B., & Floridi, L. (2016). Introduction: The philosophy of information. *Topoi, 35*(1), 157–159. doi:10.1007/s11245-016-9370-7.

BBC. (2020). Coronavirus: Why China's claims of success raise eyebrows. *BBC.* Retrieved from https://www.bbc.com/news/world-asia-china-52194356.

Bell, A. (2000). Dateline, deadline: journalism, language and the reshaping of time and place in the millennial world. *Georgetown University round table on languages and linguistics,* 46–66.

Bell, A. (2016). Media (mis) communication on the science of climate change. *Public Understanding of Science.* Sage. 3(3), 259-275.

Bell, D. (1960). *The End of Ideology: On the Exhaustion of Political Ideas in the Fifties.* New York: Free Press.

Bell, D. (1973). *The Coming of Post-Industrial Society: A Venture in Social Forecasting.* New York: Basic Books.

Bell, D. (1976). Welcome to the post-industrial society. *Physics Today, 29*(2), 46–49.

Bellamy, C., & Taylor, J. A. (1998). Governing in the information age. Open University Press, United Kingdom.

Benedictus, R., Miedema, F., & Ferguson, M. W. (2016). Fewer numbers, better science. *Nature, 538*(7626).

Bennett, P. (2010). *Risk Communication and Public Health.* Oxford University Press, United Kingdom

Bernstein, P. L. (1996). *Against the Gods. The Remarkable Story of Risk.* In, New York: John Wiley & Sons.

Berkowitz, D. A. (Ed.). (1997). Social meanings of news: A text-reader. Sage, United Kingdom.

Best, J. (2012). *Damned Lies and Statistics.* University of California Press, USA.

Bevir, M., & Rhodes, R. (2015). Interpretive political science. *Routledge Handbook of Interpretive Political Science*, Routledge, United Kingdom.

Biehler, R. (1994). Probabilistic thinking, statistical reasoning, and the search for causes— Do we need a probabilistic revolution after we have taught data analysis. *Research Papers from ICOTS, 4*, 20–37.

Blakemore, M. (1999). Working with government to disseminate official statistics. *Statistics in Society: The Arithmetic of Politics.* London: Arnold.

Blanes, J., & Kirchmaier, T. (2017). The effect of police response time on crime clearance rates. *The Review of Economic Studies.*

Blau, P. M. (1956). Bureaucracy in Modern Society. Crown Publishing Group/Random House, USA.

Blöbaum, B. (2014). Trust and journalism in a digital environment. In U. o. Oxford (Ed.), *Reuters Institute for the Study of Journalism Working Paper* (pp. 1–66). Oxford: Reuters Institute for the Study of Journalism.

Blumler, J., & Gurevitch, M. (2002). The crisis of civic communication. In *The Crisis of Public Communication* (pp. 9–16): Routledge, USA.

Blumler, J. G. (1979). The role of theory in uses and gratifications studies. *Communication Research, 6*(1), 9–36.

Bogart, L. (2004). Reflections on content quality in newspapers. *Newspaper Research Journal, 25*(1), 40–53.

Borges-Rey, E. (2016). Unravelling data journalism: A study of data journalism practice in British newsrooms. *Journalism Practice, 10*(7), 833–43.

Borges-Rey, E. (2017). Towards an epistemology of data journalism in the devolved nations of the United Kingdom: Changes and continuities in materiality, performativity and reflexivity. *Journalism*, 1464884917693864.

Borges-Rey, E., Heravi, B., & Uskali, T. (2018). Periodismo de datos iberoamericano: desarrollo, contestación y cambio social. Presentación. *La Revista ICONO 14: revista de comuncacion y tecnologias emergentes, 16*(2), 1–13.

Bovaird, T., & Löffler, E. (2003). Evaluating the quality of public governance: indicators, models and methodologies. *International Review of Administrative Sciences, 69*(3), 313–28.

Bradshaw, P. (2013a). Ethics in data journalism: accuracy. Retrieved from https://onlinejournalismblog.com/2013/09/13/ethics-in-data-journalism-accuracy/.

Bradshaw, P. (2013b). *Scraping for Journalists: How to Grab Data from Hundreds of Sources, Put It in a Form You Can Interrogate and Still Hit Deadlines.* Leanpub. www.leanpub.com

Briant, E. (2018). *Three Explanatory Essays Giving Context and Analysis to Submitted Evidence. Part 1: Cambridge Analytica, the Artificial Enemy and Trump's 'Big Lie'.* Retrieved from London: https://www.parliament.uk/documents/commons-committees/culture-media-and-sport/Dr-Emma-Briant-Explanatory-Essays.pdf.

Briggs, C. L., & Hallin, D. C. (2007). Biocommunicability the neoliberal subject and its contradictions in news coverage of health issues. *Social Text, 25*(493), 43–66.

Briggs, C. L., & Hallin, D. C. (2016). *Making Health Public: How News Coverage Is Remaking Media, Medicine, and Contemporary Life.* Routledge, USA.

Broersma, M. J. (2013). A refractured paradigm: journalism, hoaxes and the challange of trust. In C. Peters & M. J. Broersma (Eds.), *Rethinking Journalism: Trust and Participation in a Transformed News Landscape* (pp. 28–44). Abingdon, Oxfordshire: Routledge.

Brooks, B. C. (1980). The foundations of information science: Part I. J. Inform. Sci, 2(3), 4.

Browne, M. N., & Keeley, S. M. (2007). *Asking the Right Questions: A Guide to Critical Thinking.* Pearson Education. USA.

Buchler, J. (1955). Philosophical writings of Peirce. New York, USA.

Bumpstead, R., Alldritt, R., & Authority, U. S. (2011). *Statistics for the People? The Role of Official Statistics in the Democratic Debate*. Paper presented at the 58th World Congress of the International Statistical Institute, Dublin.

Burton, D. (2011). *The History of Mathematics: An introduction*. McGraw-Hill Companies, New York.

Cairo, A. (2012). *The Functional Art: An Introduction to Information Graphics and Visualization*. New Riders, Berkeley.

Cañizalez, A., & Lugo, J. (2007). Telesur: estrategia geopolítica con fines integracionistas (Andrés Cañizales y Jairo Lugo). *Temas de Comunicación* (14), 11–35.

Cañizález, A., & Lugo-Ocando, J. (2008). Beyond national media systems: A medium for Latin America and the struggle for integration. The media in Latin America, Open University Press, New York, 209-225.

Capra, F. (2009). The new facts of life: Connecting the dots on food, health, and the environment. Public Library Quarterly, 28(3), 242-248.

Castelfranchi, C., Falcone, R., & Pezzulo, G. (2003). *Trust in Information Sources as a Source for Trust: A Fuzzy Approach*. Paper presented at the proceedings of the second international joint conference on autonomous agents and multiagent systems.

Castelfranchi, C., & Poggi, I. (1994). Lying as pretending to give information. *Pretending to Communicate*, 276–91, De Gruyter Verlag, Germany.

Castelfranchi, C., & Tan, Y.-H. (2001). *Trust and Deception in Virtual Societies*. Springer, Germany.

Castells, M. (2011). The rise of the network society: The information age: *Economy, Society, and Culture* (Vol. 1). John Wiley & Sons, United Kingdom.

Cater, D. (1965). *The Fourth Branch of Government*. New York: Vintage Books.

Cervera, J. (2017). El futuro del periodismo es ciborg. *Cuadernos de periodistas: revista de la Asociación de la Prensa de Madrid, 34*, 102–9.

Chaiken, S., & Eagly, A. H. (1989). Heuristic and systematic information processing within and beyond the persuasion context. *Unintended Thought, 212*, 212–52.

Champkin, J. (2007). Henry Mayhew: The statistical Dickens. *Significance, 4*(3), 136–38.

Chen, Y., Conroy, N. J., & Rubin, V. L. (2015). *Misleading Online Content: Recognizing Clickbait as False News*. Paper presented at the Proceedings of the 2015 ACM on Workshop on Multimodal Deception Detection.

Chengalur-Smith, I. N., Ballou, D. P., & Pazer, H. L. (1999). The impact of data quality information on decision making: An exploratory analysis. *IEEE Transactions on Knowledge and Data Engineering, 11*(6), 853–64.

Chesney, T. (2006). An empirical examination of Wikipedia's credibility. First Monday.

Chibnall, S. (2013). *Law-and-Order News: An Analysis of Crime Reporting in the British Press* (Vol. 2). Routledge, United Kingdom.

Chu, B. (2007). Personal Blog. www.benchu.co.uk

Chumber, S., Huber, J., & Ghezzi, P. (2015). A methodology to analyze the quality of health information on the internet: the example of diabetic neuropathy. *The Diabetes Educator, 41*(1), 95–105.

Cohn, V., & Cope, L. (2011). News and Numbers: A Writer's Guide to Statistics. John Wiley & Sons, United Kingdom.

Coben, D. (2000). Mathematics or common sense? Researching 'invisible'mathematics through adults' mathematics life histories. In Perspectives on adults learning mathematics (pp. 53-66). Springer, Dordrecht.

Cochrane, G. (2018). Bureaucracy and Society. In *Max Weber's Vision for Bureaucracy* (pp. 117–38). Springer, Germany.

Coddington, M. (2015). Clarifying journalism's quantitative turn: A typology for evaluating data journalism, computational journalism, and computer-assisted reporting. *Digital Journalism, 3*(3), 331–48.

Cohen, E. C. (1985). Making value judgements: principles of sound reasoning, New York, USA.

Collett, A. (1989). Literature, criticism, and factual reporting. *Philosophy and Literature, 13*(2), 282–96.

Conboy, M. (2002). *The Press and Popular Culture*. Sage, United Kingdom.

Conboy, M. (2006). *Tabloid Britain: Constructing a Community through Language*. Taylor & Francis, United Kingdom.

Conboy, M. (2013). *How Journalism Uses History*. Routledge, United Kingdom

Cook, F. L., Tyler, T. R., Goetz, E. G., Gordon, M. T., Protess, D., Leff, D. R., & Molotch, H. L. (1983). Media and agenda setting: Effects on the public, interest group leaders, policy makers, and policy. *Public Opinion Quarterly, 47*(1), 16–35.

Cook, T. (2005). *Governing with the News* (2nd ed.). Chicago, IL: University of Chicago Press.

Craig, R. T. (1984). Practical criticism of the art of conversation: A methodological critique. *Communication Quarterly, 32*(3), 178–87.

Crook, T., & O'Hara, G. (2012). *Statistics and the Public Sphere: Numbers and the People in Modern Britain, c. 1800–2000* (Vol. 6). Routledge, United Kingdom.

Crook, T., & O'Hara, G. (2011). The 'torrent of numbers'. *Statistics and the Public Sphere: Numbers and the People in Modern Britain, c. 1800–2000*, 1–31.

Crosby, A. W. (1997). *The Measure of Reality: Quantification in Western Europe, 1250–1600*. Cambridge University Press, United Kingdom.

Crowe, M. J. (2007). *Mechanics from Aristotle to Einstein*. Santa Fe, California: Green Lion Press.

Crozier, M. (2008). Listening, learning, steering: new governance, communication and interactive policy formation. *Policy & Politics, 36*(1), 3–19.

Cushion, S., Lewis, J., & Callaghan, R. (2016). Data journalism, impartiality and statistical claims: Towards more independent scrutiny in news reporting. *Journalism Practice*, 1–18. doi:10.1080/17512786.2016.1256789.

Day, R. E. (2008). Works and representation. Journal of the American Society for Information Science and Technology, 59(10), 1644-1652.

De Tocqueville, A. (1982). *Alexis de Tocqueville on Democracy, Revolution, and Society*: University of Chicago Press, USA.

Dellamea, A. B. (1996). La formación de divulgadores y periodistas científicos en la Argentina. *Revista Innovación y Ciencia, 5*(4).

Desrosières, A. (2002). *The Politics of Large Numbers: A History of Statistical Reasoning*. Harvard University Press, USA.

Deutsch, K. (1985 [1963]). *Los nervios del gobierno: modelos de comunicación y control políticos*. Mexico, DF: Paidós.

Deuze, M. (2005). What is journalism? Professional identity and ideology of journalists reconsidered. *Journalism, 6*(4), 442–64.

Dewey, J., & Rogers, M. L. (2012). The public and its problems: An essay in political inquiry. Penn State Press.

Dibble, V. K. (1962). Occupations and ideologies. *American Journal of Sociology, 68*(2), 229–41.

Dorling, D., & Simpson, S. (1999). *Statistics in Society: The Arithmetic of Politics*. Arnold London, United Kingdom.

Dover, R., Goodman, M. S., & Hillebrand, C. (Eds.). (2013). Routledge companion to intelligence studies. Routledge, United Kingdom.

Drucker, P. (2012). *Post-capitalist society*. Abingdon, Oxfordshire: Routledge.

Duff, A. S. (1998). Daniel Bell's theory of the information society. *Journal of Information Science, 24*(6), 373–93.

Duffy, M. J., & Freeman, C. P. (2011). Unnamed sources: A utilitarian exploration of their justification and guidelines for limited use. Journal of Mass Media Ethics, 26(4), 297-315.

Dunwoody, S. (1982). A question of accuracy. *IEEE Transactions on Professional Communication*(4), 196–99.

Dunwoody, S. (2014). *Science journalism*. New York: Routledge.

Dunwoody, S., & Griffin, R. J. (2013). Statistical reasoning in journalism education. *Science Communication, 35*(4), 528–38.

Dyson, G. (2012). *Turing's Cathedral: The Origins of the Digital Universe*. Pantheon, USA.

Ebert, T. L. (2003). Manifesto as theory and theory as material force: Toward a red polemic. *JAC*, 553–62.

Eco, U. (1977). On the contribution of film to semiotics. London, United Kingdom.

Eco, U. (2000). *Apocalypse Postponed*. Bloomington, Indiana University Press, USA..

Ekström, M. (2002). Epistemologies of TV journalism: A theoretical framework. *Journalism, 3*(3), 259–82.

Elliott, P. A. (2010). *Enlightenment, Modernity and Science: Geographies of Scientific Culture and Improvement in Georgian England*. London: IB Tauris.

Entwistle, V., & Hancock-Beaulieu, M. (1992). Health and medical coverage in the UK national press. *Public Understanding of Science, 1*(4), 367–82.

Espeland, W. N., & Stevens, M. L. (2008). A sociology of quantification. *European Journal of Sociology/Archives Européennes de Sociologie, 49*(3), 401–36.

Esser, F. (2013). Mediatization as a challenge: Media logic versus political logic. In H. Kriesi (Ed.), *Democracy in the Age of Globalization and Mediatization* (pp. 155–76). Basingstoke: Palgrave Macmillan.

Ettema, J. S., & Glasser, T. L. (1984). On the epistemology of investigative journalism, 1–33. Retrieved from https://files.eric.ed.gov/fulltext/ED247585.pdf. (10-08-2020)

Ettema, J. S., & Glasser, T. L. (1998). *Custodians of Conscience: Investigative Journalism and Public Virtue*. Columbia University Press, USA.

Ewart, J., Cokley, J., & Coats, P. (2004). Sourcing the news: Teaching journalism students different approaches to sourcing practices. *Asia Pacific Media Educator* (15), 33.

Fawcett, L. (1993). Social scientists and journalists: Are the former really so different from the latter? *Irish Communication Review, 3*(1), 4.

Feighery, G. (2011). Conversation and credibility: Broadening journalism criticism through public engagement. *Journal of Mass Media Ethics, 26*(2), 158–75.

Fetzer, J. H. (2004). Information: Does it have to be true?. Minds and Machines, 14(2), 223-229.

Field, H. (2016). *Science without Numbers*. Oxford University Press, USA.

Figenschou, T. U., & Thorbjørnsrud, K. (2015). Faces of an invisible population. *American Behavioral Scientist, 59*(7), 783–801. doi:10.1177/0002764215573256.

Fink, K., & Anderson, C. W. (2015). Data journalism in the United States: Beyond the 'usual suspects'. *Journalism Studies, 16*(4), 467–81.

Fioramonti, L. (2013). *Gross Domestic Problem: The Politics behind the World's Most Powerful Number*. Zed Books.

Fioramonti, L. (2014). *How Numbers Rule the World: The Use and Abuse of Statistics in Global Politics*. Zed Books.

Floridi, L. (2002). On the intrinsic value of information objects and the infosphere. *Ethics and Information Technology, 4*(4), 287–304.

Floridi, L. (2004). Open problems in the philosophy of information. Metaphilosophy, 35(4), 554-582.

Floridi, L. (2010). Information: A very short introduction. OUP Oxford.

Floridi, L. (2011). *The Philosophy of Information*: Oxford University Press, United Kingdom.

Floridi, L. (2014). *The Fourth Revolution: How the Infosphere Is Reshaping Human Reality*. OUP Oxford, United Kingdom.

Floridi, L., & Illari, P. (2014). *The Philosophy of Information Quality* (Vol. 358): Springer, Germany.

Foucault, M. (2012 [1975]). *Discipline and Punish: The Birth of the Prison*. London: Vintage.

Fowler, J., Jarvis, P., & Chevannes, M. (2013). *Practical Statistics for Nursing and Health Care*. John Wiley & Sons, United Kingdom.

Frängsmyr, T., Heilbron, J. L., & Rider, R. E. (1990). *The Quantifying Spirit in the 18th Century* (Vol. 7). University of California Press, USA.

Franklin, B. (2003). *'McJournalism': The McDonaldization Thesis and Junk Journalism*. Paper presented at the Political Studies Association Annual Conference, University of Leicester, Leicester.

Franklin, B., & Carlson, M. (2010). *Journalists, Sources, and Credibility: New Perspectives*. Routledge, United Kingdom.

Freedman, D. (1999). From association to causation: some remarks on the history of statistics. *Journal de la société française de statistique, 140*(3), 5–32.

Frost, C. (2015). *Journalism Ethics and Regulation*. Routledge, United Kingdom.

FT. (2020). UK's chief scientific adviser defends 'herd immunity' strategy for coronavirus. Retrieved from https://www.ft.com/content/38a81588-6508-11ea-b3f3-fe4680ea68b5. (10-08-2020)

Fuchs, C. (2010). Labor in informational capitalism and on the internet. *The Information Society, 26*(3), 179–96.

Fukuyama, F. (1989). The end of history? *The National Interest* (16), 3–18.

Fukuyama, F. (2012 [1992]). *The End of History and the Last Man*. London: Penguin.

Gal, I., & Ograjenšek, I. (2010). Qualitative research in the service of understanding learners and users of statistics. *International Statistical Review, 78*(2), 287–96.

Gale, M. R. (2000). *Virgil on the Nature of Things: The Georgics, Lucretius and the Didactic Tradition*. Cambridge University Press, United Kingdom.

Gallagher, S. (2014). *Correlated*. USA: Penguin Random House.

Gannon, F. (2004). Experts, truth and scepticism. *EMBO reports, 5*(12), 1103–1110.

Gans, H. J. (1980). The audience for television—and in television research. Television And Social Behacior: Beyond Violence and Children. New Jersey: Lawrence Erlbaum Associates, Publishers.

Garfield, J. B. (1998). The statistical reasoning assessment: Development and validation of a research tool. Paper presented at the In the Proceedings of the 5 th International Conference on Teaching Statistics.

Garrison, B. (1998). *Computer-Assisted Reporting*. Psychology Press, USA.

Garvin, D. A. (1988). *Managing Quality: The Strategic and Competitive Edge*: Simon and Schuster, USA.

Gelman, A., & Nolan, D. (2017). *Teaching Statistics: A Bag of Tricks*: Oxford University Press, United Kingdom.

Gershkovich, E. (2020). Third Russian doctor falls from hospital window after coronavirus complaint. *The Moscow Times*. Retrieved from https://www.themoscowtimes.com/2020/05/04/third-russian-doctor-falls-from-hospital-window-after-coronavirus-complaint-a70176.

Gigerenzer, G. (2008). *Rationality for Mortals: How People Cope with Uncertainty*. Oxford University Press, United Kingdom.

Gigerenzer, G., Gaissmaier, W., Kurz-Milcke, E., Schwartz, L. M., & Woloshin, S. (2007). Helping doctors and patients make sense of health statistics. *Psychological Science in the Public Interest, 8*(2), 53–96.

Giles, C. (2020). UK coronavirus deaths more than double official figure, according to FT study | Free to read. *Financial Times*. Retrieved from https://www.ft.com/content/67e6a4ee-3d05-43bc-ba03-e239799fa6ab. (10-08-2020)

Gladney, G. A. (1996). How editors and readers rank and rate the importance of eighteen traditional standards of newspaper excellence. *Journalism & Mass Communication Quarterly, 73*(2), 319–31.

Godler, Y., & Reich, Z. (2017). Journalistic evidence: Cross-verification as a constituent of mediated knowledge. *Journalism, 18*(5), 558–74.

Gray, J., Chambers, L., & Bounegru, L. (2012). *The Data Journalism Handbook: How Journalists Can Use Data to Improve the News*. O'Reilly Media.Ireland.

Griffiths, D., Irvine, J., & Miles, I. (1979). Social statistics, towards a radical science. Demystifying social statistics. London: Pluto.

Guénon, R. (2017 [1945]). *Le Règne de la Quantité et les Signes des Temps*. Paris: Omnia Veritas.

Guerra, J. L. (2010). Sistema de Gestão de Qualidade aplicado ao Jornalismo: possibilidades e diretrizes. In E-Compós (Vol. 13, No. 3).

Habermas, J. (1978). Knowledge and human interests. John Wiley and Sons, United Kingdom.

Habermas, J. (1991). *The Structural Transformation of the Public Sphere: An Inquiry into a Category of Bourgeois Society*. MIT press, USA.

Habermas, J. (1996). *Between Facts and Norms: Contributions to a Discourse Theory of Law and Democracy*. Mit Press, USA.

Hacking, I. (1982). Biopower and the avalanche of printed numbers. In *Humanities in Society*,5, 279-295.

Hajer, M. A. (2009). *Authoritative Governance: Policy Making in the Age of Mediatization*. Oxford University Press, United Kingdom.

Halevy, A. Y., & McGregor, S. (2012). Data management for journalism. *IEEE Data Engineering Bulletin, 35*(3), 7–15.

Hall, S. (2001). Foucault: Power, knowledge and discourse. *Discourse Theory and Practice: A Reader, 72*, 81.

Hallin, D. C., & Briggs, C. L. (2015). Transcending the medical/media opposition in research on news coverage of health and medicine. *Media, Culture & Society, 37*(1), 85–100.

Hampton, M. (2008). The "objectivity" ideal and its limitations in 20th-century British journalism. *Journalism Studies, 9*(4), 477–93.

Hampton, M. (2010). *The Fourth Estate Ideal in Journalism History*. Taylor and Francis, United Kingdom..

Hanitzsch, T. (2016). The WJS 2012–2016 Study. Retrieved from http://www. worldsofjournalism.org/. (10-08-2020)

Hansen, K. A., & Paul, N. (2015). *Information Strategies for Communicators*. University of Minnesota Libraries Publishing, USA.

Harcup, T. (2006). *The Ethical Journalist*. Sage, United Kingdom.

Harcup, T., & O'neill, D. (2001). What is news? Galtung and Ruge revisited. *Journalism Studies, 2*(2), 261–80.

Harkins, S., & Lugo-Ocando, J. (2016). How Malthusian ideology crept into the newsroom: British tabloids and the coverage of the 'underclass'. *Critical Discourse Studies, 13*(1), 78–93.

Hayat, M. J., Powell, A., Johnson, T., & Cadwell, B. L. (2017). Statistical methods used in the public health literature and implications for training of public health professionals. *PloS one, 12*(6), e0179032.

Heilbrun, K., Wolbransky, M., Shah, S., & Kelly, R. (2010). Risk communication of terrorist acts, natural disasters, and criminal violence: comparing the processes of understanding and responding. *Behavioral sciences & the law, 28*(6), 717–29. doi:10.1002/ bsl.940.

Hepp, A. (2013). *Cultures of mediatization*. Hoboken, New Jersey: John Wiley & Sons.

Herrnstein, R. J., & Murray, C. (2010). *Bell Curve: Intelligence and Class Structure in American Life*. Simon and Schuster, USA.

Hilligoss, B., & Rieh, S. Y. (2008). Developing a unifying framework of credibility assessment: Construct, heuristics, and interaction in context. Information Processing & Management, 44(4), 1467-1484.

Hindman, E. B. (1998). "Spectacles of the Poor": Conventions of alternative news. *Journalism & Mass Communication Quarterly, 75*(1), 177–93.

Hjarvard, S. (2008). The mediatization of society. *Nordicom review, 29*(2), 102–31.

Hollins, N., & Bacon, W. (2010). Spinning the media: When PR really means police relations. Australian College of Independent Journalism, 1-6.

Hope, T. (2004). Pretend it works: Evidence and governance in the evaluation of the Reducing Burglary Initiative. *Criminal Justice, 4*(3), 287–308.

Hope, T. (2005). Pretend it doesn't work: The 'anti-social'bias in the Maryland Scientific Methods Scale. *European Journal on Criminal Policy and Research, 11*(3–4), 275–96.

Howard, G., Lubbe, S., & Klopper, R. (2011). The impact of information quality on information research. *Management, Informatics and Research Design*, 288.

Howell, M. C., & Prevenier, W. (2001). *From Reliable Sources: An Introduction to Historical Methods*. Cornell University Press, USA.

Hu, W., & Feng, J. (2004). Considering norms and signs within an information Source-Bearer-Receiver (SBR) framework. In Virtual, Distributed and Flexible Organisations (pp. 183-184). Springer, Dordrecht.

Huff, D., (1954). How to Lie with Statistics. Norton & Co., Inc., New York.

Hughes, H. M. (1940). *News and the Human Interest Story* (Vol. 1): Transaction Publishers, USA.

Hulsizer, M. R., & Woolf, L. M. (2009). *A Guide to Teaching Statistics: Innovations and Best Practices* (Vol. 10). John Wiley & Sons, United Kingdom.

Hutchins, E. (1995). *Cognition in the Wild*. MIT Press, USA.

Hutton, J. L. (2010). Misleading statistics. Pharmaceutical Medicine, 24(3), 145-149.

Hyde, J. S., Fennema, E., & Lamon, S. J. (1990). Gender differences in mathematics performance: A meta-analysis. In: American Psychological Association 107(2), p.139.

Kuhn, T. S., & Hawkins, D. (1963). The structure of scientific revolutions. American Journal of Physics, 31(7), 554-555.

Illari, P., & Floridi, L. (2014). Information quality, data and philosophy. In *The Philosophy of Information Quality* (pp. 5–23). Springer, Germany.

Jacoby, R., & Glauberman, N. (1995). *The Bell Curve Debate: History, Documents, Opinions.* New York: Times Books.

James, S. (2012). *Maps of Utopia: HG Wells, Modernity and the End of Culture.* Oxford: Oxford University Press.

John Walker, S. (2014). Big data: A revolution that will transform how we live, work, and think, Taylor & Francis, United Kingdom.

Johnson, R. B., Onwuegbuzie, A. J., & Turner, L. A. (2007). Toward a Definition of Mixed Methods Research. *Journal of Mixed Methods Research, 1*(2), 112–133. doi:10.1177/1558689806298224.

Johnston, R., & Brady, H. E. (2002). The rolling cross-section design. *Electoral Studies, 21*(2), 283–95.

Josephi, B. (2009). Journalism education. In *The Handbook of Journalism Studies* (pp. 62–76). Routledge, United Kingdom.

Juntunen, L. (2010). Explaining the need for speed: Speed and competition as challenges to journalism ethics. *The Rise of 24-hour news television*, Peter Lang, Switzerland, 167–82.

Kanari, Z., & Millar, R. (2004). Reasoning from data: How students collect and interpret data in science investigations. *Journal of Research in Science Teaching, 41*(7), 748–69.

Keeble, R. (2008). *Ethics for Journalists*: Routledge, United Kingdom.

Kelly, J. (2020). That Imperial coronavirus report, in detail. *Financial Times.* Retrieved from https://ftalphaville.ft.com/2020/03/17/1584439125000/That-Imperial-coronavirus-report--in-detail-/.

Kendrick, M. (2014). *Doctoring Data: How to Sort Out Medical Advice from Medical Nonsense*: Columbus Publishing.

Klaehn, J. (2003). Behind the invisible curtain of scholarly criticism: revisiting the propaganda model. *Journalism Studies, 4*(3), 359–69.

Knightley, P. (2000 [1975]). *The First Casualty: The War Correspondent as Hero, Propagandist, and Myth Maker from the Crimea to Vietnam.* London: Prion Books.

Knowlton, S. R., & Reader, B. (2009). *Moral Reasoning for Journalists.* Santa Barbara, CA: Praeger.

Koetsenruijter, A. W. M. (2011). Using numbers in news increases story credibility. *Newspaper Research Journal, 32*(2), 74–82.

Kopf, E. W. (1916). Florence Nightingale as statistician. *Quarterly publications of the American Statistical Association, 15*(116), 388–404.

Kovach, B., & Rosenstiel, T. (2001). The Elements of Journalism. New York, USA.

Kristensen, N. N. (2006). Spin in the Media-the Media in a (self-) Spin? MedieKultur: Journal of media and communication research, 22(40), 10.

Kwartler, T. Document classification: Finding Clickbait from headlines. *Text Mining in Practice with R*, 181–207.

La-Vanguardia. (2020). Chile contabiliza a los muertos como recuperados "porque ya no pueden contagiar". *La Vanguardia.* Retrieved from https://www.lavanguardia.com/internacional/20200413/48469884428/chile-contabiliza-muertos-recuperados-no-contagiar-coronavirus.html. (10-08-2020)

Lacy, S., & Rosenstiel, T. (2015). Defining and measuring quality journalism. Rutgers School of Communication and Information, USA.

Ladyman, J. (2014). Structural realism. Online Stanford Encyclopedia of Philosophy. Retrieved from https://plato.stanford.edu/entries/structural-realism/ (10-08-2020).

Lankes, R. D. (2008). Credibility on the internet: shifting from authority to reliability. Journal of Documentation.

Larmore, C. (2003). 10 public reason. *The Cambridge Companion to Rawls*, Cambridge Univeristy Press, United Kingdom.

Lazarsfeld, P., & Henry, N. (1966). *Readings in Mathematical Social Science*. Cambridge, MA: MIT Press.

Levitin, D. (2016). *A Field Guide to Lies and Statistics: A Neuroscientist on How to Make Sense of a Complex World*. UK: Penguin.

Leonelli, S. (2014). What difference does quantity make? On the epistemology of Big Data in biology. Big data & society, 1(1), 2053951714534395.

Lepri, S., Accornero, A., & Cultrera, G. (1991). Professione giornalista: EtasLibri.

Lewis, J., Williams, A., & Franklin, B. (2008). A compromised fourth estate? UK news journalism, public relations and news sources. *Journalism Studies, 9*(1), 1–20.

Lewis, J. M. W., Williams, A., Franklin, R. A., Thomas, J., & Mosdell, N. A. (2008). The quality and independence of British journalism. Cardiff University. Retrived from http://orca.cf.ac.uk/18439/1/Quality%20%26%20Independence%20of%20 British%20Journalism.pdf (10-08-2020)

Lewis, S. C. (2015). Journalism in an era of big data. *Digital journalism, 3*(3), 321–30. doi:10.1080/21670811.2014.976399.

Lewis, S. C., & Westlund, O. (2015). Big data and journalism: Epistemology, expertise, economics, and ethics. *Digital Journalism, 3*(3), 447–66.

Lincoln, B. (2014). *Discourse and the construction of society: Comparative studies of myth, ritual, and classification*. Oxford University Press, United Kingdom.

Lindberg, S. M., Hyde, J. S., Petersen, J. L., & Linn, M. C. (2010). New trends in gender and mathematics performance: A meta-analysis. In: American Psychological Association.

Lippmann, W. (1946). Public opinion (Vol. 1). Transaction Publishers.

Livingston, C., & Voakes, P. S. (2005). *Working with Numbers and Statistics: A Handbook for Journalists*: Routledge, United Kingdom.

Lowenstein, R. L., & Merrill, J. C. (1976). National Survey Shows: Most Journalism Schools Require Student Evaluations of Faculty. The Journalism Educator, 31(3), 16-17.

Lugo-Ocando, J. (2013). Reflexivity in the digital world: Rethinking journalism teaching and learning in an interactive world. *Journal of Applied Journalism & Media Studies, 2*(2), 207–14.

Lugo-Ocando, J. (2014). *Blaming the Victim: How Global Journalism Fails Those in Poverty*. London: Pluto Press.

Lugo-Ocando, J. (2017). *Crime Statistics in the News: Journalism, Numbers and Social Deviation*. In: Palgrave Macmillan.

Lugo-Ocando, J., & Faria Brandão, R. (2016). Stabbing news: Articulating crime statistics in the newsroom. *Journalism Practice, 10*(6), 715–29.

Lugo-Ocando, J., & Lawson, B. (2017). Poor numbers, poor news: The ideology of poverty statistics in the media. In A. Nguyen (Ed.), *News, Numbers and Public Opinion in a Data-Driven World*. New York: Bloomsbury Publishing.

Lynch, M. D., Kent, B. D., & Carlson, R. P. (1967). The meaning of human interest: Four dimensions of judgment. *Journalism Quarterly, 44*(4), 673–78. doi:doi:10.1177/107769906704400407.

MacDonald, Z. (2002). Official crime statistics: Their use and interpretation. *The Economic Journal, 112*(477).

MacDowall, I. (1992). *Reuters Handbook for Journalists*. Oxford/Boston: Butterworth-Heinemann.

Mack, R. W. (1957). Occupational ideology and the determinate role. *Social Forces*, *36*(1), 37–44.

Mai, J.-E. (2016). *Looking for Information: A Survey of Research on Information Seeking, Needs, and Behavior*. Emerald Group Publishing, United Kingdom.

Mai, J. E. (2013). The quality and qualities of information. *Journal of the Association for Information Science and Technology*, *64*(4), 675–88.

Maier, S. R. (2000). Digital diffusion in newsrooms: The uneven advance of computer-assisted reporting. *Newspaper Research Journal*, *21*(2), 95–110.

Majesty, E. S. t. t. T. b. C. o. H. (1998). Statistics a matter of trust. A Consultation document. Retrieved from https://www.gov.uk/government/uploads/system/uploads/attachment_data/file/260823/report.pdf (10-08-2020)

Maki, A., Evans, R., & Ghezzi, P. (2015). Bad news: analysis of the quality of information on influenza prevention returned by Google in English and Italian. *Frontiers in immunology*, *6*.

Mannheim, K. (2015 [1929]). *Ideology And Utopia: An Introduction to the Sociology of Knowledge*. Eastford, CT: Martino Fine Books.

Maras, S. (2013). *Objectivity in Journalism*. John Wiley & Sons, United Kingdom.

Marcinkowski, F., & Steiner, A. (2014). Mediatization and political autonomy: A systems approach. In H. Kriesi (Ed.), *Mediatization of Politics: Understanding the Transformation of Western Democracies* (pp. 74–89). Basingstoke: Palgrave MacMillan.

Martinisi, A., & Lugo-Ocando, J. (2015). Overcoming the objectivity of the senses: Enhancing journalism practice through Eastern philosophies. *International Communication Gazette*, *77*(5), 439–55.

Martišius, S.-A., & Martišius, M. (2008). Information society and statistics. *Inžinerinė ekonomika* (5), 16–23.

Mathieu, D. (2015). Audience research beyond the hermeneutics of suspicion. *International Journal of Media & Cultural Politics*, *11*(2), 251–58. doi:10.1386/macp.11.2.251_3.

Mattelart, A. (2000). *Networking the World, 1794–2000*. University of Minnesota Press, USA.

Mattelart, A. (2003). *The Information Society: An Introduction*. Sage, United Kingdom.

Mattelart, A. (2019a). For an archaeology of the cult of the number. *Digitalization of Society and Socio-political Issues 1: Digital, Communication and Culture*, 1–14.

Mattelart, A. (2019b). For an Archaeology of the Cult of the Number. In È. George (Ed.), *Digitalization of Society and Socio-political Issues 1: Digital, Communication and Culture* (pp. 1–14). Hoboken, New Jersey: Wiley.

Maxwell, R. (1978). Henry Mayhew and the life of the Streets. *Journal of British Studies*, *17*(2), 87–105.

Mayhew, H. (2010 [1851]). *London labour and the London poor*. Oxford: Oxford University Press.

Mayo, J., & Leshner, G. (2000). Assessing the credibility of computer-assisted reporting. *Newspaper Research Journal*, *21*(4), 68–82.

McDevitt, J., Balboni, J. M., Bennett, S., Weiss, J. C., Orchowsky, S., & Walbolt, L. (2003). Improving the quality and accuracy of bias crime statistics nationally. *Hate and Bias Crime: A Reader*, 77.

McNair, B. (2006). Cultural chaos: journalism and power in a globalised world. Routledge, United Kingdom.

McQuail, D. (1992). *Media Performance: Mass Communication and the Public Interest*. Sage, United Kingdom.

Media-Management-Centre. (2000). Managing for excellence – measurement tools for quality journalism. Retrieved from https://www.slideshare.net/victori98pt/measurement-tools-for-quality-journalism. (10-08-2020)

Meehan, A. J. (2000). The organizational career of gang statistics: The politics of policing gangs. *The Sociological Quarterly, 41*(3), 337–70.

Meer, T. G. L. A. v. d., Verhoeven, P., Beentjes, J. W. J., & Vliegenthart, R. (2017). Disrupting gatekeeping practices: Journalists' source selection in times of crisis. *Journalism, 18*(9), 1107–24. doi:10.1177/1464884916648095.

Mellado Ruiz, C. (2010). La influencia de CIESPAL en la formación del periodista latinoamericano. Una revisión crítica. *Estudios sobre el mensaje periodístico, 16*, 307–18.

Mencher, M., & Shilton, W. P. (1997). *News reporting and Writing*. Brown & Benchmark Publishers, United Kingdom.

Merrill, J. C. (1968). *The Elite Press*. Pitman, United Kingdom.

Meyer, P. (2002). *Precision Journalism: A Reporter's Introduction to Social Science Methods*. Rowman & Littlefield, USA.

Meyer, P. (2009). *The Vanishing Newspaper: Saving Journalism in the Information Age*. University of Missouri Press, USA.

Meyer, P., & Kim, K.-H. (2003). *Quantifying Newspaper Quality: I Know It When I See It*. Paper presented at the meeting of the Association for Education in Journalism and Mass Communication, Kansas City.

Miller, C. (2017). Can data save journalism? Retrieved from https://www.bbc.co.uk/blogs/academy/entries/a5947c13-50d0-4c33-af41-efcc106b4520. (10-08-2020)

Miller, D. (2004). Information dominance: The philosophy of total propaganda control. War, media, and propaganda: A global perspective, 7-16.

Miller, D., & Dinan, W. (2007). A century of spin: How public relations became the cutting edge of corporate power: Pluto Press, United Kingdom

Minnameier, G. (2010). Abduction, Induction, and Analogy. In *Model-Based Reasoning in Science and Technology* (pp. 107–19). Springer

Mitchell, S. (2009). Victorian journalism in plenty. *Victorian Literature and Culture, 37*(1), 311–21.

Mommsen, W. J. (1974). *The Age of Bureaucracy: Perspectives on the Political Sociology of Max Weber*. Blackwell, USA

Morrow, D. R., & Weston, A. (2015). *A Workbook for Arguments: A Complete Course in Critical Thinking*. Hackett Publishing, USA.

Mort, D. (2006). *Sources of Non-Official UK Statistics*. Gower Publishing.United Kingdom.

Narisetti, R. (2013). To save journalism, news needs to buy into data. Retrieved from https://digiday.com/media/data-save-journalism/ (10-08-2020)

Nerone, J., & Barnhurst, K. G. (2003). US newspaper types, the newsroom, and the division of labor, 1750–2000. *Journalism Studies, 4*(4), 435–49.

Nestor, P. G., & Schutt, R. K. (2014). Research methods in psychology: Investigating human behavior: Sage, United Kingdom.

Neubauer, R. (2011). Neoliberalism in the information age, or vice versa? global citizenship, technology, and hegemonic ideology. *TripleC: Communication, Capitalism & Critique. Open Access Journal for a Global Sustainable Information Society, 9*(2), 195–230.

Newman, N., Fletcher, R., Kalogeropoulos, A., Levy, D. A., & Nielsen, R. K. (2017). Reuters Institute Digital News Report 2017.

Nguyen, A., & Lugo-Ocando, J. (2016). The state of data and statistics in journalism and journalism education: Issues and debates. *Journalism, 17*(1), 3–17.

Nichols, T. (2017). *The Death of Expertise: The Campaign against Established Knowledge and Why It Matters*. Oxford University Press, United Kingdom.

Nobles, R., & Schiff, D. (2007). Misleading statistics within criminal trials. Medicine, science and the law, 47(1), 7-10.

Nordenson, B. (2008). Overload! Journalism's battle for relevance in an age of too much information. In (Vol. 47, p. 30): Columbia University, Graduate School of Journalism.

Olcott, A. (2012). Open source intelligence in a networked world (Vol. 7). A&C Black, United Kingdom.

O'Neil, C. (2016). *Weapons of Math Destruction: How Big Data Increases Inequality and Threatens Democracy*. London: Broadway Books.

ONS. (2020). Methodology topics and statistical concepts. Retrieved from https://www.ons.gov.uk/. (08-10-2020)

Orr, K. (1998). Data quality and systems theory. *Communications of the ACM, 41*(2), 66–71.

Osborn, B. (2001). Applying total quality management in the media organization. *Media Management,* http://bradleyosborn.com/applying_total_quality_management_to_the_media_organization.pdf, Erişim tarihi, 10(06), 2009.

Osborne, D., & Wernicke, S. (2003). *Introduction to Crime Analysis: Basic Resources for Criminal Justice Practice*. Psychology Press, United Kingdom.

Palmer, J. (2000). Spinning into control: News values and source strategies. A&C Black, United Kingdom.

Parasie, S. (2015). Data-driven revelation? Epistemological tensions in investigative journalism in the age of 'big data'. *Digital Journalism, 3*(3), 364–80.

Partington, J. (2017 [2003]). *Building Cosmopolis: The Political Thought of HG Wells*. Abingdon, Oxfordshire: Routledge.

Paulos, J. A. (2013). A mathematician reads the newspaper. Basic Books, USA.

Penenberg, A. (2010). Viral loop: the power of pass-it-on. Hachette, United Kingdom.

Pennycook, G., & Rand, D. G. (2019). Fighting misinformation on social media using crowdsourced judgments of news source quality. *Proceedings of the National Academy of Sciences, 116*(7), 2521–26.

Perrot, J.-C., & Woolf, S. J. (1984). *State and Statistics in France, 1789–1815* (Vol. 2). Taylor & Francis, United Kingdom.

Petersen, J. H. (2003). Lippmann revisited: A comment 80 years subsequent to 'Public Opinion'. Journalism, 4(2), 249-259.

Peirce, C. S. (1966). Logic as Semiotic: The Theory of Signs in Philosophical Writings of Peirce by Justus Buchler: New York: Dover Publications.

Pirolli, P. (2007). Information foraging theory: Adaptive interaction with information. Oxford University Press.

Pfannkuch, M., Regan, M., Wild, C., & Horton, N. J. (2010). Telling data stories: Essential dialogues for comparative reasoning. *Journal of Statistics Education, 18*(1), 1–38.

Phillips, A. (2012). Sociability, speed and quality in the changing news environment. *Journalism Practice, 6*(5–6), 669–79.

Picard, R. G. (2000). Measuring media content, quality, and diversity. *Turku, Finland: Turku School of Economics and Business Administration.*

Picard, R. G., & Yeo, M. (2011). Medical and health news and information in the UK media: The current state of knowledge. *Reuters Institute for the Study of Journalism.*

Pirsig, R. M. (1999). *Zen and the Art of Motorcycle Maintenance: An Inquiry into Values*. Random House, USA.

Plofker, K. (2009). *Mathematics in India*: Springer.

Poovey, M. (1993). Figures of arithmetic, figures of speech: the discourse of statistics in the 1830s. *Critical Inquiry, 19*(2), 256–76.

Porter, T. M. (1986). *The Rise of Statistical Thinking, 1820–1900*. Princeton University Press, USA.

Porter, T. M. (1996). *Trust in Numbers: The Pursuit of Objectivity in Science and Public Life*. Princeton University Press, USA.

Prewitt, K. (1986). Public statistics and democratic politics. *Behavioral and Social Science: 50 Years of Discovery*, 113.

Price, J. E. (1966). A test of the accuracy of crime statistics. *Social Problems, 14*(2), 214–21.

Quine, W. V. (1951). Main trends in recent philosophy: Two dogmas of empiricism. *The Philosophical Review*, 20–43.

Raivio, J. (2011). Quality journalism: The view from the trenches. In *Reuters Institute for the Study of Journalism*, Oxford: University of Oxford.

Randall, D. (2000). *The Universal Journalist*. Pluto Press, United Kingdom.

Reich, Z., & Godler, Y. (2014). A time of uncertainty: The effects of reporters' time schedule on their work. *Journalism Studies, 15*(5), 607–18.

Reinhart, A. (2015). *Statistics Done Wrong: The Woefully Complete Guide*. No Starch Press, USA.

Reitz, J. M. (2004). *Dictionary for Library and Information Science*. Libraries Unlimited, United Kingdom

Renn, O., & Levine, D. (1991). Credibility and trust in risk communication. *Communicating Risks to the Public: International Perspectives, 4*, 175–218.

Renó, D. P., & Renó, L. (2017). Algoritmo y noticia de datos como el futuro del periodismo transmediaimagético. *Revista Latina de Comunicación Social* (72), 1468–82.

Restivo, S. (2013). *Mathematics in Society and History: Sociological Inquiries* (Vol. 20). Springer Science & Business Media, United Kingdom.

Richards, I. A. (2003). *Principles of Literary Criticism*. Routledge, United Kingdom.

Rieh, S. Y., & Belkin, N. J. (1998, October). Understanding judgment of information quality and cognitive authority in the WWW. In Proceedings of the 61st annual meeting of the american society for information science (Vol. 35, pp. 279-289).

Ritzer, G. (1983). The 'McDonaldization' of society. *The Journal of American Culture, 6*(1), 100–7.

Rlindlof, T. (1988). Media audiences as interpretive communities. *Annals of the International Communication Association, 11*(1), 81–107.

Roberts, D. (2011). *Fatal Invention: How Science, Politics, and Big Business Re-create Race in the Twenty-First Century*. New York: New Press/ORIM.

Rodny-Gumede, Y. (2018). A teaching philosophy of journalism education in the global South: A South African case study. *Journalism, 19*(6), 747–61.

Romizi, D. (2012). Statistical thinking between natural and social sciences and the issue of the unity of science: From Quetelet to the Vienna Circle. In *Probabilities, Laws, and Structures* (pp. 443–55). Springer, United Kingdom.

Rosenberg, H., & Feldman, C. S. (2008). *No Time to Think: The Menace of Media Speed and the 24-hour News Cycle*. A&C Black, United Kingdom.

Rosenstiel, T., & Kovach, B. (2001). *The Elements of Journalism*. New York: Crown.

Ross, E. (1998). *Malthus Factor*. London: Zed Books.

Roten, F. C. v. (2006). Do we need a public understanding of statistics? *Public Understanding of Science, 15*(2), 243–49. doi:10.1177/0963662506061883.

RSS. (2020). Public courses. Retrieved from https://www.rss.org.uk/RSS/Training/Public_courses/RSS/pro_dev/RSS_training_courses_sub/public_training.aspx?hkey=80752d6b-205c-4865-8068-ab827079ced2. (10-08-2020)

Rudin, R., & Ibbotson, T. (2002). *An Introduction to Journalism: Essential Techniques and Background Knowledge*. Taylor & Francis, United Kingdom.

Ruggiero, T. E. (2000). Uses and gratifications theory in the 21st century. *Mass Communication & Society, 3*(1), 3–37.

Ruminski, H. J., & Hanks, W. E. (1995). Critical thinking lacks definition and uniform evaluation criteria. *Journalism & Mass Communication Educator, 50*(3), 4–11.

Russell, B. (1910). *Knowledge by Acquaintance and Knowledge by Description*. Paper presented at the proceedings of the Aristotelian Society.

Russell, R. S., & Taylor, B. W. (2005). *Operations Management: Quality and Competitiveness in a Global Environment*. Wiley, United Kingdom.

Russial, J., Laufer, P., & Wasko, J. (2015). Journalism in crisis? *Javnost–The Public, 22*(4), 299–312.

Russ-Mohl, S. (2006). The economics of journalism and the challenge to improve journalism quality. A research manifesto. Studies in Communication Sciences, 6(2), 189-208.

Ryten, J. (2012). Credibility and interference in official statistics: opposites at war. *Realidad, Datos y Espacio. Revista Internacional de Estadística y Geografía, 3*(1), 5–13.

Sabillon, C. (2005). *World Economic Historical Statistics*. Algora Publishing, USA.

Saetnan, A. R., Lomell, H. M., & Hammer, S. (2010). *The Mutual Construction of Statistics and Society*. Routledge, United Kingdom.

Saini, A. (2019). *Superior: The Return of Race Science*. London: Fourth Estate.

Sainsbury, P., & Jenkins, J. (1982). The accuracy of officially reported suicide statistics for purposes of epidemiological research. *Journal of Epidemiology & Community Health, 36*(1), 43–48.

Santos, G. (2013). Numbers and everything. *Philosophia Mathematica, 21*(3), 297–308.

Savolainen, R. (2011). Judging the quality and credibility of information in Internet discussion forums. Journal of the American Society for Information Science and Technology, 62(7), 1243-1256.

Sauder, M., & Espeland, W. N. (2009). The discipline of rankings: Tight coupling and organizational change. *American Sociological Review, 74*(1), 63–82.

Scannapieco, M., Missier, P., & Batini, C. (2005). Data quality at a glance. *Datenbank-Spektrum, 14*(January), 6–14.

Schatz, R., Hoßfeld, T., Janowski, L., & Egger, S. (2013). From packets to people: Quality of experience as a new measurement challenge. In *Data traffic Monitoring and Analysis* (pp. 219–63). Springer, United Kingdom.

Schlesinger, P. (1978). Putting 'Reality' together: BBC news series. *Communication and Society*. London: Constable.

Shoemaker, P. J., & Reese, S. D. (1996). Mediating the message (pp. 781-795). White Plains, NY: Longman.

Scholar, M. (2009). *Code of Practice for Official Statistics Report on the Consultation and the Principles and Procedures for Assessment*. Retrieved from: http://www.statisticsauthority.gov.uk/reports---correspondence/reports/report-2.pdf. (10-08-2020)

Schrott, A. (2009). Dimensions: Catch-all label or technical term. In K. Lundby (Ed.), *Mediatization: Concept, Changes, Consequences* (pp. 41–61). Bern: Peter Lang Publishing.

Schudson, M. (1978). The ideal of conversation in the study of mass media. *Communication Research, 5*(3), 320–29.

Schudson, M. (1994). Question authority: A history of the news interview in American journalism, 1860s–1930s. *Media, Culture & Society, 16*(4), 565–87.

Schulz, W. (2000). *Preconditions of journalistic quality in an open society.* Paper presented at the Ponencia presentada en la Conferencia Internacional News Media and Politics–Independent Journalism, Budapest.

Seyb, R. (2015). Trouble with the statistical curve: Walter Lippmann's blending of history and social science during Franklin Roosevelt's first term. *American Journalism, 32*(2), 138–60.

Shapiro, I. (2010). Evaluating journalism: Towards an assessment framework for the practice of journalism. *Journalism Practice, 4*(2), 143–62.

Shapiro, I., Brin, C., Bédard-Brûlé, I., & Mychajlowycz, K. (2013). Verification as a strategic ritual: How journalists retrospectively describe processes for ensuring accuracy. *Journalism Practice, 7*(6), 657–73.

Sheley, J. F., & Ashkins, C. D. (1981). Crime, crime news, and crime views. *Public Opinion Quarterly, 45*(4), 492–506.

Silverman, A. (1992). The naming of nature and the nature of naming. Plato's *Cratylus.*

Sjøvaag, H. (2010). The reciprocity of journalism's social contract: The political-philosophical foundations of journalistic ideology. *Journalism Studies, 11*(6), 874–88.

Slack, N., Chambers, S., & Johnston, R. (2010). Operations management. Pearson education, USA.

Slater, M. D., & Rouner, D. (1996). How message evaluation and source attributes may influence credibility assessment and belief change. *Journalism & Mass Communication Quarterly, 73*(4), 974–91.

Spencer, S. J., Steele, C. M., & Quinn, D. M. (1999). Stereotype threat and women's math performance. *Journal of Experimental Social Psychology, 35*(1), 4–28.

Starkman, D. (2010). The hamster wheel. *Columbia Journalism Review, 49,* 24–28.

Stigler, S. (2010). Darwin, Galton and the statistical enlightenment. *Journal of the Royal Statistical Society: Series A (Statistics in Society), 173*(3), 469–82.

Stigler, S. M. (1986). *The History of Statistics: The Measurement of Uncertainty before 1900.* Harvard University Press, USA.

Stocking, S. H., & Gross, P. H. (1989). How do journalists think? A proposal for the study of cognitive bias in newsmaking. ERIC Clearinghouse on Reading and Communication Skills, 2805 E. 10th St., Smith Research Center, Suite 150, Bloomington, IN 47405.

Streckfuss, R. (1990). Objectivity in journalism: A search and a reassessment. *Journalism Quarterly, 67*(4), 973–83.

Strömbäck, J. (2005). In search of a standard: Four models of democracy and their normative implications for journalism. *Journalism Studies, 6*(3), 331–45.

Tait, W. W. (1986). Truth and proof: The platonism of mathematics. *Synthese, 69*(3), 341–70.

Taleb, N. N. (2007). Black swans and the domains of statistics. *The American Statistician, 61*(3), 198–200.

Tateno, S., & Yokoyama, H. M. (2013). Public anxiety, trust, and the role of mediators in communicating risk of exposure to low dose radiation after the Fukushima Daiichi Nuclear Plant explosion. *Journal of Clinical Outcomes Management, 12*(2), 1–22.

Taylor, C. (1984). Foucault on freedom and truth. *Political Theory, 12*(2), 152–83.

Taylor, A. D., & Pacelli, A. M. (2008). Mathematics and politics: strategy, voting, power, and proof. Springer Science & Business Media.

Thorsen, E., & Allan, S. (2014). *Citizen Journalism: Global Perspectives- Volume 2*: Peter Lang, Switzerland.

Tooze, A. (2001). *Statistics and the German State, 1900–1945: The making of Modern Economic Knowledge* (Vol. 9). Cambridge University Press, United Kingdom.

Tooze, A. (2006). The wages of destruction. *The Making and Breaking of the Nazi Economy.* London: Viking.

Tormala, Z. L., Briñol, P., & Petty, R. E. (2006). When credibility attacks: The reverse impact of source credibility on persuasion. *Journal of Experimental Social Psychology, 42*(5), 684–91.

Tuchman, G. (1972). Objectivity as strategic ritual: An examination of newsmen's notions of objectivity. *American Journal of Sociology, 77*(4), 660–79.

Tukey, J. W. (1977). Exploratory data analysis (Vol. 2, pp. 131-160).

Turner, P., & Turner, S. (2009). Triangulation in practice. *Virtual Reality, 13*(3), 171–81. doi:10.1007/s10055-009-0117-2.

Ullah, A. (1998). *Handbook of Applied Economic Statistics.* CRC Press, USA.

Underwood, D. (1988). When MBAs rule the newsroom. *Columbia Journalism Review, 26*(6), 23.

UNESCO. (2017). Model curricula for journalism education. Retrieved from: https://unesdoc.unesco.org/ark:/48223/pf0000151209. (10-08-2020)

Vehkoo, J. (2010). What is quality journalism and how it can be saved, Reuters Institute fellowship paper. Oxford, United Kingdom.

Van Dijk, T. A. (2006). Discourse and manipulation. Discourse & society, 17(3), 359-383.

Van Eemeren, F. H., & Grootendorst, R. (2004). *A Systematic Theory of Argumentation: The Pragma-Dialectical Approach* (Vol. 14): Cambridge University Press, United Kingdom.

van Elsland, S., & O'Hare, R. (2020). COVID-19: Imperial researchers model likely impact of public health measures. Retrieved from https://www.imperial.ac.uk/news/196234/covid19-imperial-researchers-model-likely-impact/.

Vehkoo, J. (2010). What is quality journalism and how it can be saved. *Reuters Institute for the Study of Journalism. Recuperado de: http://links.uv.es/IvkCt2Q.* (10-08-2020)

Virgillito, A., & Polidoro, F. (2017). Big data techniques for supporting official statistics: The use of web scraping for collecting price data. In *Data Visualization and Statistical Literacy for Open and Big Data* (pp. 253–73). IGI Global, USA.

Weitkamp, E. (2003). British newspapers privilege health and medicine topics over other science news. Public Relations Review, 29(3), 321-333.

Wessler, H., & Rinke, E. M. (2014). Deliberative performance of television news in three types of democracy: Insights from the United States, Germany, and Russia. Journal of communication, 64(5), 827-851

Wahl-Jorgensen, K., Berry, M., Garcia-Blanco, I., Bennett, L., & Cable, J. (2016). Rethinking balance and impartiality in journalism? How the BBC attempted and failed to change the paradigm. *Journalism,* 1464884916648094.

Waisbord, S. (2018). Truth is what happens to news: On journalism, fake news, and post-truth. *Journalism Studies, 19*(13), 1866–78.

Wand, Y., & Wang, R. Y. (1996). Anchoring data quality dimensions in ontological foundations. *Communications of the ACM, 39*(11), 86–95.

Wang, R. Y. (1998). A product perspective on total data quality management. *Communications of the ACM, 41*(2), 58–65.

Ward, S. J. (2015). *The invention of journalism ethics: The path to objectivity and beyond* (Vol. 38). McGill-Queen's Press, USA..

Watts, G. (2020). How China hid 'tens of thousands' of virus deaths. *Asian Times.* Retrieved from https://asiatimes.com/2020/04/how-china-hid-tens-of-thousands-of-virus-deaths/

Weber, M. (1946). *Characteristics of Bureaucracy*. From *Max Weber: Essays in Sociology*, 327-334

Weinberg, S. (2004). Can science explain everything? Can science explain anything? *Explanations: Styles of Explanation in Science*, 23.

Wells, H. (2014 [1903]). *Mankind in the Making*. Auckland, New Zealand: The Floating Press.

Wessler, H., & Rinke, E. M. (2014). Deliberative performance of television news in three types of democracy: Insights from the United States, Germany, and Russia. *Journal of Communication*, *64*(5), 827–51.

Westerståhl, J. (1983). Objective news reporting: General premises. Communication research, 10(3), 403-424.

Whitney, D. C. (1981). Information overload in the newsroom. *Journalism Quarterly*, *58*(1), 69.

WHO. (2020). Coronavirus disease 2019 (COVID-19). Situation Report – 85. Retrieved from https://www.who.int/docs/default-source/coronaviruse/situation-reports/20200415-sitrep-86-covid-19.pdf?sfvrsn=c615ea20_4. (10-08-2020)

Wien, C. (2005). Defining objectivity within journalism. *Nordicom review*, *26*(2), 3–15.

Wiener, N. (1948). *Cybernetics or Control and Communication in the Animal and the Machine*. New York: Technology Press.

Willenborg, L., & de Waal, T. (2001). Application of Non-Perturbative Techniques for Tabular Data. In Elements of Statistical Disclosure Control (pp. 175-217). Springer, New York, NY.

Williams, R. (1989). *The Politics of Modernity*. London: Verso.

Woodcock, G. (1984). Henry Mayhew and the undiscovered country of the poor. *The Sewanee Review*, *92*(4), 556–73.

Wootton, D. (2015). *The Invention of Science: A New History of the Scientific Revolution*. UK: Penguin.

Xie, I., & Joo, S. (2009). Selection of information sources: Accessibility of and familiarity with sources, and types of tasks. *Proceedings of the Association for Information Science and Technology*, *46*(1), 1–18.

Yalch, R. F., & Elmore-Yalch, R. (1984). The effect of numbers on the route to persuasion. *Journal of Consumer Research*, *11*(1), 522–27.

Yaqub, M., & Ghezzi, P. (2015). Adding dimensions to the analysis of the quality of health information of websites returned by Google: Cluster analysis identifies patterns of websites according to their classification and the type of intervention described. *Frontiers in Public Health, 3*.

Yavchitz, A., Boutron, I., Bafeta, A., Marroun, I., Charles, P., Mantz, J., & Ravaud, P. (2012). Misrepresentation of randomized controlled trials in press releases and news coverage: a cohort study. *PLoS Medicine, 9*(9), e1001308. doi:10.1371/journal.pmed.1001308.

Zelizer, B. (1993). Journalists as interpretive communities. *Critical Studies in Mass Communication*, *10*(3), 219–37. doi:10.1080/15295039309366865.

Zuberi, T. (2001). *Thicker Than Blood: How Racial Statistics Lie*. Minneapolis, Minnesota: University of Minnesota Press.

INDEX

www.ingramcontent.com/pod-product-compliance
Lightning Source LLC
Chambersburg PA
CBHW030836300326
41935CB00036B/234